ugly freedoms

ELISABETH R. ANKER

ugly free doms

DUKE UNIVERSITY PRESS Durham and London 2022

Printed in the United States of America on acid-free paper ∞
Project Editor: Lydia Rose Rappoport-Hankins
Designed by Aimee C. Harrison
Typeset in Portrait Text and SangBleu Sunrise
by Westchester Publishing Services

Library of Congress Cataloging-in-Publication Data
Names: Anker, Elisabeth R., author.
Title: Ugly freedoms / Elisabeth R. Anker.
Description: Durham : Duke University Press, 2022. | Includes
bibliographical references and index.
Identifiers: LCCN 2021020941 (print)
LCCN 2021020942 (ebook)
ISBN 9781478015161 (hardcover)
ISBN 9781478017783 (paperback)
ISBN 9781478022404 (ebook)
Subjects: LCSH: Liberty. | Political culture—United States—History—
20th century. | United States—Politics and government—Philosophy. |
BISAC: PHILOSOPHY / Political | POLITICAL SCIENCE / History &
Theory
Classification: LCC JC585 .A534 2022 (print) | LCC JC585 (ebook) |
DDC 320.97301/1—dc23
LC record available at https://lccn.loc.gov/2021020941
LC ebook record available at https://lccn.loc.gov/2021020942

Cover art: Dalia Baassiri, *Dust Wander*, 2017. Dust, wipes, glue, and
acrylic primer on canvas, 47⅕ × 63 × 1⅗ inches. Courtesy Mansour
Dib, private collection.

To the loves of my life:
Matthew, Daniel, Lilah

contents

acknowledgments

One of the best parts of taking years to finish this book is that I have so many people to thank. Without the fertile connections, discussions, debates, critiques, and collaborations with friends and colleagues, this book would not have come into being. I am so grateful for all of it.

Many people read and commented on these chapters in various iterations. I thank Asma Abbas, Ali Aslam, Lawrie Balfour, Lisa Beard, Cristina Beltrán, Jane Bennett, Rom Coles, Bill Connolly, Kate Destler, Shirin Deylami, Joshua Dienstag, Tom Dumm, Kevin Duong, Loubna El-Amine, Michaele Ferguson, Jason Frank, Jill Frank, Samantha Frost, Neve Gordon, Alex Gourevich, Lindsey Green-Simms, Ayten Gundogdu, Nina Hagel, Vicki Hsueh, Turkuler Isikel, Sharon Krause, Alex Livingston, Eric MacGilvray, Patchen Markell, Lori Marso, Ben McKean, Amber Musser, Jennifer Nash, Johann Neem, Paulina Ochoa Espejo, Davide Panagia, Samantha Pinto, Mark Reinhardt, Neil Roberts, Jen Rubenstein, Sara Rushing, Shalini Satkunanandan, Joel Schlosser, George Shulman, Jeff Spinner-Halev, Calvin Warren, and William Youmans. Wendy Brown helped me clarify everything at a crucial stage. Bonnie Honig read the whole manuscript at the last minute and helped me tie it all together. Andrew Dilts and Lida Maxwell gave the gift of public and published commentary, and changed the way I think about pleasure and enjoyment (even during the Kavanaugh hearings, which is saying something). Hagar Kotef went above and beyond: reading chapters, debating freedom, and inviting me to London, an event which would shift the trajectory of this book. Gayle Wald, Ingrid Creppell, Hatim El-Hibri, Steve Johnston, Melani McAlister, Char Miller, and Matt Scherer read the entire manuscript at an early stage and spent a full day discussing it over lots and lots of food; my gratitude to them is overflowing.

For invitations to present and share this work, I thank the organizers and audiences at American University of Beirut, Amherst College, Brown University, Columbia University, Cornell University, Duke University, Emory University, Frederich-Alexander University of Erlangen-Nuremberg, Georgetown University, Mount Holyoke College, New York University, Ohio State University, Simon's Rock at Bard College, SOAS University of London, University of Alabama, University of Basel Switzerland, University of California–Los Angeles, University of Chicago, University of Colorado–Boulder, University of Hawai'i, University of Illinois–Urbana Champaign, University of Maryland, University of North Carolina–Chapel Hill, University of Utah, University of Wisconsin–Madison, Uppsala University Sweden, and Western Washington University.

For the hallway, dinner, bar (and Zoom) conversations that indelibly shaped my project, I thank Jodi Dean, Noura Erekat, Kennan Ferguson, Michael Illuzi, Jennifer James, Dan Kapust, Lisa Lowe, Dana Luciano, Utz McKnight, Ella Myers, Jennifer Nedelsky, Anne Norton, John Protevi, Smita Rahman, Camille Robcis, Melvin Rogers, Kyla Tompkins, Inez Valdez, Rob Watkins, and Liz Wingrove. My DC reading group has been a source of generativity and joy, and I'm grateful for the comradeship of Melani McAlister, Ilana Feldman, Andrew Zimmerman, Johanna Bockman, Dina Khoury, Mona Atia, Despina Khakoudaki, and K-Sue Park.

George Washington University has supported this project in many ways, and I especially thank the University Facilitating Fund, the Columbian College Facilitating Fund, and the Humanities Facilitating Fund for support of this book. I thank the gods of academia that I am in the American Studies Department with excellent colleagues: David Bjelajec, Jamie Cohen-Cole, Tom Guglielmo, Chad Heap, Nicole Ivy, Melani McAlister, Terry Murphy, Amber Musser, Dara Orenstein, Suleiman Osman, and Gayle Wald. Our graduate students always teach and challenge me. Special thanks to Craig Allen, Sarah Asseff, Jackie Bolduan, Zach Brown, Eric Cheuk, Lindsay Davis, Thomas Dolan, Chelsey Faloona, Molly Henderson, Michael Horka, Scott Larson, Shannon Mancus, Justin Mann, and Zaynab Quadri.

Working with Duke University Press is consistently fantastic. I want to thank Courtney Berger, editor extraordinaire, for supporting this book before it was even on the page, and for her great advice over many delightful dinners. Sandra Korn and Lydia Rose Rappoport-Hankins gracefully shepherded the manuscript through revision and production. Aimee Harrison's cover design captured the book beautifully. Derek Gottlieb created the detailed index. The two anonymous reviewers gave excellent suggestions for revision and reorganization.

My family is simply the best. My mom, Carol Anker, is a goddess of generosity, care, and strength, and I love her more than words can say. Jonathan Anker is the coolest, bar none. He's got more juice than Picasso's got paint. I am so grateful to Patricia and Oscar Scherer for their unwavering love. The Ankers, Teigs, Havekosts, and Barnetts mean everything to me. Michael Kutno brings warmth to every family occasion. I hope that by the time this book is out we will all be able to be together again. The matriarch of my family, my 106-year-old grandma, Lillian Anker, passed away as I was finishing up this book. She modeled courage and humor in the face of life's many challenges, and I miss her so much. My cousin Stacy Anker passed away too soon, and I am proud of her for following her dreams before she left us. May their memories be a blessing. My father, the late Donald Jay Anker, is in my thoughts every moment, and I look to him all the time for inspiration, wisdom, and laughter. Even though I did not grow up to be the next pianist for the Allman Brothers Band, I know I've made him proud. He's still a part of all that I do.

I dedicate this book to Matthew Scherer, my partner in everything and the best friend I could have ever asked for in this gift of life. I also dedicate it to Daniel Jay Anker-Scherer and Lilah Eve Anker-Scherer, the most joyful, most creative, and wildest children on the planet, who make every moment rich beyond measure. My love for you is universes wide and older than the stars. I am the luckiest person ever to share the world with you.

introduction

Ugly Freedoms

DURING THE US WAR TO ANNEX THE PHILIPPINES, American soldiers employed a special method of torture against Filipino captives resisting US occupation. Standing on their arms to hold them in place, the soldiers thrust a running water hose down their captives' throats to simulate the feeling of drowning. This method, known as the "water cure," was intended to both punish individual insurgents and compel the larger Filipino population to submit to imperial occupation. When stories of the water cure returned to the US mainland, the technique was condemned as an obscene act abhorrent to American political values, and it was eventually prohibited. Yet for the soldiers on the ground, who continued to perform it, the water cure was viewed not as the opposite of American political values but as an expression of them. One soldier wrote a song, "The Water Cure in the P.I.," that expressed this view:

> Get the good old syringe boys and fill it to the brim
> We've caught another nigger and we'll operate on him
> Let someone take the handle who can work it with a vim
> Shouting the Battle Cry of Freedom.
>
> Hurrah. Hurrah. We bring the Jubilee.
> Hurrah. Hurrah. The Flag that Makes him free.

Shove the nozzle deep and let him taste of liberty,
Shouting the Battle Cry of Freedom.[1]

In this song, torture is a battle cry of freedom. It is a jubilee celebration—a joyful and world-historic liberation—best practiced by an enthusiastic torturer, someone "who can work it with a vim." Water is transformed into an instrument of torture by the syringe nozzle, and in this form it provides a "taste of liberty." According to the song's sadistic lyrics, once water is forced into Filipinos, it *becomes* liberty—it is what liberty tastes like for the tortured subject. Freedom, for Filipino captives, is experienced sensorially as drowning by torture. This practice of freedom targets the subject of a violent racial slur, so it draws on and extends long-standing American patterns of racialized violence against nonwhite people. Deployed at home against Black and Native peoples, this brutality is now projected abroad against the people of the Philippines, newly designated as subjects of American racial empire.[2] The song's imperative to "shove the nozzle deep" sexualizes the violence that marks the water cure as a form of control akin to rape. Freedom for the Filipinos challenging US occupation means being subjected to torture, and freedom for white American soldiers entails a celebratory practice of violent and sexual domination over resistant brown bodies in the service of imperial annexation.

There is no higher value than freedom in American politics and political thought. It is the foundational value that the country embodies, that citizens desire, and that the state is said to defend. For historian Eric Foner "no idea is more fundamental to Americans' sense of themselves as individuals and as a nation than freedom."[3] It is considered a universal yearning for all people, so unquestionable is its practice. According to the revolutionary claims in the Declaration of Independence, all people are endowed with liberty. It is an inalienable right that cannot be granted or taken by others, and part of what makes the American people coalesce into a polity is that they together hold the truth of inalienable freedom so obvious as to be self-evident. Throughout US history, what people mean by freedom has differed dramatically—it has included uncoerced action, political equality, emancipation from slavery, participation in governing, nondomination, individual responsibility, the abolition of tyranny, and revolutionary collective action to bring a just and equal society into being. Freedom is a notoriously contested concept, as its meaning continuously shifts in different historical moments. But across different uses, freedom has always signified the highest of human aspirations. Even with the multiplicities of freedom, the insistence in "The Water Cure in the P.I." that torture is a practice of freedom would seem impossible, nonsensical, or profoundly and unsettlingly wrong.

Many critics condemned the brutality of the water cure during the Filipino-American war, as did critics one hundred years later in another war that promised freedom through occupation—the War on Terror—in which the signature method of torture, waterboarding, echoed the water cure. In both cases, critics argued that torture and freedom were opposites, and therefore that supporters of water torture were morally bankrupt and politically misguided because they presumed that it could serve freedom. This comforting response defended the virtue and purity of freedom while separating it from the ugliness of imperialist, cruel, and racist torture practices. But what if the soldier's song bluntly articulates a paradoxical and unsavory truth? What if torture *is* a practice of American freedom? What if popular forms of freedom have entailed not merely the celebrated practices of individual liberty, rule of law, or shared participation in collective governance, but also torture, dispossession, and racial domination?

Ugly Freedoms interrogates practices of American freedom to examine the oppressions they legitimate as principled ideals. Throughout US history, freedom has taken shape as individual liberty and emancipation from tyranny, but it has also taken shape as the right to exploit and the power to subjugate. The American Revolution is perhaps the archetypal expression of political freedom in the United States, when former colonial subjects liberated themselves from the yoke of unjust monarchy in a radical act of political world-making. The founders brought a new democratic society into being, and galvanized a form of free subjectivity beyond individual rights to include the shared making of politics. Yet this liberation was only possible because of widespread land theft from indigenous peoples who had inhabited the land upon which they declared independence. Violent and world-destroying acts of dispossession were practiced by the founders as freedom: the freedom of settlers to take land in order to instantiate a new government, the freedom to cordon off native territory by labor, treaty manipulation, murder, and fiat in order to exercise independence.[4] This practice of freedom disrupted indigenous political systems and land relationships in order to be free from monarchy, a freedom that continues to this day in ongoing settler practices of land appropriation and cultural erasure.

The American Revolution also relied on and was funded in part by the enslaved labor of millions of Africans and their descendants. Slavery, legalized by US juridical processes, was interpreted by enslavers not as the opposite of liberty but as a practice of liberty. Some colonialists' desire to practice enslavement unregulated by the British Crown was precisely what led them to support the self-rule of national independence.[5] Political theorist and slaveholder John C. Calhoun, like many others in his milieu, argued that slavery was necessary for freedom.[6] It entailed the freedom of local control and citizens' self-rule. Slavery comprised the freedom to improve the land in an orderly fashion as well as the freedom of private property, as it authorized white property owners to use the labor of their Black human property largely as they decided. Slavery was the basis for free white institutions, and it provided his fellow enslavers the freedom of mastery, prosperity, and leisure, including the leisure to write treatises on liberty.[7] The system of slavery was thus not merely considered the opposite of freedom but also a practice of freedom: the freedom of the master.

At other moments in US history, freedom was a legitimating factor when the United States entered the second world war, helping to mobilize the fight against the genocidal authoritarianism and violent territorial expansion of the Nazis. Yet US efforts to support global freedom also legitimated imperial wars like those in the Philippines and Vietnam, as well as more recent neoimperial wars in Afghanistan and Iraq. The War on Terror was explicitly called a war for "Freedom against Fear" as President George W. Bush articulated, liberating both the United States and other countries from the specter of terrorism. Even its military operations were titled "Operation: Enduring Freedom" and "Operation: Iraqi Freedom" to emphasize the centrality of freedom as a guiding principle. The War on Terror killed hundreds of thousands of people, destroyed the infrastructure of both Afghanistan and Iraq, installed crony capitalists as leaders, and siphoned both countries' natural resources and national industries for the benefit of US-based multinational corporations.[8] Within the United States, the War on Terror justified pervasive domestic surveillance, widespread and ongoing state harassment of people with Arab or Muslim backgrounds, and the mass securitization of public space, each in the name of American freedom.[9] Throughout US history, the pursuit of freedom has legitimated democratic revolution, slave emancipation, labor organizing, and social justice movements for gender, sexual, and racial equality, but it has also legitimated slavery, indigenous dispossession, environmental destruction, sex and gender oppression, and the violent machinations of a "free" market that enable the powerful few to accumulate vast wealth amid widespread poverty and homelessness. Practices of freedom include enslavement and exploitation as much as independence and emancipation.

Freedom is thus, at once, the highest ideal in American politics and also the most brutal. This ambivalent legacy demands a full reckoning. Celebrated practices of freedom like self-rule, full participation in governance, and non-domination are crucial for understanding the complexity and possibilities of freedom. But systems of domination like imperialism or capitalism have also unfolded in freedom's name. Capitalism's economic exploitation is justified as an engine of freedom for individual and global prosperity, and imperial control of other states is understood by its practitioners to bring freedom to unfree peoples. Freedom is not the overarching driving force that constitutes these different systems of power, but its tenets are capacious enough to justify each one of them. It is too reassuring to claim that these systems are only falsely justified as freedom, that they only fabricate or dissimulate their connection to freedom as a fig leaf to cover true motives. This claim preserves freedom as a righteous, hallowed ideal. But the trouble is not that these practices demonstrate a failure to embody the correct ideal of freedom. Nor is it that the virtue of freedom is tragically subverted by bad actors who erroneously use freedom to legitimate their predation. The trouble is that ideals of freedom can be produced out of and within what Saidiya Hartman calls "scenes of subjection"—that freedom can legitimately be practiced as subjugation.[10] Freedom can entail both nondomination and domination, both worldmaking and world destruction, both challenges to and impositions of unjust authority. Rather than disavowing this dynamic to discard subjugating freedoms as either insincerity or false consciousness, I take the ambivalence and violence of freedom's expression seriously. *Ugly Freedoms* de-idealizes freedom and its entailments.

This book examines four specific iterations of modern freedom, with a focus on how they take shape in the United States from colonization to the present: first, freedom understood as the practice of individual liberty alongside a liberal civilization that codifies it. This iteration of freedom envisions continual human progress toward peace through individual self-possession, noncoerced activity, rule of law, and economic prosperity, but often excludes vast populations as unable to achieve self-possession, while it depicts nonliberal polities as barbaric and nonwhite peoples as requiring discipline or eradication in the service of liberty. Second, it challenges freedom understood as the historic emancipation from slavery, a presumed past political process that ended Black slavery and paved the way for inexorable progress toward racial equality. This version of freedom continues to identify freedom with mastery, thus enabling new forms of racial domination bound to the dynamics of slavery that continue into the present. Third, it challenges freedom interpreted as private property and individual choice in economic markets, an iteration of freedom now closely associated with neoliberal capitalism. This version of freedom values individual control over the property one owns, and offers individuals unfettered access to a competitive marketplace in which all presumably have equal capacity to trade and profit, even when their lives are otherwise riven by material and social inequality. This freedom entrenches poverty and inequality across the globe, while impelling people to reject supportive relations with others, condemn public life as domination, and structure their lives as a series of capital investments. Last, it challenges freedom understood as rational thought and human exceptionalism, an iteration that grounds freedom in the sovereign will of a logical and reasonable subject who overpowers the limits of nature to dictate her own destiny. This type of freedom often justifies violence over nature, over other animals, and over people deemed irrational. It destroys habitable environments while entrenching hierarchies of living creatures, and it hastens global warming.

I name these freedoms "ugly freedoms." By using the term *ugly* to describe freedom, I draw partly from an aesthetic category of interpretation to name an affective experience of antipathy or dissonance, and a judgment of offensive action. Ugliness as an aesthetic judgment attaches to things with subjectively determined displeasurable properties that work in multiple sensory registers of vision, smell, and taste when experiencing something disturbing, a sensorial multiplicity that is important throughout this book.[11] At one level, I draw on these aesthetic categories in a political way by examining how they connect to political and economic deployments of freedom.[12] Primarily, however, ugliness, as I use it to describe freedom, specifically challenges the claim that what it judges is an ideal and is universally desirable. To call these four varieties of freedom and their offshoots ugly is to emphasize how a celebrated value of nondomination or uncoerced action can be practiced as brutality, which also leaves this brutality discounted or disavowed. For freedom is ugly not only when it legitimates mass harm but also when its practitioners and tenets disregard these harms to uphold freedom as an always celebrated virtue. This disregard is central to freedom's status as a universal ideal. "The Water Cure in the P.I." song is atypical in this sense, in that it makes the link between freedom and torture explicit and celebrates rather than dissimulates their connection. Typically, to call a political action "free" means that this action is principled and noble, in the best interest of all people, and the most desirable choice in a field of options. Ugliness as a political assessment targets how principles and actions of freedom are granted preeminence even when they support widespread subjugation. The ascription "ugly" draws attention to this disregard and disavowal, gnawing away at the ceaseless affirmation of freedom's virtue, challenging the veneration of actions practiced under its mantle.

The injuries produced by the pursuit of modern freedom are well documented in feminist, Black, indigenous, and anticolonial thought, among others, which detail how philosophies of free practice can rely on a metaphysics of gender, race, and civilizational enlightenment that harm and exclude those considered too dependent or barbaric to practice freedom or be worthy of its responsibilities.[13] Ugly freedoms rely on those formative accounts while arguing that those harms and exclusions are not only the violent effects of freedom *but can also be considered free practice*. The water cure, for one, was a practice of freedom for American soldiers who enacted it. They did not invent this claim on the fly or justify their violence erroneously, but they drew from long-standing ugly freedoms practiced for centuries in the United States to interpret torture against people of color as an exercise of freedom. Freedom as subjugation is also found in the aptly named "Ugly Laws," laws created around the turn of the twentieth century in various American cities to forbid visibly poor or disabled people from inhabiting public space. Ostensibly to celebrate and beautify public life by removing "an unsightly and disgusting object . . . an improper person to be allowed in public," as the language of one municipal code explained, the Ugly Laws generated free movement in public by denying power to, and disavowing from public consciousness, the people whose poverty and physical struggles emerged out of war, industrialization, bodily difference, and immigration.[14] As Susan Schweik has analyzed, Ugly Laws constructed a political sphere organized specifically by excising "unsightly beggars"—people whose workplace and war injuries or malnutrition revealed in physical form the effects of capitalism and imperialism. The Ugly Laws named these conditions unworthy of and disconnected from American political experience, while deeming nonnormative bodies and unfamiliar cultural practices unsuitable for public life.[15] Many Ugly Laws were not overturned until the mid-twentieth century. The Ugly Laws made explicit one logic of ugly freedom: instantiating public freedom by refusing access to and practicing violence upon bodies deemed unworthy, while also denying those bodies political legibility. It also, I would suggest, inadvertently condemned the freedoms it enabled as "ugly."

Ugliness has historically served as a social and political judgment, one that in Euro-American philosophy has often appraised the worth of peoples and cultures in a hierarchical fashion, placing elite European-derived practices and features as the standard for the beautiful and desirable. Aesthetic claims of the beautiful and the ugly frequently map onto constructed political distinctions: modern and backwards, rich and poor, white and Black, Christian and Jewish and Muslim, pure and dirty. By the eighteenth and nineteenth centuries, aligning with systems of enslavement, industrial capitalism, and colonialism, ugliness became attached to non-Western cultural behaviors and nonwhite physical features, whereby features associated with wealthy white European Christians became the beautiful, and ugliness attached to Blacks, Jews, poverty, disability, and indigenous peoples. Designations of ugliness helped to lubricate the politics of servitude and extermination. As in the Ugly Laws, ugliness derived not merely from subjective judgments of the repulsive or obscene, but importantly from the copresence of things that were expected to be segregated: ideal and degenerate, normative and abnormal, and racial and religious diversity.[16] Ugliness invoked the discomforting presence of the deviant thing next to the object that signified rectitude, symmetry, and beauty when undesirable bodies and practices rubbed up against those deemed desirable and demanded to be reckoned with.[17] Ugliness derives from diverse political orders that produce encounters with difference, diversity, and interconnection as undesirable and suppress the granting of power to those who deviate from the standard or are considered unworthy, inadmissible, or just plain gross. Calling freedom ugly highlights how freedom is imbricated in politico-aesthetic judgments of degeneracy, worth, and power, judgments that cultivate xenophobia, political separations of peoples, and the rejection of collective mutuality.[18]

The anti-mask protests during the COVID-19 pandemic demonstrate key problems of ugly freedom. Anti-mask protestors rejected the mask wearing and social distancing required to stop the spread of the deadly new virus, and did so as a principled stance of individual freedom against government paternalism. The freedom to flout health recommendations, named "health freedom" by its supporters, relies on principles of individual sovereignty and limited government power over personal decision-making. It also relies more subtly on freedom as the capacity to refuse dependence, and on nonresponsibility for the world outside one's constructed private sphere. The refusal to distance or wear masks disregards the copresence of others, which makes all other people around the anti-mask protestors much more vulnerable to the virus while it actively thwarts public health efforts to prevent mass death. Health is a socially interconnected phenomenon that depends on public measures, environmental regulation, and economic distribution at a widespread level. The anti-maskers fantasize away these interconnections in order to recuse themselves from both individual and collective responsibility for stanching the crisis. Freedom here means to be free from the burden of others' vulnerability—to be free from recognizing one's complicity in making others vulnerable. It is to be free from the shared burden of public care by imagining health is only a personal concern. Their freedom entails a performance of invulnerability through the presumed capacity to reject interdependence by sheer force of will.

The "health freedom" of the anti-mask protestors led to the rapid spread of COVID-19 across populations and some of the highest COVID death rates in the world. Anti-mask protestors did not call for a freedom that would prevent mass death by demanding free healthcare, or housing for all people, or robust public resources to fund vaccines and solutions, which would rely on a version of freedom grounded in shared interdependence, collective accountability, and a bodily dignity that stands in solidarity with the most vulnerable as an expression of mutuality. It therefore reveals the necropolitical underpinnings of their ugly freedom, as the freedom of mask-free masculinity sacrifices the lives of the elderly and immunocompromised, as well as poor, minority, and immigrant populations more vulnerable to COVID-19 both because they are more likely to be "essential" workers forced to work during the crisis, and because of long-standing racialized health inequities. By making vulnerable people even more vulnerable, the anti-maskers enact the domination they claim to reject. The COVID warriors practice a freedom to expose others to death, and indeed to be free *from* them.

Ugly freedom entails a dynamic in which practices of freedom produce harm, brutality, and subjugation *as freedom*. I use the language of ugliness to push past the positive agencies and idealized practices that are the supposed exclusive provenance of "freedom" to see what forms of damage they legitimate or incorporate. Ugliness names disruptive experience, and I deploy it to disrupt the exclusively positive way freedom is typically understood to highlight the domination practiced in its name.[19] The explosive growth of housing evictions in the United States reveals this ugliness in our present moment. Eviction, as the freedom of landlords to remove nonpaying tenants from their property, draws from freedom as ownership and as the capacity to make a profit in a free market, two of the central tenets of liberal freedom in capitalism. It involves a landowner's freedom to control private property and to acquire economic independence by renting land.[20] In a neoliberal era when wages are depressed, state support for impoverished families is minimal, and rent prices have skyrocketed in a deregulated housing market, the entire housing system prioritizes owners' profit over renters' lives. Landlords also benefit from freedom as the rule of law, as in this case the law is tilted toward ownership rights over the rights of those who rent property. The law thus deepens asymmetries of power that force people with low incomes to pay extraordinary amounts for housing or become unhoused. The freedom of landlords to evict poor tenants both requires and disregards systems of political economy that make one person's poverty a source of profit for others. Those evicted are primarily poor women and their children—especially Black and brown women—who cannot make enough money in minimum-wage jobs to both support their family and pay high rent, nor do they have enough legal or social backing to stay housed in one of the most economically unequal countries in the industrialized world. Evictions damage the lives of those who are evicted, destroying the stability and connection provided by housing and familiar neighborhoods while thrusting vulnerable people into dangerous situations. Evictions, and their support in legal policies and law enforcement, show how the legacies of dispossession, mastery, and patriarchy are not historical embarrassments but present structures of power that continue to be practiced as freedom.

The freedom to evict is similar to the freedom of gun ownership, enshrined as a core individual freedom in the United States and practiced in a more explicitly violent way.[21] Gun ownership carries the promise of strengthening personal freedom as individual sovereignty. If sovereign power, classically defined, is the final authority to make decisions about life and death within a given sphere, then gun ownership allows owners final say in deciding who shall live and who shall die within their personal radius. It allows owners, especially the white men who make up a vast majority of the gun-owning population, the promise of control over life and death on their own terms. Individual freedom practiced through gun ownership constructs political relationships through analytics of control and threat assessment rather than equality or cooperation. It is not a new phenomenon, as it reflects what Nikhil Singh describes as a historical inheritance "that invested every white person with the sovereign right to kill," a form of individual freedom derived from indigenous dispossession and slave ownership that I examine in chapter 1.[22] Combined with new statutes like Concealed Carry and Stand Your Ground laws that allow people to carry guns in public and claim self-defense in offensive murder, guns now deepen a sense of freedom as individual capacity to control the life and death of others, especially the racialized and immigrant others so often deemed a threat to stability and order in US political discourses.

Evictions, anti-mask protests, and gun carrying entail practices of freedom that only exist through violent power unevenly distributed to the people who already have relatively higher access to it. All of these ugly freedoms have historical antecedents in US politics even when they take new and innovative form. Within their fashioning of individual freedom, the harm principle—the central tenet of freedom in liberal theory—is reconfigured: individual freedom does not stop if one harms another, countering what John Stuart Mill would claim to be the limit of freedom's expression. Rather, through gun carrying and anti-masking, individual freedom is now expressed by the very capacity to harm another. Evictions operate similarly, in that the freedom of a landlord's property ownership reaches full expression in the life-damaging power of eviction. Chandan Reddy has shown how state bestowals of freedom for some can unleash state violence on others, especially minority populations, a dynamic that is made clear in the ugly freedoms practiced by landlords, gun carriers, and COVID anti-maskers.[23] In addition, in these examples the same people accorded freedom are those also granted the capacity to injure others. Indeed, their freedom is expressed through the individual capacity to enact harm. Reddy persuasively argues that freedom often comes with violence, and *Ugly Freedoms* argues further that freedom often *is* a form of violence.

YET THE UGLINESS OF FREEDOM IS ONLY HALF THE STORY. The obverse of ugly freedom is not beautiful freedom, as if the capacity for shared world-making grounded in free action, collaborative flourishing, and equal power for all is an act of beauty, an ideal vision of purity, or an object for disinterested contemplation as in Kantian aesthetics. Instead, I want to emphasize a second and different type of ugliness. From the perspective of the visions of freedom outlined above, there are political and economic conditions deemed "ugly" and undesirable precisely because they seemingly cannot offer opportunities for freedom: these include deep dependence, obstructed agency, and moral debasement. In response, I examine what is possible *within* these rejected conditions for cultivating less conventional yet generative practices of freedom. If most versions of freedom construct boundaries that exclude reliance on others or dissolute behavior and relegate weakness to the category of unfreedom, I examine what unexpected freedoms can be found in those exclusions. What freedoms are found in the discarded places that the Ugly Laws, for one, rejected as unfree, the spaces cordoned off for "unsightly," "improper," and "disgusting" life? What freedoms are cultivated by and within these putatively ugly conditions, practices that might otherwise seem too disturbing, minor, or compromised to qualify for the grand descriptor of "freedom"?[24] Can these practices, rejected by conventional perspectives on modern freedom, actually offer less brutal and more life-upholding visions of what freedom can entail?

The critique of certain forms of freedom as "ugly" lays the foundation for examining practices of freedom that these very forms would otherwise denigrate as ugly and unfree. I explore the copresence of alternative freedoms, overlooked as unworthy or demeaning by conventional standards of freedom's exercise. Practices shunted to the undesirable part of the spectrum can showcase undervalued and uncelebrated modes of freedom. In the context of my critique of neoliberalism's violent takeover of politics, I see communities also finding petty and peculiar ways to reject neoliberal rationality as a governing ideal. They craft unconventional ways of living habitably with others off the radar—ways often seen as too uninspiring to be interpreted as freedom. I highlight how Black emancipation generates new forms of white supremacy, a key dynamic of ugly freedom in this book, while also exploring the unsettling actions that thwart structures of antiblack domination, even when these activities do not look like resistance or agency. Alongside practices of individual responsibility and human exceptionalism that further climate change, we can also find experimental freedoms in toxic waste zones and dank bodily registers like guts, which emphasize distributed agencies across many species and nonliving matter. Together these more-than-human collective subjects can creatively revitalize their decimated polities—polities that necessarily include the land and all it sustains.

The phrase "ugly freedom" thus has a double meaning in this book. In its first meaning it is an attack on certain freedoms understood as unproblematic political ideals. In its second meaning it is a generative resource for identifying alternative visions of freedom in practices rejected or disparaged by the first version of ugly freedom—freedoms that might otherwise be deemed too inconsequential, repellant, or deflating to qualify as such. Aristotle claimed that beauty is an ideal that marks something as distinctively attractive, and that the disagreeableness if not repulsion of ugliness is its opposing category.[25] But ugliness as I use it disrupts the boundary that demarcates desirable from undesirable things, ideal from nonideal instantiations, pleasurable from unpleasurable sensations, or perfect from debased forms.

There is a minor tradition in political theory of learning from the ugly as both a vital resource for political critique and a site of expansive possibilities for divergent sensorial experiences that can contribute to a more equal polity.[26] Theodor Adorno, for one, emphasizes the diagnostic qualities of ugliness; the world is full of injustice and barbarity, and this demands sustained attention to the things and people deemed degenerate and despised, since those affective judgments often indicate problems of social subjugation. Adorno argues that ugliness "stands witness for what domination represses and disavows" and thus attends to those discarded by violent social ideals of worth and beauty. Disruption of the "beautiful" is a key aspect of ugliness's power. In a few short pages nestled within *Aesthetic Theory*, Adorno suggests that to probe the ugly is not to languish in the cruelty or suffering brought on by the dismissal of things and people judged to be ugly, but to understand and denounce the violence that underpins it.[27] In provoking dissonance with social ideals, ugliness therefore "refuses to affirm the miserable course of the world as the iron law of nature," and in this way holds open a space for rejecting that course and even, perhaps, for imagining emancipation from it. Ugly freedom as a concept draws from this dynamic to delegitimize claims of freedom as always ideal and to tarry with the critical generativity of ugliness.

Leah Hochman's study of Jewish philosopher Moses Mendelssohn argues that his experience as designated ugly and deformed allowed him to generate a politico-aesthetic philosophy in which encounters with ugliness—with the things and peoples labeled repulsive, irrational, and outmoded—can supersede socially produced revulsions and inspire social conviviality through difference.[28] As ugliness "was one of the means of framing judgments about minority participation in modern civil society," Mendelssohn aimed to revalue politico-aesthetic categories that valued uniformity over difference to instead encourage diversity over purity, disorder over order. He aimed to both generate access for "ugly" minority participation in the social, and produce new forms of sociality that did not rely on aesthetic hierarchies of beauty and virtue.[29] For Mendelssohn, open encounters with ugliness spur a revaluation of prejudicial values, promote mutuality across variance without devolving into claims of abstract sameness, and cultivate pleasure through encounters with variety—even when the actions or peoples deemed ugly do not and will not reflect idealized forms of action or beauty.[30]

For both Adorno and Mendelssohn, encounters with ugliness do not confirm but disturb what Jacques Rancière has called the partition of the sensible, which include perceptual-political processes that determine what is deemed sensible and regulate what objects, persons, and ideas are worthy of representation.[31] Encounters with ugliness can instigate new ways of perceiving practices of political violence traditionally conceived as imperceptible or unfit for attention, as Adorno demands. And also, as Mendelssohn calls for, encounters with ugliness can help to imagine, articulate, and *feel* what a polity disentangled from domination and constituted by diverse mutuality might be. Their challenges to "ugliness" do not turn the peoples or situations deemed ugly into ideal, pure, or normatively beautiful subjects, however. They do not aim to shoehorn what is deemed ugly into established standards of beauty. Instead, they challenge the very ascription of "the beautiful" as a form of political violence.

In this second way of using the term *ugly* to identify unvalued freedom, I am specifically interested in forms of freedom that arise out of ambivalent situations, uncelebrated actions, and moments of "suspended agency," similar to those Sianne Ngai examines in her book *Ugly Feelings*, from which my own title riffs.[32] Ngai uses ugliness to flag undesirable affective states and marginal agencies, which inspires my own political interrogations of modern freedom. Ngai upends aesthetic theory's focus on the beautiful and iconic by emphasizing the petty and the trivial, what she terms the "weaker and nastier" realm of aesthetics, and this is the ugliness I draw from when examining otherwise discarded practices of freedom: the nonprestigious, the uninvigorating, the seemingly weak. These freedoms take shape not as the most powerful or cathartic enactments of liberation, but as more ambivalent, trivial, or uneasy expressions. They dwell in the gulf between powerlessness and heroic expressions of untrammeled agency. And just as importantly, they show how free action need not be a hallowed or monumental practice. Ugly freedom in this second valence does not require a virtuous actor, an upstanding citizen, or an ideal political subject explicitly yearning for liberty. Insistence on moral purity, as James Baldwin argued, can be a violent and dehumanizing expectation that denies the lived experience of moral complexity and grants worthiness only to those who demonstrate virtuous victimization for others' sentimentalized salvation.[33] Instead, I focus on practices of freedom in the muddle of situations deemed unvaluable because they do not conform to aspects of freedom deemed ideal, because the people practicing them do not fit neatly into familiar categories of exemplary political subjectivity, or because they can thrive in mediocrity and disgust.

Both uses of ugly freedom aim to revise the typical terms of freedom. In the first, I use ugliness to disrupt and de-idealize iterations of freedom. In the second, I identify practices of freedom in the discarded spaces and disparaged practices of the freedoms reflexively deemed ideal, in order to highlight the productive work of uninspiring, deviant, and displeasurable acts, those seen as unworthy of reverence. The freedoms in this second category often exemplify freedom as collective work to compose a shared world across difference without exploitation or domination, but they can take marginal if not disconcerting form. If the first use of ugly freedom turns an ideal into a degenerate practice, the second turns degenerate practices not precisely into ideals, but into actions worthy of acknowledgment as freedom. I ask how these seemingly undesirable practices might reflect versions of freedom like nonhierarchical mutuality, the collective composition of a shared world alongside others, and the eradication of exploitation.

While some ugly freedoms in the second use of the term emanate from pettiness or weakness, others bide their time for the right moment to strike, or operate under the expectation of powerlessness to carve out an obscure space of self-governance, or locate expansive potential in being undervalued, or strategically ignore the very terms on which ideal freedoms are envisioned. In *Wayward Lives, Beautiful Experiments*, Saidiya Hartman examines this second meaning of ugly freedom as she studies how poor young Black women in the early twentieth century experimented with freedom in ways deemed unacceptable, disrespectable, and insignificant amid poverty and what she explicitly describes as the "ugliness" enforced by white supremacy.[34] These freedoms, which include "the errant path taken by the leaderless swarm," free love, and "the right to opacity," constitute what Hartman calls a revolution in a minor key. She points to freedoms overlooked because they either do not take place in celebrated spaces of public freedom, because the actions may seem too insignificant, or because the Black women experimenting do not conform to whitened images of universal personhood. They are generated by people driven into dingy urban tenements, which then become the site of freedom's practice: "A small rented room was a laboratory for trying to live free in a world where freedom was thwarted, elusive, deferred, anticipated rather than actualized . . . the hallway, bedroom, stoop, rooftop, airshaft and kitchenette provided the space of experiment."[35] Wayward Black women at the start of the twentieth century harnessed the resources at hand in the spaces they were relegated to, from the kitchenette or airshaft, spaces of hurt and disappointment, to seize and invent freedoms enacted by those dismissed either as unfree or as having nothing to offer free practice. These freedoms are particular to the context of their enactment and to the people practicing them. Hartman is not arguing that discarded spaces and dingy tenements are always the space of freedom; she does not romanticize the poverty produced by white supremacy. Yet on her reading these wayward acts repudiate the ascription of "ugly": the ugliness of freedom in this case refers to something else that is crafted in worlds disparaged as ugly, forms of agency that might seem errant or nonspectacular, but are daring worldmaking practices, in ongoing efforts to fight for a livable world.

Ugly Freedoms thus shifts the study of freedom to both interrogate its subjugating practices and broaden its exercise to ignored or maligned registers of action. I do not adjudicate whether different actions practiced as freedom are or are not "real" freedom, but question what versions of freedom must be fought against, and what are worth fighting for. *Ugly Freedoms* calls some idealized practices of freedom *revolting* and then examines seemingly displeasurable or denigrated ways of *revolting* against them. I am not arguing that practices of freedom cannot be grand, that desires for freedom should not be expansive or motivated by large-scale visions for how to produce and live in a more just and nurturing world. But I am arguing that the sole focus on freedom as a majestic practice both ignores the appalling violence that traffics under its name and discounts many ways that freedom can be exercised productively in otherwise dispiriting, opaque, or "uncivilized" ways. This project is thus a companion to, not a rejection of, those offering more invigorating visions. Ugly freedom finds inspiration in actions and alliances dismissed as worthless, or as being too ineffectual to build common worlds, or too miniscule compared to vaunted acts of revolutionary transformation. It broadens what can be considered freedom.

The etymology of *ugly* is "to be feared or dreaded."[36] Its origin is in the Norse term *ug*, which also roots current use of the interjection *ugh*. When people and practices deemed ugly claim public space or exercise power never granted to them, this can appear reflexively fearful or dreadful to those unaccustomed to or antagonistic to more equitable social relations. The exercise of power by the putatively undeserving or unworthy can evoke the "ugh," as those actions seem chaotic or repulsive compared to established hierarchies of power and desert.[37] This dread and repulsion is precisely what the Ugly Laws aimed to excise from politics. The "ugh" is a response from a position of power to the second type of ugly freedom, as it denigrates ways of acting freely by people who are not at liberty to do so. The actions I examine in the book as free practice in this second valence of ugly freedom can seem perplexing or repulsive from the perspective of conventional discourses of freedom: a thwarting of neoliberal governance by overbloated municipal bureaucracies; a self-governing Black polity that sets fire to white supremacy and heteropatriarchy through gamesmanship, sex, and theft; an agentic environmental subject made up of multispecies bodies, land, dust, feces, and trillions of microbiota as an acting collective against environmental degradation. Each of these practices of freedom embody aspects of ugliness: (1) they might be deemed "unruly" by traditional gatekeepers to politics; (2) they are "matters out of place"—when being in place requires obedience to standard practice, to established hierarchies of power, or to the sensible; (3) they are, in the case of the third example, human-animal hybrids, one of the central forms of ugliness stemming from medieval and renaissance visions of monstrosity, which also attaches to the Western degradation of blackness as animality.[38] Many of the commonplace descriptors for ugliness are even the same descriptors for radically democratic rule used by those who condemn it: disorderly, offensive, and obscene. This is not to say that designations of disorder or obscenity are merely false judgments of democracy, and the truth of democratic freedom is a beautiful and well-ordered polity. Alexis de Tocqueville warns of the dangers of that presumption.[39] It is, rather, to press disorder or obscenity in new directions, to see how ugliness generates different understandings of what free action might be.

Negative politico-aesthetic experiences are valuable for freedom in their own right, without having to reclaim them as beautiful or grand for this to be the case. *Ugly Freedoms* does not argue that the practices it investigates only have value once they are recategorized as beautiful. Instead, it finds worth in actions otherwise derided as ugly without recouping them back into standard categories of beauty, especially if those categories are themselves crafted out of brutal forms of power. It marinates in scenes, politics, and practices deemed "ugly" to see what possibilities for mutual transformation they incite, making a bid to transmute the reflexive "ugh" into an experience of conviviality out of enmeshment with difference, deviance, and unruliness without redefining it as necessarily ideal or beautiful. It is a common assumption that beauty gets us through the challenges and struggles of the world, but what if it is ugliness that gets us through? What if encounters with ugliness produce different ways of seeing and feeling possibilities for freedom, even or especially when they don't feel grand or inspirational?

Ugly freedoms often take the low road. By focusing on these freedoms—and their expression in denigrated or discomfiting actions that may lack ideal visions—my goal is not to narrow political horizons to the mundane or truncate political strategies to trivial and seemingly less desirable possibilities. Instead, I seek to expand them, to find allies where one might otherwise expect foes or dead weight, to locate collective support in demoralizing conditions that seem to predict defeat, and to identify generative resources in stigmatized situations, dreary institutions, and seemingly vanquished spaces. Ugly freedoms do not take refuge in a politics of "the small and weak" or languish in powerlessness.[40] It is not about settling for scraps of power or reconciling with defeat. Instead I aim to rehabilitate and revalue practices that are dismissively shunted into those categories, practices erroneously condemned as having nothing to offer freedom's expression. These manifestations are often scorned or disregarded precisely because they operate in maligned registers deemed inconsequential, gross, or embarrassing within traditional discourses of freedom. I thus examine actions and spaces traditionally considered waste, deviance, or worthy of neglect, in order to study their latent possibilities for living free.

Freedom

Throughout this book I scrutinize freedoms popular in American politics and political theory from the start of colonization to the current moment that are premised on ideal values but entail exploitation or domination. I also find practices of political freedom in activities rejected by those ideal values. They can be found in aesthetic works, bodily performances, theoretical scholarship, political projects, and historic places, some of which may initially seem bereft of freedom's possibility. These include defunct sugar refineries, multimedia artwork, the teachers' lounge, gut microbiota, southern plantations, dirty windowsills, awkward sex, and police melodramas. They showcase practices that could seem too problematic to be considered freedom, or territorially disconnected from American political practice, or too small to demonstrate freedom's exercise. Each highlights how domination has been practiced as freedom and also how freedom takes shape in chaotic, uninspiring, or even offensive actions. These freedoms call attention not to the thrilling moments or shiny objects of freedom but to the scrappy and perplexing.

Many of these manifestations challenge the familiar boundaries of freedom. When freedom is envisioned as autonomous agency or masculinist heroism, then practicing freedom through dependence and muted action might seem laughable or humiliating. Numerous practices of modern freedom are grounded in dynamics of white supremacy and Black enslavement, so enacting freedom beyond the purview of whiteness and mastery takes shape in unexpected and often undervalued ways. If freedom has been associated with a practice of sovereignty that is expressed through private property, territorial control, and human exceptionalism, then different practices of freedom enacted by bodies composed of other bodies, other animals, and the land might seem both disturbing and nonsensical. Instead, these practices draw sustenance from arguments in indigenous political thought by Glen Coulthard, Leanne Betasamosake Simpson, Kim TallBear, and others, to show how individual sovereignty and private property create disturbing and nonsensical boundaries that ignore relational connections between human and more-than-human worlds.[41] Every acting body includes billions of other entities, land particles, and social relations that together compose worlds alongside all who inhabit them. The freedoms above encompass a set of definitions that can include acts of shared worlding, undoing exploitation, overcoming oppression, or living together without domination, even as these concepts alone are insufficient for envisioning and practicing freedom at any moment. They varyingly exercise freedom as the fight for and activity of composing and caring for the world alongside others, in equality and mutuality, across and in celebration of difference.

Yet freedom does not demand the same set of practices across time and space and history and peoples. It is not an unchanging or stable state nor the special purview of "ideal theory." The water cure is certainly not a universal expression of freedom but is quite particular to the time and place of its enactment. The wandering freedom or queer loving of Hartman's wayward women is also not a universal practice but is specific to the subjects and context of their enactment; different instances of street wanderings or sexual desires need not reflect freedom's expression. Other acts of ugly freedom—a rather mundane sigh of boredom in a teachers' lounge, for example, which I examine in chapter 3—typically only signify freedom in the moment they are exercised. Not all sighs in a teachers' lounge express freedom, clearly. But in the instance I examine here, when teachers are directed to conform their teaching to neoliberal market metrics for student performance that undermine true learning, one teacher's sigh leads to another's knowing eyeroll, and contagious affects of disaffection turn into collective refusal. If conditions set the terms for freedom's practice, then the specifics of any situation matter. As Max Horkheimer and Theodor Adorno emphasize, practices of freedom are oriented by specific forms of oppression and thus are always generated out of the conditions they aim to overcome.[42] They derive from particular moments and iterations that often cannot be replicated in other contexts, even when they are guided by similar principles.[43] Freedom refers to many, many ways of attending to and tending a world, and to varied capacities for worldmaking possible in different moments.[44]

Hannah Arendt famously argued that "the raison d'être of politics is freedom," and many traditions of political thought would agree, though they would differ significantly about what freedom actually is and how and where it is exercised.[45] Conclusively defining freedom is a challenge, as it is one of the most contested concepts in the history of political thought, referring both to principles and to the actions, conditions, and spaces motivated by those principles. While it often denotes political and economic independence, release from bondage, self-determination, and/or the condition of not being subject to arbitrary control, it has never meant one thing. No theorist in the history of political thought has categorically defined its content or its boundary limit; indeed, some of the biggest arguments over centuries of political thought revolve around the meaning and practice of freedom. In versions of freedom influential just in modern Euro-American political thought alone, freedom has taken shape as unobstructed agency; intrinsic individual rights; revolutionary overthrow of tyranny; economic and political equality; participation in civic life; emancipation from slavery; consent to the laws one is governed by; self-ownership; collective control over the production of society's needs; unfettered access to a free market; self-directed labor; radical communal transformation to a world without gendered, racial, sexual, and class hierarchy; and more. Freedom has never been a universally agreed upon value, nor a universally shared one, even when it is claimed as such.

Even with the multiplicity of definitions, no tradition adequately addresses the specific problem of ugly freedoms examined here. Some categorically exclude violence from freedom and thus ignore a range of problems encountered in its practice, while most presume their favored definitions of freedom are ideal, thus delimiting the diagnosis of freedoms neither virtuous, inspiring, nor exemplary. The most widely influential theory of freedom in Western political thought is liberalism, which, as its appellation suggests, takes liberty as its central concern. Yet aspects of the liberal tradition highlight both the problems and misdiagnoses of ugly freedom. Isaiah Berlin's wide-ranging and formative inquiry into "the essence of the notion of liberty" led liberalism to embrace a distinction between negative and positive liberty that narrows understandings of free practice and disavows the dominations within liberal freedoms.[46] Negative freedom entails an absence of constraint and coercion, a condition whereby an individual is left alone to make autonomous decisions. Positive freedom is the ability to act purposively, guided by a vision for what freedom is and how to practice it, rather than merely the absence of interference. This distinction aims to distill many definitions of freedom but limits the identification and interpretation of them, as it makes unstated and unacknowledged presumptions about who can practice freedom, what traditions of thought are relevant to freedom, and whether certain actions even qualify as free.[47] Prioritizing negative freedom, Berlin's liberalism does not address how a focus on noncoercion alone enables domination to flourish outside overtly coercive forms of power, thus omitting exercises of power like exploitation, structural discrimination, or necropolitics that do not fit neatly under "coercion." It also contributes to a worldview that the realm of negative freedom, especially its key expressions individualism and capitalism, are not coercive or disciplinary, while insisting that collective political action is mainly coercive and disciplinary. It can disregard how powers not reducible to governing authority or social conformity have limiting power on freedom's exercise, including race, capital, gender, sexuality, and disability.

These concerns can be seen more explicitly in the theorist whom Berlin called the best example of negative liberty, John Stuart Mill, who galvanized modern liberal thought by arguing for universal individual sovereignty limited only by the prevention of harm. Mill stated in his treatise *On Liberty* that "the only purpose for which power can rightfully be exercised over any member of a civilized community, against his will, is to prevent harm to others." Yet he also wrote in the very next paragraph that "we may leave out of consideration those backward states of society where the race itself may be considered as in its nonage . . . despotism is a legitimate mode of government in dealing with barbarians."[48] These two claims of freedom are both central to Mill's civilizing project in which the practice of liberty includes despotic imperialism.[49] To claim that these are opposing visions, that the first argument is a universal declaration of individual freedom and the second argument for colonial despotism is an embarrassing or outdated aberration from it, disavows the many ways they are alloyed together in Mill as freedom's expression. Mill's two principles reveal both the ugliness of this type of liberal freedom and the ease with which that ugliness can be disavowed by its supporters, who in this case claim the harm principle alone is the foundational principle of liberal theory. Achille Mbembe has argued that part of colonization's staying power is that it constantly lies to itself about itself, and liberal political theory perpetuates this dynamic when it excavates and isolates Mill's claims of universal individual sovereignty out of their colonial context.[50] *On Liberty* demonstrates two core claims of ugly freedom: first, that practices of subjection and domination can be compatible with, if not constitutive of, freedom, and second, that these practices can be ignored by their supporters, who decline to own the violence their favored systems uphold.

Other prominent approaches to freedom develop more multifaceted analyses, even as they continue to separate freedom from violence and delimit the analysis of its expressions. Contemporary republican theory recovers the insights and practices of the ancient Roman Republic to shift the definition of freedom from noncoercion to nondomination. It thus postulates a more robust concept of power and emphasizes civic participation and public commitment as essential elements of freedom, against liberalism's focus on private life, markets, and individual interest.[51] It highlights the crucial role of action and engagement in freedom's exercise. Yet its emphasis on the virtuous quality of civic practices can repeat the binds of individualism by focusing too heavily on personal comportment and moral virtue to the detriment of collective activity. Combined with an emphasis on ancient Roman rather than modern Black slavery as the antithesis to freedom, republicanism can sometimes recapitulate masculinity and whiteness as virtuous forms, even as scholars work to generate republican values that are more inclusive.[52] If we still live with the remainders of freedom derived within Black slave societies, then racialized freedom should be central to any analysis of enslavement as freedom's opposing form.

Hannah Arendt's democratic theory shares with republican theorists an inspiration in ancient political practices, and she articulates a version of freedom as participation in public action that has become deeply influential in contemporary democratic political thought. For Arendt, freedom entails performing something new in the world alongside others, the action of great speech and deeds in the reciprocal creation of public life alongside fellow citizens.[53] Attentive to the violence inherent in sovereign power, she argues that freedom does not entail acts of will or sovereignty, as they demand control and obedience from others and thus negate the plurality of worldly action. Freedom as inventive nonsovereign action in public, and as political worldmaking alongside others, opens vast new possibilities for envisioning freedom's practice separate from domination and outside a dynamic of negative or positive determinations to highlight reciprocal action and political creativity. Yet it also truncates the space of politics to public action and narrows the practice of freedom to courageous and virtuous gestures modeled on a European canon of value, celebrating the individual heroics of Achilles, for instance, but disparaging the collective actions of the civil rights movement.[54] Nor does it include practices of freedom that could be grounded in ordinary daily concerns practiced outside spaces recognized as political, or that take other models for free action besides courageous speech and glorious deeds.

For all their differences, these three theoretical approaches share the assumption that freedom and violence are antagonistic, such that acts of violence are ipso facto the mark of unfreedom. Whether the argument is that freedom is limited by the harm principle, as in liberal theory, that freedom is the condition of nondomination, as in republican theory, or that violence undoes the relations of mutuality necessary for political freedom, as in Arendt, each view contends that freedom ends where violence begins. Yet by insisting that violence, domination, and harm mark the limit point of freedom, these arguments conflate normative investments in nonviolence with political analysis of modern freedom's exercise.[55] They miss a range of complex practices when freedom's exercise entails both nondomination and dominating violence. The problem is not that normative visions of freedom as nonviolent are wrong, but that when also taken for definitive limits they do not address violent forms of freedom that also operate in modern life. This perpetuates the problem of freedom's disavowed dominations by erasing the brutal practices that challenge the idealism of their preferred freedom.

Other traditions of political thought reckon with the ways that freedom's practice can entail violence, including revolutionary arguments in which violence can be part of freedom's expression when fighting against domination. These include revolutionary democratic, communist, and anticolonial political theories, though they all justify their violence as virtuous and cathartic while inadequately addressing freedom's practice in subjugating modes. The revolutionary freedom articulated in the American Declaration of Independence entails the capacity to "alter or abolish" any governing system that destroys its foundations in consent of the governed, and to mutually pledge alongside others to institute a new government for a free and equal people. Upholding neither the moral freedom of virtuous and dutiful individual behavior nor the economic freedom of financial independence, the Declaration's words articulate political freedom as a collective overthrow of tyranny to make the world anew through shared and equal power for all participants.[56] The freedoms outlined in the Declaration accept antimonarchical violence as the price for independence, yet simultaneously discount the violence that independence perpetrates against native populations while excluding a vast majority of people living in the US from its vision of shared power. The Declaration casts revolutionary violence against the British Empire as worldmaking while negating how this worldmaking devastates the worlds of indigenous and enslaved people and bars all women from its practice. If, as the Declaration implies, freedom's revolutionary violence solely targets unjust tyranny, then the Declaration can dismiss the tyranny its freedom creates and justifies.

Karl Marx's communism embraces aspects of the Declaration's definition of revolution while simultaneously arguing that political emancipation alone cannot abolish all forms of unfreedom, especially capitalism's production of economic exploitation.[57] Marx ruthlessly critiques the ugliness of a political-economic system that claims material inequality and economic exploitation are nonpolitical and thus unadjudicable. Capitalism's freedom in profitmaking and individual self-interest produce world-historic violence upon workers and the poor while all people are alienated from others and from their own work in the process of economic exchange; claims of formal equality and freedom before the law obscure and perpetuate this ruthlessness.

However, Marx too wants to preserve the righteousness of freedom by claiming that these exploitative forms of freedom are merely fake manipulation of the real thing: the freedom to sell one's labor while under the formal equality of the law is, he argues, "a mere semblance, and a deceptive semblance."[58] Yet economic exploitation is fundamentally compatible with liberty understood as freedom to buy and sell in a market regardless of external conditions outside of it. The violence of the labor contract is not a *semblance* of freedom but an *iteration* of freedom that refuses to account for power outside of the moment of exchange. Freedom can be practiced in exploitative ways while still being "freedom."

Engaging the ugliness of freedom in both valences, Frantz Fanon's anticolonial political thought examines how modern freedom has been exercised as subjugation and also finds freedom in places disparaged as inferior and worthless. Fanon diagnoses how modern Euro-American freedom sanctions racism, cruelty, and colonization, how violent acts of domination over colonized subjects are practiced as freedom by the colonizers at liberty to control them. His concern is not that this freedom is a semblance but that it has colonized what freedom is and who can practice it.[59] For Fanon, political categories of freedom and aesthetic categories of beauty work together to justify colonization; he condemns the racist ways in which freedom is exercised by colonial powers while the Western ascriptor "beauty" labels colonized people as uncivil and substandard. He rejects the violence of this type of "beauty" as a desire or aim when he states of his argument for liberation, "I want my voice to be harsh, I don't want it to be beautiful, I don't want it to be pure."[60] Like Marx and the signers of the Declaration, Fanon argues that freedom can take shape as violence when fighting against domination, but he also argues that freedom is expressed in the violence of colonial subjugation; the problem is not that colonizing freedom is a semblance but that different freedoms, originating with the colonized, must rearticulate its practice for anticolonial ends.[61] Yet although Fanon addresses the ugliness of freedom in multiple ways, he envisions anticolonial liberation to entail generally masculinist, heroic, and striking gestures that violently instantiate independence with new forms of sovereign determination. Marx and the writers of the Declaration, as much as they offer different visions of revolutionary freedom, share assumptions that freedom requires bold expressions, rousing actions, and cathartic processes of emancipation.

None of these traditions articulates precisely the freedoms that are noncathartic, minor, or compromised. Their emancipatory practices do not imagine how freedom might be found in gestures that are not boldly revolutionary or powerful, but nonheroic and even imperceptible. These include possibilities of freedom in opaque gestures, or actions that would otherwise seem demoralizing, dirty, or unelevated above the drudgework of daily life.[62] Yet what of freedoms practiced in ways that are not galvanizing, or cleansing, or grand? Or collective refusals that are not motivated by desires for sovereignty but something else entirely? How is liberation enacted in less gratifying, less potent, and more desultory ways, but still a process of freedom?[63]

Every practice of freedom has drawbacks and remainders, as no iteration of freedom is wholly pure, righteous, or free from ambivalence. And even though political theorists study the development and inheritance of different traditions of thought, practices of freedom often do not emanate from a single tradition or with loyalty to a set of cohesive arguments. They can be shaped by intermixed or even oppositional derivations and practiced in ways that contradict ideal forms. Versions of freedom that emerge in the lives of ordinary people, or in collective movements on the ground, are often philosophically disjointed, politically ambivalent, and genealogically blurred. This is not to deride those practices as bad or incorrect; to the contrary: it is to point to the real complexity and disarray of both lived practice and scholarly endeavor.[64] All forms of actually existing freedom are nonideal, either partly produced out of domination and violence, or inseparable from their remainders and losses. Ugly freedoms open to the disappointments and ambivalences of freedom's practice.

The ugly freedoms cataloged in this book may thus seem undesirable or deflating. What if freedom might look like willing participation in one's own domination? Can freedom be exercised through bureaucratic sloth? Or through something as boring as statistical manipulation of data? What if freedom is practiced in stealing? Or an eyeroll? What if the subject exercising freedom is composed of an admixture of toxic chemicals and the fecal matter of strangers? Could freedom actually be tasted—as the water cure song suggests? If Judith Butler crucially argues that "the street and the square are not the only platforms for political resistance," how can ugly freedoms both significantly expand the "platforms" available for political action beyond customary spaces, and push beyond the familiar celebrated agencies congealed into "resistance"?[65] The ugly freedoms I explore in the second use of the term, those that are unfairly maligned as unfree, do not presume that resistance always motivates freedom or that participants only qualify for freedom if they are morally upstanding or noncomplicit in unfreedom. Freedom, in this sense, is not necessarily a righteous act by an exemplary subject. Subjects practicing freedom do not need to be fully extricated from the forms of domination their actions aim to countermand. They do not have to inhabit a position of purity or honor in order to practice freedom, especially as those categories can delimit who qualifies for them in the first place.[66]

In tarrying with practices deemed unworthy or aberrant, these ugly freedoms emphasize modes of agency that may not offer desired or hoped-for visions of freedom, while still demonstrating free action. These acts can include stealing, "foot-dragging," strategic incompetence, and otherwise unremarkable actions that still retain power to push against oppression, as James C. Scott's *Weapons of the Weak* examines.[67] He calls these actions "nonspectacular forms of struggle," as they happen below the radar of expected political action and in sometimes undetectable registers of political agency. Scott, however, focuses solely on freedom as "resistance" and identifies the state as the primary source of oppression people face. When one imagines the state is always an enemy to freedom, then resistance to unfreedom inevitably takes anti-statist form. But the origins of unfreedom are not limited to the state (which is never a monolithic entity in any case) and include more nebulous formations of power that are not easily identifiable as a single source of constraint, even when they are imbricated with state power, like climate change or patriarchy. In addition, as I argue in chapter 2, state bureaucracies can be harnessed in the service of freedom. Foot-dragging and strategic incompetence can even be practiced by state institutions like schools or states attorneys as a challenge to nonstate forms of oppression. Turgid bureaucracies can be an unlikely weapon in the fight against the neoliberal decimation of public life.[68]

Ugly freedoms may not accomplish alone the transformations necessary for an equal and just society. They may not even provide what is desired or needed in the service of those visions. But their ambivalence and bewilderment can be an asset. They offer less dignified, and thus more livable, experiences of action and collectivity. Waiting around for the ennobling, the beautiful, or the heroic can contribute to melancholia, in which a better future seems unachievable and past failures remain the only vision for engaging the present. Perhaps the late twentieth-century advent of left melancholia follows not only the collapse of communist and anticolonial experiments and the rise of neoliberal capitalism as a global superpower, but also the sense that some visions of revolutionary freedom can be too unapproachable, too pure, too heroic. Perhaps paralysis or self-flagellation grows in response to a perception that heroism seems beyond the reach of ordinary people who are constantly doggie paddling just to keep their heads above water.[69] Yet the loss of a particular vision of freedom is not the same as a loss of possibility as such, and this book asks what is possible under relatively visionless conditions. In pushing freedom in different and sometimes unrecognizable directions, it asks: What transformative freedoms might develop, and develop fruitfully, without a galvanizing vision of alternative futures to guide them?

Although this book examines historical and contemporary practices of ugly freedom, its focus on derided and ambiguous acts is particularly geared toward present dilemmas, especially the conundrum of failure and impasse that make up a version of the current moment, in which promises of the American Dream and progress toward a cooperative world order that seemed achievable throughout the second half of the twentieth century are now widely seen to have slipped out of reach in the twenty-first. Part of the challenge, as differently articulated by Wendy Brown and Lauren Berlant, is that there seem to be few large-scale resources for envisioning desirable futures, as both liberal and left visions for a better world have seemingly dissipated but new large-scale visions have not yet arisen.[70] The promises that have organized liberal democracy in the past, including political progress, upward mobility, and respect for the hardworking congealed into "The American Dream," are not sustainable in our current political economic order, yet nothing else equally promising has taken their place at a societal-wide level. In addition, for Brown, left investments not only in liberal democracy but in a more radically economically and politically equitable future have also been weakened by a combination of neoliberal and authoritarian powers. Neoliberal capitalism's erosion of social support for the vulnerable, the ravages of climate change, and the struggle of Black, immigrant, gay, and feminist movements to secure full equality have dismantled many of the stories of a successful life centered around recognition and fairness. Both Brown and Berlant argue that instead of crafting large-scale new possibilities for a more vibrant and just future, people hold on to tattered promises in ways that become destructive and deflating.[71] The resurgence of white nationalism and violent xenophobia, as well as the presidency of Donald Trump, are just some of the reactionary formations arising out of these lost visions.

Ugly freedoms offer a different way of approaching these lost visions. Some of the subjects examined in this book have abandoned the tattered promises of liberal democratic capitalism altogether, even though their abandonment is unguided by a new, galvanizing social-political vision that explicates an ideal future. Their rejection of the present without an alternative vision for the future is not the demise of political action, however. Instead, it still cultivates viable and potent political acts, just in less expected registers of action. In their lack of grandeur, their drudgery, and their concessions, the practices of ugly freedom I highlight offer different ways of organizing power and community without requiring a clear vision of where they are headed. While some of the ugly freedoms I examine are guided by an explicit vision, whether that be collective mutuality for shared worldmaking, radical economic equality, the Black freedom dreams Robin Kelley details, or a rehabilitated climate, others are not. Without guiding visions they still craft practices of political freedom—and they show how a lack of vision is not the same as a lack of agency. Their practices take shape not as cruel optimism, nor as reactionary *ressentiment*, nor as mere survival, but as a disorganized combination of blithe rejection, mutual decision-making, filthy enmeshment, unruly collaboration, low-key subversion, unauthorized pleasure, and rootedness to place. They may be inchoate or fuzzy, incorporating a sense of a different and a more that is not fully articulable but still felt and desired—an expansive sense that something else is possible, even if it is yet to be carefully limned.

I am inspired by responses to an aligned debate about political vision in postcolonial scholarship, particularly in Caribbean studies, about how to manage struggles for freedom after emancipation from colonialism, once the end of colonization did not lead to a decolonized people governing their futures together but to a postcolonial order governed by predatory capitalism, racial hierarchy, and neglect. For some scholars, twentieth-century visions of decolonial freedom are no longer viable to shape political futures, yet nothing else has taken their place.[72] In response, Yarimar Bonilla reassesses the very measures used to determine the success and failure of political projects, arguing that nonsovereign and nonemancipated political actions, while seeming to carry the connotation of being nonmodern and unambitious, offer political options for thriving while still entangled in the constraints of political modernity shaped by colonialism.[73] She calls the projects she examines "disappointing," which does not mean that they have failed, only that they should be measured by different metrics of value that reveal hope for an as-yet experienced form of collective action. With an aligned focus but studying a different era, Natasha Lightfoot examines "the unfree nature of freedom" in the nineteenth-century post-emancipation Caribbean, studying how freed people navigated the challenges of an emancipation within diminished visions of possibility. She emphasizes modes of agency that may not offer desired or hoped-for visions of freedom but should still be categorized as free, and states: "the narrative of valiant and unified subaltern struggles against domination of the powerful, while recognizable and seductive, does not account for the range of acts chronicled in this book."[74] As Lightfoot and Bonilla might suggest, the second type of ugly freedoms I examine in the context of US politics are not unqualifiedly valiant and may not even be easily recognizable as freedom. They may not be satisfying, but they are significantly more prevalent than images of freedom as always ideal, ennobling, or epic. With a shift in perception they also cease to seem insignificant. They generate different responses, in which only recognizing valiant actions becomes a problem, fomenting either indifference to lived dilemmas or heroic fantasies of power that can seem unachievable.

The normative vision of "freedom" has dropped off the radar of some important twenty-first-century leftist projects, just as neoliberal and authoritarian forces try to cement freedom's meaning as individualist, free-market, entrepreneurial for the former, and both nationalist and imperialist for the latter.[75] While freedom can seem the sole purview of free marketeers, colonizers, and white supremacists, or alternately as a residue of past and outdated modes of emancipation that have failed, there are many ways that freedom takes shape before, through, and in opposition to those formations of power.[76] It is also common in parts of current humanistic inquiry to argue that agency is an unsophisticated or old-fashioned political category that ignores other ways of living in the world.[77] Of course, a sole focus on resistant individual agency as the form free subjectivity takes undermines more capacious histories of people's adjudications with domination. But challenging the hegemony of liberal visions of autonomous agency is different than collapsing all forms of agency into liberal individualism and then giving up agency as a value altogether. This is especially problematic at a moment when so many forms of dominating transnational power like global finance or fossil-fuel capital insist that resistance against them is impossible anyway. To demote freedom as a collective aspiration in favor of other values like belonging or capacity is not to be unburdened by freedom's legacy but to relinquish a vital resource to fight for a better world. Left-wing repudiations of freedom and agency surrender power and narrative to right-wing visions. As a rejoinder, I use the concept of ugly freedom to offer more textured examinations of agency and freedom, rather than ceding them either to the dustbin of history or to the limited imaginary of a sovereign subject and autonomous individual.

How we tell stories of freedom matters. If the freedom to participate in and help compose a world alongside others is premised on a subject that is not a masculinized heroic individual who self-wills his action, but a collaborative amalgamation of acts from many nonhuman and human creatures that form an agentic ecosystem, then different stories of freedom will emerge from that vision. If freedom is not a rational, self-interested personal choice made in a free market but the communal deployment of obdurate and turgid labor oriented by neighborhood care, then this might mobilize a more encompassing push against visions of marketized free action. If freedom is not a national proclamation that declares Black emancipation from slavery but rather Black freedom *from* national proclamations of formal liberty, then different politics emerge from that scenario. If freedom is not about self-making, noninterference, or sovereignty but about participatory composition, agonistic collaboration, and the hard, sometimes joyful, sometimes mundane, and sometimes ambivalent work of mutuality across difference, then an entirely different range of actions and actors come into view.[78] Tarrying with ugly freedom, not only in its first register of disavowed brutality but also in its second register of maligned action, showcases undervalued freedoms and instigates more possibilities for free action than those offered by stories of individual agency and nondomination. None of these practices of freedom claim moral purity, unimpeachable motivations, or ideal actions that gratify all those involved. None might be viable acts outside of the particular conditions they are embedded within, or even first-order desires within those conditions. None might even seem to be related to freedom traditionally conceived. But to tell stories about freedom that include these actions is to tell a different story about freedom's practice altogether, one exercised by many more of the inhabitants of our complex and violent world.

Racism, Settler Colonialism, Neoliberalism, Climate Change

Each chapter of *Ugly Freedoms* engages an iteration of ugly freedom and traces different relations of freedom in composite social, economic, and political conditions.[79] They all examine both forms of ugly freedom: both exercises of subjugation practiced as freedom, and unsettling or degraded actions that demonstrate free practice. In all of the chapters, visions of freedom are derived in part from canonical inheritances and practiced in the middle of disorganized, ambiguous, and often contradictory formations. The chapters also aim to challenge the linear temporalities unjustly imposed on the stories they tell: dispossession, slavery, neoliberalism, and climate change are understood falsely as premodern, past, present, and future events, though in truth they upend any kind of historical trajectory. These forms of ugly freedom swirl together at this very moment as the past, present, and future of freedom.

The analysis in each chapter revolves around contested objects—weird pop science, household dirt, distasteful films, putatively high-brow television shows, and pantry food staples. I also include multimedia artworks displayed to be seen, smelled, and experienced sensorially, all of which aim to create discomfort in viewers, and none of which are conventionally pleasing or conforming to aesthetic standards of beauty. Each object, as I study it, confronts freedom as a problem. And each also opens possibilities for imagining different worlds of possibility, and for thwarting standardized relations of power out of which new visions of freedom are tested, practiced, or created in action. Many might not seem traditional objects or sites for political theorizing, or even worthy of study, but I find productive engagement with objects deemed unworthy for contemplation, unrecognized as political, or seeming to desecrate freedom's hallowed ground. The works I choose are thus typically interpreted as offering no vision for freedom, or offensive visions of unfreedom, or experiences that seem too crass to even qualify for freedom's practice. Yet it is precisely their compromised and problematic status that keeps them productive and open for both readings of ugly freedom.

Chapter 1, "White and Deadly: Sugar and the Sweet Taste of Freedom," shows the historical imbrication of the three ugly freedoms I examine most in the book, white supremacy, neoliberal capitalism, and climate change, to note their germination in patriarchal systems of settler colonialism. I focus on a common pantry food staple connected to childhood innocence and pleasure—sugar—which might seem irrelevant to freedom's practice. Yet sugar offers a material and gustatory archive of freedom's violent practices, and it reveals how some US practices of race-making and freedom-making developed in the sugar plantations of the Caribbean, especially Barbados. Alongside early American figures of freedom like the self-sufficient yeoman farmer of Jeffersonian ideals, and the burly frontiersman single-handedly subduing the wild, another key figure of US freedom is the Barbados sugar plantation owner, a pioneering figure in the history of slavery and freedom whose entrepreneurial and ruthless power quickly traveled to American colonies. While the influence of the Barbadian sugar master is ignored or disavowed in histories of freedom, this figure shaped liberal futures through both practices of profitmaking and political theories of individual freedom, especially in John Locke's contribution to the *Fundamental Constitutions of Carolina*, which was created to bring Barbadian practices to North America. I examine current reverberations of sugar and modern freedom by turning to the contemporary artist Kara Walker's massive sugar sculpture, *A Subtlety, Or the Marvelous Sugar Baby*, which interrogates the ugly freedoms of sugar plantation slavery through a bittersweet sensorial aesthetics. The Marvelous Sugar Baby is birthed by the history of sugar plantation mastery but also showcases different freedoms that overpower the sugar plantation's reach. Its challenging bodily openness offers freedom untethered to slavery, pleasures untethered to racial and sexual subjugation, agency untethered to the individual, land untethered to private property, and the sweetness of liberty untethered to the horrific predations of sugar.

The following chapters disarticulate the ugly freedoms examined in chapter 1 to focus on their independent dynamics. Chapter 2, "Tragedies of Emancipation: Freedom, Sex, and Theft after Slavery," examines the ugly freedoms of slavery, racism, and Black oppression as they take shape in American narratives of slave emancipation. This chapter engages a body of scholarship in Black and postcolonial thought that I call "tragedies of emancipation," which includes seminal work by Orlando Patterson, Saidiya Hartman, and David Scott, that interprets emancipations as tragedies and attends to the unfreedoms that remain after and through slave emancipation. They ask not merely what freedom has enabled but what it has wrought, viewing emancipation events less as breaks from the past and more as shifts in the racial logics of antiblack exploitation. This chapter accepts and also presses beyond tragedies of emancipation. Its contested object is the controversial film *Manderlay* (dir. Lars von Trier, 2005), which depicts a slave plantation still operating in the US South seventy years after emancipation. On the one hand, the movie is considered by many critics a ghastly spectacle of racism. On the other hand, it has become a film in the archive of Afropessimism, as it can be read to articulate antiblackness as perpetual enslavement.[80] *Manderlay* is doing something different than either of these claims, as it depicts actions that shift the tragedy of emancipation to imagine the end of white supremacy and antiblack domination. These actions are not typical visions of emancipation, however, and might at first even seem to be their opposite. They are easily overlooked because they are small-scale, morally ambiguous, and sometimes violent performances of racialized freedom that trade on racial stereotypes of theft, sexual excess, and ignorance in order to fight for emancipation distinct from either the control of the nation-state or the abstractions of universal personhood. The freedoms they demonstrate reject possession as the hallowed ground of freedom. And they challenge the belief that Black emancipation demands the moral purity of virtuous Black actors for its practice, and for that reason are easily overlooked or derided as self-defeating and shameful. *Manderlay* suggests that there are more options than fated tragedy, ontological pessimism, or revolutionary romance for challenging white supremacy—though they may bear little resemblance to practices of freedom envisioned in the past.

The third chapter, "Thwarting Neoliberalism: Boredom, Dysfunction, and Other Visionless Challenges," examines neoliberal freedom in contemporary capitalism, noting how a range of recent political-economic developments pushing the privatization of public life, defunded social services, wealth accumulation by the powerful, and securitization of the poor through heightened police power and mass incarceration, all tender a widespread social vision in which money, rather than people, must be free. Yet for all their profound and brutal effects, neoliberal developments are weaker than they sometimes appear. Many challenges to them go unnoticed because they do not take shape as revolutionary acts of resistance, widespread protest tactics, or multilateral governing possibilities. Instead, they look like bureaucratic ineptitude, outdated technology, boredom, cheating, bleak statistical measurements, neighborhood pranks, and even competing neoliberal policies. The critically celebrated and deeply problematic television drama about urban life in Baltimore, *The Wire*, contains an archive of these challenges to neoliberal freedom. They are not robust or satisfying but rather mundane and disappointing, and thus not typically counted as available forces to confront neoliberal power. This chapter uses *The Wire* to ask: What challenges to neoliberalism are fomented by dreary institutions and defunded neighborhoods, and without compelling alternative visions of freedom?

The final chapter, "Freedom as Climate Destruction: Guts, Dust, and Toxins in an Era of Consumptive Sovereignty," argues that the ideal of freedom as it is often understood in modern Euro-American politics—encompassing control over nature, individual sovereignty, human exceptionalism, uncoerced will, and private ownership—is partly accountable for the geological upheaval and toxic pollution of climate change. This version of freedom envisions nature to be separate from the individual and composed of inert objects available for exploitation, so that control of nature becomes an indication of personal sovereignty, and collective action to care for the earth seems a coercive limit on individual agency. Different stories of freedom and subjectivity that tarry in filth and dirt can help make the vast actions required for long-term planetary survival in the face of rapid climate change come to seem both necessary and desirable. Counterstories of freedom as nonsovereign, multispecies, compositional, agonistic, and symbiotic between and within creatures both challenge many of the constituting categories of modern freedom (including individual, will, property, and reason) and ground alternative practices of freedom that could contribute to, not decimate, the ongoing livability of the planet.

This final chapter offers three alternative visions of free political subjectivity that muddle boundaries between humans and the natural world: they are found in the dank register of human guts, in the dirty register of household dust and shed skin, and in the geochemical registers of preplanetary gases and synthetic toxins, sites rarely explored for their political visions let alone for nurturing the hallowed practice of freedom. Yet each generates alternate representations of political agency, collective action, and freedom. Drawing inspiration from a combination of indigenous political thought, feminist science studies, and queer theories of the inhuman, these visions suggest that each individual and the land understood to be "private property" are made up of more-than-human ecosystems intertwined with nonliving matter, in which intimate material is constantly transformed into other creatures. They claim that the "self-determining individual" is an assemblage of microbes, stardust, feces from other humans, synthetic toxins, aerosolized pavement, and detritus constituted in inextricable webs of collective dependence. They incorporate actants from the microscopic to the cosmic to suggest that freedoms traverse everyday practices of interdependence across the widest of scales, and undo violent divides between private/public, sovereign/powerless, human/nonhuman, self/other. Freedom thus shifts within interpretations of bodies as reciprocal assemblages that together compose worlds at a visceral level—literally in the guts, in the blood, and at the boundary of skin. Ending with Lebanese artist Dalia Baassiri's *The Dust Series*, a set of multimedia paintings composed of dust and shed skin, I suggest that alternative ways of acting with others, connected by multispecies and multimatter bodies often consigned to the gross, impossible, and unfree, are effusing with possibility for practicing a freedom premised on connectedness, nonhierarchy, and place-based rehabilitation. In *The Dust Series*, disgust and ugliness support the collective and equal flourishing of life and land.

Together, all of the chapters engage with land as a practice, place, and site for freedom. They invest in, and do not take flight from, connection to place. Whether it is monoculture Barbadian sugar plantations in chapter 1, southern US agricultural farmland in chapter 2, defunded city neighborhoods in Baltimore in chapter 3, or desiccated California droughtscapes and dusty Beirut windowsills in chapter 4, each chapter examines forms of freedom that commit to rehabilitating the broken physical world they call home. In this they demonstrate a somewhat different type of freedom than *marronage*, a project of flight from racial oppression, a freedom that entails escape from systems of enslavement.[81] The ugly freedoms I elucidate are in many ways aligned with and supportive of this refusal, but they operate with a different relationship to movement and land. Rather than flight as their signature movement of freedom, the ugly freedoms I embrace in this book remain connected to place as a site of nourishment and community, even when that place has been a source of domination and dispossession, and they fight for its care. Inspired by indigenous demands to care for land and acknowledge interrelated social connections, they aim to rehabilitate the fecundity of land and neighborhood from the destructive practices of the plantation, dispossession, neoliberalism, and climate change. Their practices of freedom emphasize unruly yet collaborative practices of worldmaking that are less about finding refuge than about cultivating worlds by living and flourishing together.

In an era in which the world is burning and neoliberalism plus climate change are together rapidly destroying the habitats of life across the world—whether for generic glass skyscrapers that decimate poor neighborhoods to build investment properties for the global elite, or chemical factories that poison ecosystems—this commitment to the land is specifically connected to twenty-first-century problematics in which there is no place to escape or find refuge, elite fantasies of secret bunkers or a Mars colony notwithstanding. It entails a full rejection of the thoughtless trashing of the earth and its inhabitants. These practices fight for relationships to others and to the land that sustain the long-term viability of our shared world, even amid spaces discarded as worthless. They enact freedoms that do not rely on others to exclude or oppose, that build from social interdependence rather than its destruction, that cultivate shared and equal worldmaking to rejuvenate our stressed planet, and that could help stop the devastation that occurs under freedom's mantle before the world goes up in flames.

white and deadly   1

Sugar and the Sweet Taste of Freedom

Most men today cannot conceive of a freedom that does not involve
somebody's slavery. They do not want equality because the thrill of
their happiness comes from having things that others have not.
—W. E. B. DU BOIS, *Darkwater*

What is it about icing that links it to joy, to empire and excess and
the sovereign tongue?
—LAUREN BERLANT AND KATHLEEN STEWART, *The Hundreds*

THE STORY OF MODERN FREEDOM is often recounted as the progress of political ideals of individual liberty, rule of law, and consent. Freedom initially
spread from Enlightenment centers in Europe, to the United States, and then
to the rest of the globe. It transformed civilization from barbarity to reason,
as it shifted political regimes from absolute monarchy to universal suffrage
and equality before the law. This chapter retells the story of modern freedom through the commodity of sugar, which is tied to centuries of brutality,
indigenous dispossession, environmental destruction, and racial hierarchy.
Sugar might seem nonpolitical: it is a delicious treat, available anytime, that
satisfies taste buds across the world. It is a source of immediate pleasure, delightful to children and adults alike. Yet sugar uniquely makes palpable, and

palatable, the interconnections between stated values of modern freedom, including individual personhood, self-rule, free trade, and private property, with the ugly freedoms I explore in this book: enslavement, settler colonialism, climate change, patriarchy, and economic inequality. A focus on sugar offers both a challenging story of freedom and a gustatory archive of ugly freedoms that cascade into the present.

The history and production of sugar is brutally violent, as scholars of Caribbean history, colonialism, and Africana studies have long detailed, yet this violence also served as fertile ground for political theories of freedom influential in liberal democratic thought. Theories of liberty as individual self-possession, of legitimate government as based in consent, of self-rule as a rejection of state tyranny, and of economic freedom as uncoerced labor and trade have links to the production of sugar. The study of freedom through the material of sugar takes inspiration from Lisa Lowe's argument that the complex and contradictory inheritance of liberal freedom is fruitfully explored through material commodities and aesthetic objects, as they can sometimes best reveal the interconnections of European wealth and practices of self-rule with African enslavement, North and South American indigenous dispossession, and Asian labor and imperial governance. Lowe argues that this transcontinental history of liberalism chronicles a more complex and insidious account than the story of freedom outlined above. It is often known but "unthought" in liberal political discourse, yet material and aesthetic objects that circulate globally contain this account and reveal its details.[1] In focusing on sugar, I am interested, like Lowe, in how tactile material or seemingly irrelevant "texts" offer complex theories of freedom, or offer new perspectives on settled stories of liberal progress.[2] Sugar encompasses the unthought register of modern freedom; it links individual freedom to plantation mastery, self-rule to enslavement, and independence to environmental destruction. It is the sweetest object of ugly freedom.

Cuban artist Maria Magdalena Campos-Pons's multimedia artwork *Sugar/Bittersweet* uses sugar to render visible these ugly freedoms.[3] She creates a Caribbean sugar field using African spears as cane, recalling the geographical origins of sugarcane laborers and the violence that enslaved them. Chinese weights to measure the harvest surround the spears, recalling the indentured laborers from Asia positioned to mediate between freed Blacks and white landowners (figure 1.1). Chinese and African wooden stools center the cane, and refer to the transcontinental intermixing of peoples in the cane fields. Stacks of raw sugar confections of varying levels of refinement symbolize both the different peoples involved in its trade and the plantations' racialized

1.1 Maria Magdalena Campos-Pons, *Sugar/Bittersweet* (2010).

hierarchies, in which sugar is more pure, prized, and valuable the whiter and more refined its texture.[4] These stacks in turn are pierced by the spears, symbolizing the inseparability of sweetness and violence, as well as the global upheavals that enabled sugarcane production to dominate Cuba. Lowe argues that *Sugar/Bittersweet* reveals a violent history of liberalism that entails both Cuban sugar and the transcontinental shifts of labor, people, and industries that make up a circuit of liberal modernity. Indeed, this history is brought into the present as the room that houses the artwork of *Sugar/Bittersweet* visually recapitulates this original colonial dispossession. The art objects are far removed from the lands that generated them, dislocated from sustaining social relations, and replanted in a geometric grid in an antiseptic art space, connected only as cogs in the sugar production process.

This story told about sugar in *Sugar/Bittersweet* is also a story of *freedom*, though it may not appear so at first. Yet the artwork might just as accurately be titled *Liberty* as *Sugar/Bittersweet*, so intertwined and co-constitutive are their historical trajectories. The violent sugar industry throughout the Caribbean unfolded within familiar practices of modern freedom, including the following:

1   The pursuit of independence through landowning and economic prosperity

2 Individual freedom to acquire private property through agricultural development on occupied but uncultivated land
3 Self-rule in colonies, including local autonomy to make governing decisions rather than being subjected to a distant monarch's declarations
4 The right of personal authority over one's property—including enslaved people
5 The capacity to spread freedom by imposing dictatorial norms on non-European peoples who do not (yet) value private property and individuality
6 The control and subordination of nature for profitable extraction
7 The right to engage in free trade and participate in international markets

Sugar/Bittersweet depicts the sugar plantation as a pioneering scene of brutal domination and dispossession, as well as an outgrowth of owners' particular practices of freedom. For the sugar planter, freedom from necessity, freedom to own land, freedom to trade, and freedom of economic independence were gained on the backs of those forced to supply necessities and relinquish land: those forced into dependence. The practice of freedom in this context *requires* theft and domination. Freedom shifts in relation to sugar; it becomes not only a European-originating political ideal of the individual protected from and by state power, but also a practice that enables and sustains colonization, slavery, and economic exploitation.[5]

Sugar/Bittersweet suggests that the story of freedom is not merely a ruse to conceal enslavement and domination. Instead, it suggests that *practices of modern freedom include enslavement and dispossession.* On the sugar plantation, planters' individual freedom and autonomy take shape through slavery and dispossession. The wealth generated by Caribbean sugar plantations enabled Euro-American experiments with democracy and self-rule, and those very practices of self-rule and independence entailed domination over others. The title of Alejandro de la Fuente's curatorial notes for *Sugar/Bittersweet* gestures to this: "On Sugar, Slavery, and the Pursuit of (Cuban) Happiness" offers a biting inverse of both John Locke's and the Declaration of Independence's story of emancipation from tyranny, suggesting that modern freedom's exercise emanates in part from the bitter violence of sugar.[6] *Sugar/Bittersweet* reveals this known but unthought aspect of modern freedom—freedom is not the antithesis of the sugar plantation, but encompasses the sugar plantation. The artwork also shows how different ugly freedoms like racism, economic exploitation, and environmental destruction are imbricated with one another, which I examine here before separating them out for closer analysis in other chapters. Achille Mbembe has argued that the antebellum United States cultivated a "proslavery democracy" out of antiblack racism; here, on the Caribbean sugar plantation, we see an aligned development of what I would call a proslavery freedom.[7]

Caribbean sugar plantations are a key site for studying the simultaneous development of racial slavery, indigenous dispossession, and modern liberal freedom. Sugar was different from other New World agricultural commodities from the start. It required larger plots of land and significantly more capital investment than tobacco or cotton. Cultivating sugar, as opposed to other crops, demanded more of everything: more money, more labor, more land, more inputs like water and energy. It was also the most profitable of all New World commodities; indeed it was the first crop to render colonization profitable. And its production was uniquely destructive to the land, destroying more native landscapes than all other crops. Sugar was also highly destructive to people; the first legal categories instantiating enslavement as a perpetual, lifetime condition for Blacks came from sugar plantation societies. C. L. R. James argued that many modern social and economic practices originate in the Caribbean, and we could say the same for practices of freedom.[8]

The foremost place for understanding the initial development of freedom through sugar is the Caribbean island of Barbados. Barbados was the first English colony to successfully cultivate and market sugar, and it was the most important colony for the early expansion of British Empire.[9] Indeed, its success with sugar created the first large plantations and the first Black slave society in the world.[10] In emphasizing the role of sugar in the construction and practice of modern freedom, this chapter traces the influence of the Barbadian sugar plantation on liberal democratic theories of freedom, especially upon liberalism's foundational early theorist, John Locke. Barbados's formative status is well studied in histories of slavery and the plantation but ignored both in political histories of self-rule and in political theories of modern freedom. Like sugar, Barbados is virtually absent from the study of Western freedom. Yet many key practices of modernity developed in Barbados, as historian Richard Sheridan explicates: its landowners were the first to develop enslavement as a mass labor practice, the first to create large-scale plantations, the first to invent a vast monoculture regime for international markets, and it was the first settlement to have a self-governing political system dominated by a few plantation owners.[11] Locke knew all of this well and encouraged it as England's Secretary to the Council of Trade and Plantations. The many new practices generated on Barbados deserve sustained attention for understanding modern Anglo-American conceptualizations of freedom, as they not only influenced Locke but more broadly traveled across the New World, especially to North American colonies. Many key practices of race-making and freedom-making in the United States were transplanted from the sugar plantations of Barbados.

The importance of Barbados to the history of liberal freedom may be comparable with that of England, France, and the North American colonies, or at least deserves more sustained scholarly focus in political theory.[12] The Barbadian sugar master is a key figure of modern freedom. He invented the gang-style system of mass slavery that became the backbone for the next two hundred years of enslavement in the Americas. He also created the first slave code in the English-speaking world, which was later copied in North American colonies. He built profit and pleasure on the lifelong domination of other humans in producing sugar for international markets. Barbadian sugar plantation masters were, at the same time, free and independent subjects who organized local self-rule against the colonial metropole, prioritized independence and self-interest in juridical relations, and developed an island-wide ethos of entrepreneurialism. The Barbados sugar plantation master is a pioneer figure rather than an exception, innovating modern freedoms shared and revised as they circulated in the New World. The freedom of the Barbadian sugar master, composed of local autonomy, democratic rule among a restricted citizenry, systemic and legal antiblack racism, unacknowledged indigenous dispossession, and the wholesale destruction of ecosystems for short-term prosperity, would become a pattern for many modern freedoms.

The innovations of the Barbadian sugar plantation master were translated directly to the North American colonies, their point of insertion being Carolina. Carolina was intentionally created to bring highly profitable Barbadian practices of slavery to North America. More than cotton or tobacco, the plantation crops most studied in the history of North American slavery, a focus on sugar shows how American freedoms emerged beyond North American and European influences; they must include Caribbean innovations. The Carolina colony was founded by successful Barbadian plantation masters looking to expand their territory and duplicate their distinctive model of production. As historian Betty Wood describes it, Carolina "was as much a Barbadian as it was an English creation."[13] Often forgotten today, Barbadian sugar plantation mastery influenced the shape of ugly freedom in Carolina, which eventually extended throughout the United States. Unsurprisingly, Americans have long preferred to imagine the archetypes of their freedom differently: the self-sufficient yeoman farmer, the sturdy frontiersman, or the resistant taxpaying colonial subject who yearns for independence from the British Crown. If Americans continue to venerate the figure of the self-sufficient Virginia farmer, then the Barbadian sugar master is American freedom's unthought forebear.

In this chapter, I first examine the broad history of sugar in the early British Empire to retrace early connections among freedom, enslavement, settler colonialism, and capitalism. I then narrow my focus to Barbados and Carolina to highlight how nascent practices of liberal freedom particularly influential in the United States developed there, and how they also place John Locke's writings on freedom in a new light. Sugar helps to show how what might appear to be incompatible claims in Locke's work—which supports both individual sovereignty and native dispossession, both natural equality and enslavement—cohere in a vision of freedom as the New World sugar plantation owner. I conclude by turning to Kara Walker's thirty-five-foot sugar sculpture, *A Subtlety, Or the Marvelous Sugar Baby* (2014), to bring the ugly freedoms of sugar dynamics into present aesthetics. The Marvelous Sugar Baby discloses more of the "unthought known" connections between ugly freedoms and sugar plantation slavery through a bittersweet sensorial experience. The piece addresses both forms of ugly freedom—both freedoms practiced as subjugation and freedoms found in practices otherwise denigrated as useless or unfree. The Marvelous Sugar Baby emerges out of slave plantation mastery, but also embodies different productive practices of freedom. These are freedoms that are not categorized by self-ownership and self-mastery—ideals still trapped in a sugar plantation dynamic in which mastery, possession, and property are the forms freedom takes.[14] Instead, the figure of the sugar baby invites viewers to envision (and smell) a freedom divested from control, mastery, and possession altogether. It is literally overwhelming to process, because it intimates that freedom is significantly larger than individual bodies but committed to individual flourishing, and practiced by diverse and erotic solidarities connected across geographical space and historical time. If sugar's delight on the tongue overpowers other critical sensations to render its ugly freedoms palatable, the Marvelous Sugar Baby catalyzes different sensorial registers of smell and sight to interpret freedom differently. The freedoms emerging from the Marvelous Sugar Baby, envisioned in both her sugared labia and formidable figuration, advocate not the pleasures of domination or industrialized sweetness but the pleasures and challenges of radical openness in composing a shared world alongside diverse others. It is a freedom built of sugar that strips the Barbadian plantation master of his reach.

Sugar and Freedom in the New World

Sugar interlinked with modern freedom after it arrived in Western Europe around 1400 via the Pacific Islands and Middle East, and was quickly adopted by wealthy royal households on account of the exquisite gustatory pleasures it provided. Sugar's rarity and enormous expense made it an emblem of power, status, and majesty in Europe.[15] This potent substance was typically boiled and carved into elaborate displays or "subtleties," which portrayed animals, flora, biblical scenes, genitalia, and other spectacular decorations that would be displayed during court feasts and royal celebrations. Sugar subtleties were especially desirable for marking enthronings, weddings, and military victories. One of Henry VIII's subtleties depicted a forest with each animal embellished with the king's coat of arms. He also once held a large banquet that centered around a sugared re-creation of a dungeon, a particularly vivid combination of sugar and sovereignty.[16]

By the eighteenth century this once royal preserve had become available worldwide for consumption by common people, but the democratization of sugar was only made possible by the advent of plantation slavery and European settler colonialism in the Caribbean Islands.[17] Sugar and New World settler colonialism were entangled from the outset. Before his voyages to the New World, Christopher Columbus had worked for a company that dealt in sugar, and he knew its commercial potential. In scouting the Caribbean islands, he assessed their potential for sugar production, and he brought the first sugar cuttings to the New World on only his second voyage in 1493.[18] Along with firepower and weaponry, sugar was a key resource in colonizing the New World.[19] Having decimated indigenous populations in murderous conquest raids and metals mining, settlers were growing the first profitable sugarcane on Hispaniola by 1509, and by the 1650s the cultivation of sugar in the Caribbean was arguably the most profitable industry in the world.[20]

The English began to colonize the Caribbean in the early 1600s, roughly a century after the Spanish and Portuguese, but they became the largest global producers of sugar by the end of the century. Initially the English experimented with diverse crops in attempts to grow foodstuffs and commodities for profit. Once they realized the profit potential of sugar, everything changed.[21] Sugar production was notoriously difficult. It needed more people, more land, more water, and more time than any other crop, and it required many laborers to coordinate their actions over many precise steps. Sugar processing demanded a fourteen-month cane growing cycle, then entailed cutting the cane, crushing and juicing it, boiling it, and skimming impurities, all in a tight timeframe; all were difficult and exhausting practices.[22] From the start sugar required more investment capital than other crops, as it needed multiple buildings and material to get off the ground, including a sugar mill, huge pots for boiling, tubes for transferring liquid in various stages, vast tracts of land for the sugarcane, and separate houses for milling and curing.[23] Sugarcane was also the most dangerous commodity of all the New World crops, as laborers would routinely get infections while tending the sharp cane spears, lose limbs in sugar mill machines, or fall into boiling vats of sugar.

Laborers on sugar plantations were primarily indentured and enslaved since the work was so difficult and dangerous that most people would only undertake it when coerced. Alongside indentured servants, usually Irish or English, the settlers often enslaved native people. When they refused enslavement by this system and fled, or were murdered, and when European indentured laborers also would not come to the Caribbean because the labor was too taxing, the settlers began to import enslaved Africans to make up the labor shortage.[24] With the advent of gang-style slavery, production dramatically increased, and the consumption of Caribbean sugar in European markets rose twentyfold from the late seventeenth to the late eighteenth century.[25]

Sugar by many accounts, including Sidney Mintz's formative history, was the specific commodity that gave impetus to the system of mass plantation slavery.[26] Enslaved Africans were brought by the millions to New World colonies to produce sugar, and the cost of producing sugar quickly fell, not because of increased productivity or new time-saving methods, but solely because of mass unpaid slave labor. The use of enslaved people on sugar plantations spread so quickly that their number doubled every few years.[27] Sugar plantations at scale consumed vast reserves of free labor and land. Land was prepared for mass cane growth using slash-and-burn methods that eradicated the local ecology, transforming tropical rainforests into monoculture plots. Because it consumed so much land so quickly, sugar was the most destructive crop introduced in the New World. Sugar, an unnecessary food additive, was the most damaging and most valuable commodity in world trade by the eighteenth century.[28]

Many scholars agree with the argument of Eric Williams's *Capitalism and Slavery* that the plantation system is the origin of capitalist industry, but it is important to note that Williams argues it is specifically the sugar plantation that served as capitalism's foundation.[29] Capitalism's industrial prototypes were, among other things, found in the repetitive and coordinated labor of the sugarcane fields. Industrial factories were patterned on their routinization and alienation, in which labor only worked on a coordinated mass scale, was broken down into parts, and was disconnected from the final product.[30] The work was brutal and presupposed the disposability of laborers, who often died within a few years of being kidnapped to work on sugar plantations, only to be replaced. In engendering the plantation system, English sugar planters in pursuit of profit in the British West Indies "created one of the harshest systems of servitude in Western History."[31] As James argues in *The Black Jacobins*, "Wherever the sugar plantation and slavery existed, they imposed a pattern. It is an original pattern, not European, not African, nor a part of the American main, not native in any conceivable sense of that word, but West Indian, sui generis, with no parallel anywhere else."[32] The sugar plantation in the West Indies invented a new type of social and economic power, generating huge profits for a few families through standardized labor production that relied on both stolen indigenous land and the enslavement of millions of Africans to produce profits in transcontinental trade markets.

As depicted in Campos-Pons's artwork, sugarcane fields replaced wild lands with geometric monoculture plots, and the ecological destruction they wrought paralleled the destruction of indigenous social worlds. The sugar plantation soon generated some of the most widespread destruction of native ecosystems the world had yet seen, exchanging them for nonnative monocultures that colonized the land's resources for life. Anna Tsing describes the process clearly: "exterminate local people and plants; prepare now-empty, unclaimed land; and bring in exotic and isolated labor and crops for production."[33] Even the newly planted sugarcane stalks were uniformly homogeneous. Each cane stalk was a clone of all others, so successful plantations did not even require intraspecies sugarcane diversity; planters would simply stick new sugar cuttings derived from old ones into the ground in regularly spaced intervals. The sugar plantation thus destroyed wide swaths of complex biodiverse ecosystems and replaced them with uniform monocrops. Richard Dunn called it "murdering the soil for a few quick crops and then moving along."[34] Sugar plantations were an early experiment in what Macarena Gómez-Barris identifies as extractive zones, material changes in the land resulting from resource extraction and soil depletion that violently reorganize social and ecological life.[35]

This world-historic destruction impelled by sugar production created what Donna Haraway has termed the "plantationocene," the groundwork for existing forms of climate violence that destroy functional ecosystems through standardized, abstract labor with no sustaining interspecies relations: a "devastating transformation of diverse kinds of human tended farms, pastures, and forests into extractive and enclosed plantations, relying on slave labor and other forms of exploited, alienated, and usually spatially transported labor."[36] The plantationocene was predicated on destroying indigenous land relationships and life worlds, in which, as indigenous scholars Robin Wall Kimmerer, Glen Coulthard, and Leanne Betasamosake Simpson argue, the land was not viewed as an inert resource for the extraction of profit but as part of a mutually sustaining relationship bred from people's obligations to land, animals, trees, water, and other people—relationships that generated reciprocal obligations from the land to support living creatures over many generations.[37] The plantationocene instantiated a structure of dispossession that uprooted that view and generated a new relationship to land as one not of interdependence but control, not of sustenance but exploitation. The plantationocene thus entwined the ugly freedoms of indigenous dispossession, antiblack domination, economic exploitation, and climate destruction to generate financial prosperity and individual liberty for European sugar plantation masters settled in the Caribbean and those across the globe who provided the investment capital.

Part of the novelty of the sugar plantation was the sheer size and scale of it. W. E. B. Du Bois succinctly observed, "The using of men for the benefit of masters is no new invention of modern Europe, it is quite as old as the world. But Europe proposed to apply it on a scale and with an elaborateness of detail of which no former world had ever dreamed. The imperial width of the thing—the heaven defying audacity—marks its modern newness."[38] The system of mass enslavement combined breathtaking scale of "imperial width" with minute detail of labor process micromanagement to produce a new mass commodity for an emergent global market. Some scholars even argue that the taste for sugar, rather than a preexisting or timeless craving that profiteers came to satisfy, is itself learned, cultivated, and created out of the mass plantation production of sugar. "An entirely new taste for sweetness manifested itself" that was not an innate desire for blasting sweetness waiting to be satisfied, but rather a new taste, generated into being out of sugar's mass availability.[39] The desire for sugar thus came about as a geopolitical-economic effect. The popular craving for sugar is arguably an effect of the plantationocene.

Sugar production changed political systems to authorize ongoing slave labor, and it did so through the colonies' self-rule and local autonomy. Many colonies that supported sugar plantations were proprietary, so they were not funded by the Crown but by the individual proprietors who received the charter for the land; proprietary colonies were understood as private investments created for the pursuit of profit. They were given more autonomy than elites on the English mainland and eventually were able to craft laws and policies created by and for the landholders in the colonies.[40] Laws created on many proprietary Caribbean colonies were organized by sugar processing and plantation life, including legal structures protecting private property and enslavement.[41] Local laws began to regulate the lives of free people and enslaved people in fundamental ways, dividing them into separate legal classes in which white landowning settlers participated in representative governance, white servants had some rights but no representation, and enslaved people were categorized as chattel economically, yet responsible and thus culpable legally.[42] By the late 1600s, racialized slavery was practiced on many colonized islands in the British West Indies such that only indigenous people and Africans could be enslaved; all other laboring classes were indentured servants or tenant farmers and thus not property.[43] As Sylvia Wynter describes it, "the peoples of the militarily appropriated New World territories (i.e., Indians), as well as the enslaved peoples of Black Africa (i.e., Negroes) were made to reoccupy the matrix slot of otherness—to be made into the physical referent of the idea of the 'irrational/subrational human other.'"[44] This irrational-subrational other became the modern vision of unfreedom, and subduing the other or harnessing its land and labor became part of the practice of freedom.

While Mintz and Williams have argued sugar reveals how capitalism was tied up with colonialism and slavery from the start, sugar also shows how *freedom* was tied to colonialism and slavery from the start. To be free in the British West Indies meant to have economic independence and to possess a plantation, which qualified one to participate in the collective freedom of self-rule. Freedom was gained in the West Indies through possession of other persons, and acquisition of land for agricultural profit-generation.[45] Owning land (which in the New World was always appropriated) and controlling others' labor meant that one did not labor for others and was not dependent on waged labor, and therefore self-reliant.[46] Self-reliance meant the capacity to harness the labor of others, to have others do the work of sustenance. In this sense freedom on the sugar plantation highlights the necropolitics of modern freedom; for Mbembe, necropolitics "means the capacity to define who matters and who does not, who is disposable and who is not"—a dynamic of sovereign power that accurately describes freedom as possessing and disposing others' labor and lives.[47]

Freedom for the sugar plantation owner entailed personal control over many aspects of one's life, not only control over labor, as freedom was more commonly defined in the English metropole at that time.[48] It also required governmental noninterference inside plantations, and it meant that neither the Crown nor local law could dictate policies for regulating the master's use of slaves. Whereas philosophical distinctions between freedom as noncoercion and freedom as self-rule are important and reflect different historical conditions of labor and political autonomy in different places like the colonies or the mainland of England, those concepts are more muddled and contiguous in practice, especially on the sugar plantation where they were practiced simultaneously by landowners. The sugar plantation influenced life in England too, of course, as sugar generated enormous wealth and prosperity for English people in England, vitalized English workers who consumed it for energy to work, and fueled an English middle class ready to experiment with parliamentary power, one of whom was John Locke.[49] I next turn to sugar's specific developments in Barbados, its influence on Locke, and its travels to Carolina.

Sugar Plantation Freedom: Locke, Barbados, Carolina

The British colony island of Barbados, and its influence in the North American colony of Carolina, are key to understanding sugar's contributions to modern freedom. Barbados was the first polity in the English-speaking world to place racial hierarchies into law; one of the first sites of colonial self-rule as autonomous local governance; one of the first places to instantiate limited government control over household property; and a leader in the mass ecological destruction that would ground extractive capitalism. The innovations of the Barbadian plantation master traveled to other British colonies, especially Carolina, and also played a role in John Locke's analyses of freedom. They influenced a new vision of modern freedom that combined aspects of self-rule, private property, racial domination, entrepreneurialism, settler colonialism, and patriarchal mastery, all of which grew in the social world supporting and extending sugar production.

BARBADIAN SUGAR PLANTER FREEDOM

When English settlers first arrived in 1627, Barbados was uninhabited land. The indigenous Taino and Kalinago inhabitants had been routed by Spanish slave-raiding missions before the English arrived.[50] Barbados in this sense was pre-dispossessed. The English settlers, by and large, were thus spared the violence of conquest and dispossession, which likely helped facilitate Anglo-American political fantasies of dispossession as a natural process, both necessary and easily subsumed by myths of the New World as empty of inhabitants.

It made the dispossession of Barbados invisible, both physically and ideologically, just like the vacant places later imagined in Locke's *Two Treatises of Government*. Barbados propelled a sense of the New World as a vacuum domicilium, a "wasteland" just waiting for industrious individuals with the right methods of cultivation to extract profit and make the land useful.

By the 1640s, only twenty years after settlement, this small island, only fourteen miles by twenty-one miles, was already the most densely populated English-speaking settlement in the world outside London. By the 1660s Barbados had its "sugar revolution" and became the most productive and profit-generating sugar plantation society in the world.[51] Sugar from Barbados was more valuable than the exports of all other crops in the English empire combined.[52] Many of the innovations in sugar production detailed in the previous section originated in Barbados and in the Barbadian plantation master's experiments with cultivation and processing. In addition to these industrial innovations, as early as 1639 the Barbadian colonists had developed a burgeoning system for self-rule by establishing a House of Assembly, one of the first parliamentary democracies in the New World with a measure of autonomy from the Crown.[53] By 1650s the island was run by larger planters who extended this experiment in self-rule by creating their own local laws to support their enterprise in sugar. Barbados's governing practices rose out of the creation and development of the sugar plantation. Its labor organization, profit generation, crop management, market reach independent of the Crown, rule without significant input from England, and simultaneous development of race and racism into law, all stemmed from a social world generated in large part through sugar.

By design, the local government established on Barbados did not regulate or manage the internal workings of plantations, so planters had almost unchecked power to govern the lives of servants and slaves. As early as 1630, plantation owners expected to govern their households without any interference.[54] Enslavers could treat laborers as they chose, dispense justice, regulate food and allowances, and control the property of the people on their land. It was a huge expansion of planters' discretionary power over the work, sleep, nourishment, and lives of others, significantly more powerful than English landowners in England had over their servants. It was a "major extension of patriarchal authority," according to historian Gary Puckrein, the very power of the West Indies planter that Locke would later detail in his *First Treatise of Government*.[55] Attempts by Crown-appointed governors to reduce planter authority over workers generally failed: "Plantation owners, for their part, had grown accustomed to dominating the island's government, and they viewed their households as their own private domain where they alone made and enforced rules."[56] English settlers were thus able to, at once, resist the centralizing power of the English Crown over local governance and establish personal control over their plantations and over the people who lived there. In these twinned practices of rejecting the authority of monarchy to pursue local autonomy and insisting that the plantation is a private space where the government generally cannot reach, the planters developed practices of freedom specific to the conditions of the islands.

Barbados's "sugar revolution" would soon become a world-historic revolution in politics, economy, labor, and ecology, oriented to support the profits generated out of sugar. The planters on the island invented the gang labor system of Black slavery in their pursuit of capital through sugar.[57] Barbados became "the first Black slave society" in world history, according to Barbados historian Hilary Beckles, the first society to be thoroughly dominated by and fully organized around racialized master-slave relations.[58] From the 1640s through the 1660s the number of slaves on the island increased from less than one thousand to twenty-seven thousand. The forms of enslavement developed on Barbados by English settlers differed from past slaver practices. Portuguese settlers in South America first used slave labor for sugar cultivation in their own nascent sugar industries before the English boosted it to vast new scales. Portuguese sugar in South America was a self-sufficient agricultural enterprise, as landowners produced not only sugar but all the necessities and foodstuffs for people working there. In addition to tenants renting land the Portuguese had slaves and servants, and they viewed their relationships to their various laborers in more of a lordship or paternalistic way, interpreting it as their role to provide food as well as social services like religion and education for their enslaved workforce, in recognition of a kind of codependent though deeply hierarchical and coercive relationship.[59] The Barbadian system diverged from this model, and oriented around a different value system.

The Barbadian planters did not deem it their responsibility to care for their workers, all of whom were eventually enslaved and treated as commodities and property rather than people with needs and desires. Barbadian planters thus became known throughout the British Empire as the harshest enslavers.[60] As Beckles shows, these planters subordinated enslaved Africans using militia regiments, imperial troops, and legal machinery, all oriented to Black subjugation and sugar profit.[61] Their brutality was detailed as early as Richard Ligon's 1657 book about his visit to the island.[62] Unlike the Portuguese, Barbadian masters provided no services to their enslaved workers and explicitly banned education for enslaved people by the 1700s.[63] Barbados was an incredibly dangerous colony, with one of the highest mortality rates for indentured and enslaved people in the Western Hemisphere. Given the harsh conditions and difficulties of sugar processing, in the early years of the colony a quarter of enslaved people died in the first three years of bondage, and most lived to just seven years, a horrific number.[64]

In addition, unlike those of Portuguese settlers, Barbadian plantations were not designed for self-sufficiency; instead, to maximize profit in the burgeoning sugar market, planters used every available inch of their land for sugarcane.[65] They relinquished the capacity to provide for themselves and chose to import not just luxuries but basic food necessities and supplies needed for survival, such as timber and coal. It was this strategy that would soon bring them to North America in the form of the Carolina colony. In its rush to sugar, Barbados became the first colony to lose self-sufficiency, and the environmental costs were devastating. The landowners quickly deforested Barbados, eliminating virtually all natural flora and fauna on the island by 1665. The settlers created a new ecological world, generating enormous profit by cultivating short-term extractive relationships to the land.

Barbadians crafted a distinctly individualistic, competitive, and highly materialistic society, representing a new social way of being that connected individual freedom with personal traits that enhanced profitmaking, and their pioneering focus on profit became legendary throughout the British Empire.[66] Many seventeenth-century traders who stopped in Barbados were shocked by the "unusual acquisitiveness of the people, a trait that seemed to know no moral boundary." As an observer from 1654 succinctly described it, "They came here in order to become wealthy."[67] One Barbadian advised his brother about a financial matter on the island, in another precursor of liberal capitalism's emphasis on rational self-interest as the cornerstone of free practice, to "fairly and soberly consult your own interest."[68] The planter elites in Barbados cultivated what Beckles calls "unaccountable entrepreneurial aggression."[69] They soon became the richest inhabitants of the British Caribbean, and all of the New World. The colony was known for the most ostentatious displays of money in the British Empire, and the planters threw parties renowned for their lavishness and excess.[70] By one 1665 account, "The gentry here doth live far better than ours do in England."[71] These traits collectively contributed to Barbados's rapid wealth, for which it soon became "the Brightest Jewel in our Crown of Trade."

Barbadian planters created the first English-language slave code in the world.[72] Early sugar planters in the 1630s and 1640s employed white indentured servants from the British Isles, and they treated them so much more violently than servants were treated in England, due in part to the difficulties of sugar planting and in part to burgeoning colony mores for how people could be used in the service of profitmaking, that servants refused to come to Barbados anymore. Many servants only came when kidnapped, a practice that became so common and so feared it led to a new word: to be "Barbados'd."[73] In 1649 there was an island-wide white servant rebellion, and it drove the planters' skyrocketing use of African slave labor in the following decades.[74] The planters were fearful of rebellions by their majority-enslaved population, so in 1661 the Barbados Assembly passed a world-historic slave code titled "An Act for the Better Ordering and Governing of Negroes." It officially legalized slavery on the island, which had long been practiced, and stripped people who were enslaved of all rights. It allowed masters to kill enslaved people with few repercussions and encoded the power to torture the enslaved, elaborating a variety of allowable mutilations, including slitting nostrils, branding, and laceration. Very different punishments were instantiated for the same crimes committed by Black slaves or by white servants, who were regulated under a newly created servant's code. The slave code squelched early alliances between Irish and Black laborers coming together to fight for better living conditions, in an early example of crushing multiracial solidarity by bestowing rights and gifts to white people solely on the basis of race while enforcing greater harm on Black people.[75] Enslaved people were denied all rights under English common law while indentured servants gained new rights including trial by jury.

The Barbadian slave code thus inaugurated antiblack racism into English-language law. Edward Rugemer compellingly argues that when creating the first Black slave code the Barbados Assembly made a "conscious effort to establish the guidelines of New World mastery."[76] The slave code separated out who could be enslaved by racial categories, not only by designations of "heathen" practices or contractual status, which had previously defined differential punishment structures.[77] Defining the status of slave as a racial category by connecting "negroes" to slavery in its very title, the code justified both racialization and slavery by arguing that "their slaves their Negroes [are] an heathenish brutish and uncertaine dangerous kinde of people." It thus initiated in English jurisprudence the process of legally attributing deviant characteristics to Black people based on the forced condition of enslavement. It postulated a central facet of colonial modernity, as Wynter describes it, by connecting the juridical rights of Europeans (including landowning, people-owning, and sovereign power) to the negative qualities of people being controlled by them (e.g., heathenish, brutish, dangerous).[78] The code further made slave control and punishment central to public order. Any free white person could discipline and punish any Black slave for a perceived infringement of the code. Whiteness entailed, from the start, the surveillance and control of Black bodies.[79] The slave code was an integral dimension of the new collective and public practices of Barbadian freedom in which masters and free whites enacted their freedom by monitoring and controlling the behavior of Black people in public spaces.

In the Barbados slave code, then, both slavery and freedom became racialized. Barbadian slavery thus differed from predecessors in multiple ways, not only in mass, gang-style plantation labor practices, but also that it legally encoded a racial division of humans based on enslavement. This racial division was enforced publicly, as a shared system of governance by whites. Slavery was coterminous with blackness only, and free status entailed the power of whites to control the behavior of Blacks. To be white, here—or more precisely at this time before the concept of whiteness fully came into use, to be "Christian," which implied European, a term that in later codes would be replaced directly by "white"—meant to be free to never be enslaved.[80] It was to be assured of nonenslavement, but also to be assured that one had dominion over the enslaved.

The Barbados slave code was created by the colony's legal practices of self-rule, indeed it was a primary example of Barbadian self-rule. The development of self-rule and local autonomy on Barbados emerged with and through the legalization of Black slavery. Because the slave codes were produced on the islands by planters and not by lawmakers in England, the laws were even more harsh in their treatment of enslaved people; autonomy from the Crown and local self-rule enabled more brutal and violent laws.[81] The Barbadian settlers did not view the enslavement they practiced as an affront to liberty, or as an ancillary matter, but instead they knew that their practices of freedom were built upon their mastery of slaves, and that practicing freedom meant the ongoing and active individual ownership—as well as collective domination—of enslaved peoples. Barbadian sugar freedom was a proslavery freedom.

The Barbadian slave code also, crucially, shifted the role of enslaved Black women by making enslavement a lifetime condition passed down through generations in perpetuity through the maternal line, which subjected Black women to increased and systemic rape and sexual violence. As Jennifer Morgan has detailed, Black women's enslaved labor in Barbados both produced commodities and reproduced the pool of enslaved laborers. This "doubled labor power" of women, both as workers of the land and producers of new slaves, combined planters' demands for "plantation labor with sexual gratification, reproductive gain, and an inexplicit level of social control."[82] Reproductive labor extracted value from women's bodies' ability to produce life. Black women were central both to plantation masters' pleasure and to wealth creation. Alys Weinbaum writes, "in vivo reproductive labor was deemed alienable and slaves were bred not only for use and prestige (as they were in the ancient world) but also expressly for profit."[83] Rape became institutionalized as a practice of plantation life, not just as an act of violence committed by the prerogative of the master, but as a built-in and persistent part of sustaining the production process for sugar.[84]

Rape became a key practice of the ugly freedom of plantation mastery. It entailed dominion over Black women's bodies for the extraction of profit and pleasure. For the sugar masters, sexual assault marked dominion, generated control, and bolstered economic independence. Marisa Fuentes notes in her study of women in early Barbados that gender and sexual violence were central to plantation life yet little mentioned in the archives, which shows how thoroughly normalized this violence was and how disposable Black women's bodies seemed, a disposability that undergirded the freedom of white masters.[85] As Fuentes further notes, the control of Black women's bodies also increased the independence and economic power of white women. At the intersection of patriarchy, white supremacy, and a burgeoning racial capitalism, white women could secure a measure of relative independence though the control of Black women, whether through direct ownership, through exploitation of Black women's labor and reproductive status, through their own ability to reproduce whiteness, or through the increase in social status that slave ownership enabled.[86] All of these shifts were enabled or strengthened at least in part by the Barbados slave code, which became the basic social and economic legal code governing the island. The code was so popular that its 1688 version lasted 150 years until emancipation in the 1830s.[87] The Barbadian slave code became the basis for multiple slave codes across the Caribbean and in North America, especially Carolina, which later cribbed from its description of Black characteristics and instantiated the same practices of Black surveillance and reproductive violence.

JOHN LOCKE AND THE WEST INDIES SUGAR PLANTER

John Locke's life and work developed connections between Barbadian sugar and liberal freedom, a freedom of New World sugar masters that influenced liberal modernity in general and North American iterations of freedom in particular. Locke's theories of freedom and property, his creation of colonial policy in Carolina, and his belief that colonization supports freedom, are all shaped in part by sugar (both its embodied commodity form and its practical arrangement as a mode of production). In addition, what may seem to be contradictory arguments in Locke's work—on the one hand for individual freedom, release from arbitrary will, and natural equality; and on the other hand, for dispossession and enslavement—cohere within a theory of freedom as the freedom of a sugar plantation master.[88]

Political theorists and historians have grappled with both Locke's personal involvement in colonialism and slavery and with the implications of this involvement for the theories of liberal government that grew from his work.[89] This includes the justification for slavery in his *Second Treatise of Government*, his role in crafting juridical norms for the appropriation of native lands in the New World, and his hand in penning the *Fundamental Constitutions of Carolina*, which instituted both slavery and rule of law in the American colony of Carolina. Aziz Rana has importantly argued that North American settlers developed self-rule and property acquisition through the subjection of indigenous and enslaved people, what he calls the two faces of American freedom, and that Locke's work plays a role in this construction. For Rana, American freedom connects liberty and suppression, free citizenship and subject communities, generating "frameworks of exclusion" that support imperialism and subordinate Black and Native Americans.[90] A focus on sugar in Locke's work relies on these claims but also complicates them, showing first how American frameworks for understanding freedom must include Caribbean formations. Second, it shows how this freedom entails not just racist or imperial exclusion from universal values, but a normative framework of whiteness, mastery, property, and domination that continues to be influential as freedom.

For much of his adult life, Locke was involved as an administrator, a financial backer, and a direct beneficiary of the colonial sugar industry. He invested in two enslaving companies that made sugar cultivation in the Caribbean possible. One was the Royal Africa Company, a slave-trading company that had monopoly over the English slave trade and eventually transported over ninety thousand people kidnapped into slavery from Africa to English colonies across the New World. He also invested in the Bahamas Adventurers, a company which acquired and traded slaves in the Bahamas in order to stimulate the planting of successful crops in the Caribbean, especially sugar.[91] The Bahamas was a central nodal point for the burgeoning sugar industry, and Locke was considered an expert in its natural environment.[92] He supported and defended colonial settlement in the New World in both his financial investments and political writing, even when a majority of English people at the time were opposed to colonization.[93]

Locke's support for colonization is reflected in his *Second Treatise of Government*, where he famously argues that all individuals are free, equal, and endowed with power of self-governance, and that government is created to marshal political power from consenting individuals to protect individual property. Yet Locke's theory of property acquisition—a key aspect of freedom which argues that uncultivated land can be appropriated for private ownership by the industrious, whose improvement of the land by labor is a form of freedom—justified the dispossession of indigenous New World inhabitants.[94] Locke's doctrine that property rights stem from improvement of land through enclosure and industry, not occupancy of land, was one of the key arguments underwriting Europeans' freedom to acquire land occupied but "unimproved" by Native Americans.[95] Locke's example of waste ripe for appropriation is specifically America: "I ask whether in the wild woods and uncultivated waste of America . . . a thousand acres yield the needy and wretched inhabitants as many conveniences of life as ten acres of equally fertile land do in Devonshire, where they are well cultivated."[96] For Locke, the freedom of men to become sovereign individuals, and to be motivated by rational self-interest in the pursuit of property, implied the failed sovereignty of others, on account either of their failed performance of property acquisitiveness or their own supposedly violent and wasteful activity.[97] The *Second Treatise* also makes land in America appropriable because it does not recognize indigenous political systems as legitimate, so practices of rule on the continent are considered to be nonpolitical: "in many parts of America, there was no government at all."[98] Freedom as property appropriation is made possible by "no government" in the New World that settlers would need to respect, an argument that Locke did not invent but that was directly used to justify the removal of native peoples from their lands, and to negate treaties first made with indigenous peoples who had occupied but otherwise did not have relationships to place considered "ownership" or governing systems considered political.[99] As Richard Tuck notes, Locke "made clearer than anyone had hitherto done the right to settle in the 'vacant places' of America."[100]

Property ownership is at the heart of Locke's theory of freedom, and the colonial predicament of establishing settlers' rights to land is arguably at the forefront of his theory of property. It is particularly telling that, as Locke openly acknowledges, his theory that property rights inhere to labor, industry, and enclosure were all but irrelevant to England at the time of his writing—this theory could only be applied in a New World context of settler colonization. The meteoric success of England's sugar plantations at the time of Locke's writing likely factor into these claims about property acquisition for profit and legitimate land relationships in "America," which extended beyond North America to include the Caribbean. Waste was land that did not generate profit, and the most profitable land in the world at that time was on Caribbean sugar plantations. In Locke's famous passage arguing that labor increases the value of land, sugar is a key example: "It is labor indeed that put the difference of value on everything; and let anyone consider what the difference is between an acre of land planted with tobacco or sugar, sown with wheat or barley; an acre of the same land lying in common, without any husbandry upon it, and he will find that the improvement of labour makes the far better part of the value."[101] The reference to sugar points explicitly to Caribbean plantations, which were significantly more productive and profitable than any tobacco, wheat, or barley in North America at the time. When Locke is writing of "vacant places" for colonial settlement, the spectacular profits and ingenuity of the West Indies sugar plantations, well-known parts of his own portfolio, surely informed his analysis.

Between the 1660s and 1690s, when Locke wrote, sugar from West Indies plantations was the single most important commodity in the British Empire. Sugar was more profitable than tobacco or any other colonial commodity. Throughout the late 1600s sugar was more profitable to Britain than the imports of all other colonial produce combined.[102] And Barbados sugar was the crown jewel of the empire, its profits and innovations renowned throughout the English-speaking world. The Barbadian sugar plantation was "a far more advanced and complex industrial enterprise than any in England at the time," according to historian Susan Amussen.[103] These are all things Locke knew well, as he served for two years as Secretary for the Council of Trade and Plantations (1673–74), which managed England's colonial plantations, and served again later on the Board of Trade (1696–1700). He also served as Treasurer to the Council, which gave him deeper knowledge of sugar plantations' profitability than virtually any other Englishman at the time.

The example of sugar in the *Second Treatise* is thus no abstract speculation on Locke's part, as he knew sugar plantations' profitability and process well. Given Locke's intricate knowledge, the world-altering success of West Indies sugar, especially in "the Crown Jewel" of Barbados, surely informed his political vision for freedom gained through property acquisition by laboring on waste land.[104] When Locke writes of sugar, Barbados is at the forefront of sugar development, and sugar's huge profitability in Barbados came from the appropriation of huge agricultural tracts of land and massive importations of slave labor. Slavery plays a part in most New World property acquisition, as many of England's settler colonies were, from the start, connected with enslavement; the costs and risks of colonial settlement would not be profitable without enslaved labor.[105] Locke's defense of New World colonization is therefore a defense of chattel slavery, as Robert Bernasconi and Anika Maaza Mann have argued.[106] Locke even explicitly connects settler colonialism, slavery, property ownership, and freedom in the *Two Treatises:* he does so through the figure of the West Indies plantation owner.

Locke's argument in the *First Treatise* is generally understood as a rebuttal of the absolute sovereignty accorded to monarchs, but his specific examples include "a planter in the West Indies" who can make war on indigenous inhabitants as reparation for past injuries, or on determination of their "enmity." This is not a casually chosen example, for Locke draws from West Indies planters' power to construct a version of individual freedom as an alternative to monarchical sovereignty, an example that was most powerful in Barbados. He writes:

> May not therefore a man in the West Indies, who hath with him sons of his own, friends, or companions, soldiers under pay, or slaves bought with money, or perhaps a band made up of all these, make war and peace, if there should be occasion, and "ratify the articles too with an oath," without being a sovereign, an absolute king over those who went with him? . . . None can make war or peace but that which has the direction and force of the whole body, and that in politic societies is only the supreme power. In voluntary societies for the time, he that has such a power by consent may make war and peace . . . where they have no superior to appeal to."[107]

For Locke the West Indies planter has power to declare war, even if he is not a monarch. This is at one level an argument for individual and political authority in the New World. Locke, of course, does not recognize the sovereignty of indigenous political systems, claiming no "Superior to appeal to" to settle disputes, and thus leaving the planter with the individual power to determine war and peace. In Europe, sovereigns hold a right to make war so this situation would be irrelevant. But in Caribbean colonies, settlers arrogate this right and with it a measure of sovereignty. It entails a theoretical transfer of power from king to individual only possible in a settler colony. Planters can make war on their own individual determination when they are not in the metropole or another European state ruled by acknowledged governing systems.[108]

Locke writes that the West Indies planter is the master of a "voluntary" society, which means that all the people he controls, including servants and slaves, are there by "consent." Locke designates the plantation a consent-based society. Slaves have, according to Locke's just-war theory, consented to the terms of their enslavement, even as Locke suggests in the *Second Treatise* that colonial enslavement is not oriented by conquest so would not be subject to just war norms.[109] Thus, even though the planter does not head a political society, he still heads a voluntary one that others have chosen to join and consented for him to lead. Crucially, part of what grants the West Indies planter the power to make war is his very ownership of land and slaves. Locke writes, "Is it not possible for a man to have 318 men in his family without being heir to Adam? A planter in the West Indies has more, and might, if he pleased (who doubts?) muster them up and lead them out against the Indians to seek reparation upon any injury received from them, and this without the 'absolute dominion of a monarch' . . . since the title to the power the master had in both cases, whether over slaves or horses, was only from his purchase."[110] The planter's freedom to raise an army and determine which Indian is an enemy is acquired specifically through "his purchase" of people, not because he is an heir to Adam, that is, royally ordained by god.

In claiming that there is no superior political body to appeal to in the West Indies and that the planter is the head of a voluntary society that includes enslaved people, Locke is at once divesting indigenous inhabitants and enslaved people of recognizable political subjectivity as he is vesting the freedom to make war in enslavers and settlers—who individually acquire this power "by purchase" and subsequent consent. In this argument, the Caribbean planter's sovereign decision-making about war and peace is justified in part because he is the master of a household that has purchased slaves who have voluntarily consented to his rule. The planter's freedom derives from his purchase of individuals in forming a plantation. This is no mere speculative fantasy of individuals in the state of nature. It is Locke's codification of a practice of freedom already established and observable in Barbados and other West Indies islands.

Locke's legitimation of land use only when it is cultivated by European methods of agricultural farming also undergirds the massive environmental disruption upheld by this version of freedom. He articulates the relationship of planters to the land as primarily about domination and control: "subduing or cultivating the earth, and having dominion, we see are joined together. The one gave Title to the other. So that God, by commanding to subdue, gave authority so far to appropriate."[111] Land in the West Indies becomes valuable only when its biodiverse "waste" is subdued by mass agricultural monoculture embodied in the plantation system. This theory of property connects plantation agriculture to individual freedom and thus, at once, divests native people practicing forms of sustainable use from claiming land and legitimates as freedom biodiverse ecosystem destruction across the settler colonies. These relationships of mastery are as damaging to nonhuman worlds as they are to human worlds. In both, to labor in order to create property and wealth—that is, to practice freedom—is to subdue, to have dominion, and to appropriate. All of these practices have been ongoing for decades by Barbados sugar masters by the time of Locke's writing; this is precisely what made them so successful in profitmaking, and why Locke supported them in his secretarial positions.

Yet the arguments in the *Treatises*, Locke's own secretarial positions in support of colonial sugar plantations, and his personal profit from the sugar slave trade are not Locke's only investments in sugar. Sugar also bridges his investments in the West Indies and North America. Carolina was colonized in large part to provide commodities and food for sugar plantations in Barbados.[112] From 1668 to 1675, Locke provided well-regarded service as Secretary for the Lords Proprietors of Carolina (the Lords Proprietors were the original English families granted the royal charter to colonize Carolina for profit). He was noted for "the zeal shown by him in endeavoring to secure the property of the settlement."[113] Carolina was colonized in large part to support Barbados, the sugar capital of the empire, with food and other commodities, and also to replicate its success. Locke was also one of the main authors of the colony's first constitution, the *Fundamental Constitutions of Carolina*, with what historian David Armitage has called "a major supervisory role."[115] The *Fundamental Constitutions* legalized slavery at the same time that it instituted the rule of law in the founding of Carolina.[114] Although scholars have yet to determine which lines Locke specifically wrote, they know that he had a hand the clause granting planters "Absolute dominion and power over slaves" in its first version in 1669. Locke worked side by side with Peter Colleton, a leading Barbadian planter, to craft the *Fundamental Constitutions of Carolina* and establish planter freedom in North America.[116]

Peter Colleton—the patriarch of a Barbadian plantation family whose wealth, power, and status derived from sugar and the slave trade—was Locke's companion and correspondent while Locke was secretary to the Lords Proprietors. He and Locke were the only two people who coauthored both the 1669 and 1682 versions of the *Fundamental Constitutions*.[117] Locke and Colleton understood that Carolina would grow the food and commodities for Colleton's and others' plantations on Barbados, and it would be populated with less prosperous whites from Barbados in pursuit of their own fortunes.[118]

Barbadian planter freedom sets the political and economic course of Carolina, and through that part of American freedom. Locke's theory of freedom crystallizes aspects of Barbadian political practices, which are also put into the *Fundamental Constitutions* and then gain broader expression in North America.

Carolina was deliberately structured to replicate the Barbadian plantation system of profiting from large-scale and enslaved labor agriculture. Carolina has been referred to as "a colony of a colony" of Barbados, so tied was its founding to Barbadian models and markets.[119] Given its heavy Barbadian influence, we could say that Carolina was creolized from the start.[120] Although the settlement was first tasked with providing diverse foodstuffs and timber for trade with Barbados, by the early 1700s the same methods of gang labor enslavement and vertical integration used in Barbadian sugar plantations were deployed in tobacco plantations in the north and rice plantations in the southern Carolina low country. The settlers in Carolina copied the infamously harsh disciplinary tactics of the Barbadian sugar planters, especially their military-like rule over enslaved Africans. They also deployed the doubled labor of enslaved Black women from the very start of the colony.[121] Like Colleton and Locke, many of Carolina's Lords Proprietors were familiar with these practices of enslavement. Seven of the early governors of South Carolina had backgrounds in Barbados, and almost half of Carolina's initial settlers were Barbadian.[122]

Peter Colleton aimed to bring Barbadian methods to American colonies, and the Carolina constitution he and Locke cowrote, along with Locke's patron Ashley Cooper (later the Earl of Shaftesbury and also at one time a Barbadian plantation owner) instantiated into law the enslaving practices begun on Barbados's sugar plantations. The Constitution they created in 1669 not only legalized chattel slavery but allowed "every free man to have absolute dominion and power over his negro slaves."[123] "Every free man" was granted sovereign authority, including the power of life and death, over "his negro slaves," thus from the outset of the colony racializing free subjectivity and authorizing Blacks as enslaved property. For new settlers, the more slaves a planter imported to Carolina, the more land that person received for settlement, thus encouraging enslavement, expansion, and settler colonialism simultaneously.[124] The freedom that Locke, Colleton, and Cooper granted to proprietors was the power that plantation masters carved out for themselves in Barbados.[125] It included local autonomy, "absolute dominion" over Black slaves, and little interference over the land they appropriated as their own. While subsequent generations would condemn the *Fundamental Constitutions* for its cruelty and hierarchies, Armitage argues that Locke "seems to have taken pride in the *Fundamental Constitutions* right up to his death in 1704."[126]

The Carolina constitution was a step in translating Barbadian sugar masters' freedom into modern liberal freedom, including the sorting of free and slave persons by race and property, as well as a mass production plantation economy organized by racial divisions for a landed aristocracy investing in agricultural commodities. For Bernasconi and Mann, the *Fundamental Constitutions* reveals how Locke's political norms of individual freedom and property were tethered to norms of Black enslavement and native dispossession.[127] Neither Locke nor the Carolina constitution invented these racialized norms, but they enabled dictatorial and race-based politics in North America alongside a liberal constitutional system for religious toleration, secret ballots, and the rule of law. Tellingly, the section in the first 1669 *Fundamental Constitutions* establishing absolute dominion over negro slaves (Sec. 110) appears between two of the most lauded features of the constitution: Section 109 legalizes freedom of religion, and Section 111 insists on trial by a jury of one's peers.[128] The Carolina constitution incorporates all the contradictions of ugly freedom, supporting both the rule of law and legal enslavement, both local autonomy and land appropriation, both religious toleration and racial hierarchy.[129] All were crucial to plantation practices of freedom from Barbados that entail what Mbembe names "the impossibility of sharing freedom" as a core part of liberal freedom's practice.[130]

The *Fundamental Constitutions* were initially published in 1669, yet the first permanent settlement in Carolina was not established until 1670. The *Fundamental Constitutions* were thus created before settlement. It was not a law made by and for people already living there, but a lure to convince settlers to live there. It provided white settlers with a blueprint for expected economic prosperity: land appropriation and plantation slavery. Carolina depended on these measures for its existence and it was the only North American colony founded on slavery, as other colonies began to enslave Africans and Indians after settlement.[131] By translating Barbadian slavery into its fundamental law, the constitution clearly signaled to its potential settlers that the new colony would extend Barbados's pattern of building great wealth by human bondage, and the sugar masters' practices of freedom would continue apace on the North American mainland. While it has been noted that white Barbadians emigrated to Carolina "bringing with them ideas, institutions, and ideologies first developed in Barbados during the sugar boom," it is also important to note that many of those practices were already established in Carolina at the drafting of the constitution.[132]

Settler dispossession by the English was more violent and juridical in Carolina than in uninhabited Barbados. Many different native nations including Yamahsee, Stono, and Kiawah lived on land appropriated as Carolina and were soon forced out. Whereas Barbados may have appeared as a blank slate, with no indigenous people to contest settler appropriation by the time of English arrival, in Carolina the land was clearly not a vacuum domicilium. Claims of uninhabited land did not apply here. Yet the settlers still invested in what Nikhil Singh has called the "blank slate" vision of settler freedom, the fantasy of "cheap, empty, exploitable lands and resources that must be cleared of any competing interests" as a practice of freedom.[133] The Carolina settlers soon depopulated the land through a combination of conquest, trade, and wars geared toward taking control of territory.[134] They directly assaulted indigenous worlds, viewing their assault at one level as a necessary and natural process of clearing settlement and at another level as an exercise of their own freedom to gain independence.[135] What Robert Nichols calls "theft as property" came into play in Carolina where it did not in Barbados, as indigenous land was taken and only recognized legally as property retroactively, after it had been stolen.[136] In Carolina the direct theft of native land instantiates settler property relations for the region.

Barbados and Carolina are but two early strands in the complex braid of sugar and freedom that spread across continents. Beckles writes, "slavery, Barbados style, became a celebrated global brand . . . wherever there was money to be made in the empire, the model was exported."[137] Profits from sugar, and later from tobacco, rice, and cotton grown on the plantation model innovated in Barbados, generated European opulence, colonization, and enslavement across the Americas. To sketch the traveling entwinement of sugar and freedom very briefly, the wealth generated by early plantation masters made other forms of commodity agriculture possible, underwrote challenges to monarchical demands, and allowed settlers to embrace self-rule (understood as the self-rule of white masters).[138] As Edmund Morgan famously put it, the profits generated by slave labor enabled the financial ground for the United States' experiments in individual freedom and mass democracy.[139] While Barbadian methods were adapted and revised across New World colonies, they also met with mass resistance and multiple revolts from those enslaved on sugar plantations, especially on Jamaica and Haiti.[140] By the late 1800s many abolitionist and labor movements organized around the brutal conditions of labor in the sugar industry, and in the United States the sugar plantation became a key site for organizing Black politics during Reconstruction.[141]

By the early twentieth century in the United States, individual sugar plantations in Florida and Louisiana soon consolidated into "US Sugar," which became a corporate trust as big and powerful as US Steel and Oil. The pursuit of sugar profit contributed to US imperialist wars in Cuba, Puerto Rico, Hawai'i, and the Philippines, all of which were occupied in part to grow sugarcane.[142] Across the planet, the planting of sugarcane caused greater loss of global biodiversity than any other single crop. It contributed heavily to world deforestation, and to the drying up of waterways and desertification that plague the world today.[143] The rise of industrially processed food in the mid-twentieth century only intensified these trends. Sugar transformed from a food enhancer to an independent source of calories, even a food substitute, even though knowledge of its toxicity was rampant. Its mass consumption has particularly affected poor people across the world, who rely on its cheapness to satisfy hunger and invigorate themselves for physically laborious work. The material of sugar, its addictively gratifying taste, still contains the ugly freedoms of Barbadian plantation mastery, all concealed within its familiarity and sweetness, its cheap ubiquity and easy pleasure.

White and Deadly: The Marvelous Sugar Baby

Against this backstory, what do we make of individual liberty, rule of law, and promises of uncoerced agency, tethered as they have been to circuits of racism, theft, and land exploitation? Seen through the lens of sugar, freedom entails forms of self-governance, private autonomy, and entrepreneurial self-interest that take shape through mastery, which includes domination of others and destruction of land. Freedom includes a racial parsing of peoples into those whose appearance and practices normatively qualify for individual personhood and those whose bodies must be either be exploited or eliminated to enable individual norms of individuality, mastery, and property that constitute freedom's universal form. Like the industrial practices that sift and refine sugar, modern freedom has often functioned as a sorting mechanism. As sugar in its final stage of refinement is white and considered free of impurities, so too with the story of freedom derived from sugar plantations. Sugar, in this sense, is one of freedom's material forms. Sugar, perhaps, is freedom's digestible form.[144] If the archives of freedom are a multisensory experience, as Lowe suggests by conceiving of archives differently, then sugar is one way to answer the question of what freedom *tastes like*.

It is no wonder sugar is called "Pure, White and Deadly," the title of an early history of sugar's health effects from the 1970s.[145] If whiteness is a structure of power that sorts people into hierarchies of freedom and prizes those people whose racialized image mirrors the personhood of independent landowners, acquisitive planters, and uncoerced individuals, then white and deadly describes both sugar and freedom. What does it look like to confront the horrors of these ugly freedoms, to engage them directly, and to work collaboratively to overcome their subjugating horror? How do people craft alternate systems of politics and practices of freedom that are not just antagonistic to sugar plantation freedom but are dissociated from the slave dialectic altogether? This freedom is beautifully articulated by a person formerly enslaved on a sugar plantation: "all we ask . . . is to be rid forever of MASTERISM."[146] What does it look like to be rid forever of masterism? It presumably entails being rid not only of plantation masters, but also of freedoms still wrapped within dynamics of mastery, including those understood as self-mastery, self-possession, or inclusion into the terms of plantation freedom. I spend much of the rest of this book examining this question, but here I look at two specific examples that crucially come from the Caribbean sugar plantation.

Neil Roberts's *Freedom as Marronage* offers one path forward, articulating a theory of freedom as a flight from slavery that originates *within* Caribbean experiences of enslavement on sugar plantations.[147] Marronage offers a version of freedom emanating out of the Caribbean islands grounded in enslaved people's refusal of white domination. Roberts importantly argues, inspired by Orlando Patterson, that freedom's practices are best articulated by the very people who have been denied its practice in conventional versions of freedom's form. As a practice of fugitivity, marronage draws on flight from plantation enslavement as the ground for freedom, rather than on abstract concepts of personhood or individual sovereignty. It is, at one level, a historic practice in which enslaved Afro-Caribbean people ran away from plantations to create autonomous and self-sustaining communities. Marronage is also, at another level, a normative and transhistoric project of flight from racial oppression still necessary today, guided by what Roberts describes as "a total refusal of the enslaved condition."[148] While some marronage communities in the Caribbean recapitulated labor hierarchies or gender-based domination, in its most democratic forms, the freedom of marronage has included community, creativity, and resistance, when maroon communities together interpret freedom as a processual action of shared worldmaking on collectively controlled land.

Marronage as a theory and practice does not seek to discard freedom or to idealize it but to expand its imaginative possibilities. It is generated by the people who best know the brutality of plantation freedom and can thus best articulate alternate forms of freedom's value. In this sense marronage expresses ugly freedom in both of its valences—in the first it offers a scathing critique of the ugliness of modern freedom, and in the second it offers an alternative freedom created by people and found in spaces disparaged as deviant by standard iterations of modern freedom, but aim to compose a shared world away from masterism. Maroonage fully rejects the plantation and its practices of enslavement; however, it does not eliminate the slave dialectic or eradicate the plantationocene, in part because the freedom marronage entails is specifically flight from slavery. A *maroon* is an escaped slave, so the freedom of marronage does not make sense without the slave plantation to escape from, even when marronage is importantly reimagined for the present as a strategy to challenge ongoing antiblack racism through evasion and flight.[149] In this sense marronage remains connected, however oppositionally, to plantation dynamics. And yet marronage envisions how to practice freedom in ways that do not presume private property, sovereignty, or a figure of whiteness as the universal foundations of freedom. It explicitly rejects these forms to imagine new social worlds that reject the violence of masterism, and directly engages the history of sugar as a starting point.

Kara Walker's enormous sugar megasculpture offers another intervention that challenges the disavowals of modern freedom, using sugar both to emphasize the ugliness of freedom as mastery and to locate alternative freedoms in spaces and bodies deemed inadequate to freedom's majesty. Titled *A Subtlety, Or the Marvelous Sugar Baby, an Homage to the unpaid and overworked Artisans who have refined our Sweet tastes from the cane fields to the Kitchens of the New World on the Occasion of the demolition of the Domino Sugar Refining Plant* (2014), it was created as a site-specific installation in the abandoned Domino Sugar refinery factory on the New York City waterfront. Inside, Walker crafted a thirty-five-foot-high and seventy-five-foot-long sculpture of a nude Black woman in a sphinx position (figure 1.2). It was made out of forty tons of white refined sugar over Styrofoam. Accompanying the sphinx were life-size sculptures of Black children scattered around her feet, crafted from hardened unrefined brown sugar and molded into the shape of Blackamoor figurines. *A Subtlety* interrogates the violent history of the sugar plantation, its pleasures and its oppressions, and in so doing attends to freedom's white and deadly expression. Like marronage, it too offers both versions of ugly freedom, both a critique and reimagination. The work creates a *sensorial narrative* of ugly freedom, forcing the unthought known of sugar's disavowals into perception, provoking an experience of what ugly freedoms of the sugar

1.2 Kara Walker, *A Subtlety, Or the Marvelous Sugar Baby* (2014).

plantation feel like and smell like. It also, however, moves beyond plantation dynamics in all their forms, including self-mastery and self-possession,
which merely transfer slave dynamics internally without undoing them.
In asking what it might feel like to be rid forever of masterism, the Marvelous Sugar Baby generates different sensorial encounters with freedom's
possibilities.

A *Subtlety* is a reference to the earliest history of sugar's travels to the European continent as decorated "subtleties," like Henry VIII's dungeon, luxuries only available for consumption to white Europeans with title and power.
Walker gestures to sugar's congealing of power into objects that elites consume in a show of victory, delight, and dominion. This marvelous subtlety
too contains sugar as sovereign power, as mechanism and justification for
the "absolute dominion" of enslaved Blacks as the *Fundamental Constitutions
of Carolina* states, for the justification of indigenous dispossession, and for
the absolute dominion over nature, all seen as necessary to generate freedom of mastery and economic prosperity. The sugar planter's sovereignty
over nature, land, and bodies shapes the Marvelous Sugar Baby; Walker refers to the sculpture as a "monument to the quest for whiteness . . . this ideal
of mastery over continents, peoples, body, ecology."[150] Whiteness here is a

quest for mastery over the earth as it takes shape on the sugar plantation. Walker's subtlety points to extant forms of modern freedom as whiteness, dispossession, and mastery, but she confronts these forms through the figure of an enormous nude Black woman sphinx, and in this way offers a different version of what power, and freedom, might be.

Walker's subtlety is not a subtle presence. Her sugared body towers over all who cross her path in the refinery. Kyla Wazana Tompkins argues that sugar has been historically linked to blackness in Anglo-American culture, both through the Black laborers who made the sugar and because sugar's quick energy was considered "dangerously animating of whiteness." The link was also and alternately made by abolitionists who would not eat sugar because it was a commodity "soaked in the blood and death" of the enslaved.[151] A Subtlety plays with these racialized links of labor, animatedness, and blood, while also challenging their terms. The enigmatic sphinx is both, at once, a marvel and a danger, animated and eternally frozen, pure white and blood-soaked. She is created by a material of "blood and death" that is refined to whiteness, a process that whitewashes the brutal conditions of production into visual purity. White sugar is exchanged for Black bodies, an exchange which is literalized in the Barbados slave codes that listed punishment for killing Black people in terms of pounds of sugar. The Marvelous Sugar Baby inhabits that exchange and challenges their popular disavowal by insisting that racialized bifurcations are contiguous and codependent. She is both Black and white simultaneously. She is a Black figure made of pure white sugar, reflecting Fernando Ortiz's argument that "sugar was mulatto from the start, for the energies of Black men and white always went into its production."[152] Mutually constituted, the sphinx amalgamates rather than seg-regates racial categories to show their historic indissociability. As a sphinx she is naked and unprotected, but she also has the answers and solves the riddles that bedevil the mortals scattered at her feet. These riddles reveal the plantationocene's codependence of freedom and slavery, whiteness and Blackness, brutality and sweetness.

The smell of the art installation is something that many attendees noted, and itself told a story of sugar's ugly freedom in an olfactory register. The first smell from the factory was sweet, a sugary perfume wafting from the ex-hibit to the outside line. Once inside, it soon became an overpowering sickly sweetness.[153] It then turned rancid, rotten, and industrial as one settled into the exhibit, all of the decades-old molasses still seeping—or as Walker provocatively noted, "weeping"—from the walls. Within a few minutes the sweetness mixed with rot, putrefaction, and corroded metal, and in this way offered a shifting sensorial narrative that evoked the fullness of sugar's ugly freedom. The smells undid and transformed binaries between sweet and rancid, freedom and enslavement, just as the sphinx transformed them in a visual register. In turning sugar from something tasted to something seen and smelled, Walker suggests that the taste of overpowering sweetness obscures the conditions of sugar labor, in which profit and pleasure excuse the horrific predations of production, in which many people to this day discount the conditions that power their pleasure and their freedom. The refinery's sensorial effects generate a challenge to Rancière's partition of the sensible, in that the first and overpowering encounter of its sweetness is soon experienced as nauseating and dominating through a different, olfactory, sensorial register, revealing, or at least smelling, sugar's "unthought known." It immerses audiences' sensorium into the world that it, like marronage, decries.

Like Campos-Pons's sugared sculpture, and Robert's theory of marronage, this artwork interrogates the conditions of the sugar plantation as a grounding location for modern freedom. Yet it works differently from both in its relations to figuration and land. Campos-Pons takes the spectacle of violated human bodies out of her representation of racism, settler colonialism, and ecological destruction. She shows the violence of sugar plantation freedom without depicting suffering Black and brown bodies, a spectacle that Saidiya Hartman argues both exposes racialized violence and "secures the enjoyment, sovereignty, and bodily integrity of man and master."[154] Walker, by contrast, risks that exposure by figuring the bodily violence of the Marvelous Sugar Baby and the little children at her feet, though on my reading she also refuses the spectacle of bodily suffering. She insists that the figuration of Black women and the doubled labor they are tasked to perform on the sugar plantation can be visually interrogated without reproducing the spectacle of their pain (even when audiences try to reproduce it themselves, as I discuss later). She challenges the alienability of bodies from the labor they are forced into, while arguing for bodies that have a different relationship to power, pleasure, and freedom. And unlike marronage, The Marvelous Sugar Baby's bodily movement is not in flight, but in fixity. Her overwhelming presence does not suggest an escape from masterism so much as a reclamation of the spaces it had colonized and trashed. Her relationship to place is thus less about finding refuge than about constructing reciprocity. It is a reclamation not only of space but of relationships that are not based on exploitation, extraction, and destruction, but on nourishment and community. The Marvelous Sugar Baby reclaims the fecundity of the places and peoples destroyed in the pursuit of sugar plantation mastery for these alternate values.

1.3 The sugar babies of the Marvelous Sugar Baby.

The molasses sugar babies next to the Sphinx carry harvest baskets, but rather than fruits and vegetables, they contain sugared arms, legs, and other broken body parts. The sugar babies construct a brutal image demanding attention to the brutality of enslaved children's lived experiences (figure 1.3). Popular ideologies link sugar consumption to simple childhood pleasures, but rather than consuming sugar, these children are instead consumed *by* sugar, their bodies broken and melting in the sweltering refinery.[155] These babies are birthed by sugar, as the Sphinx's exposed vulva suggests, gesturing to the long history of rape and sexualized brutality of the cane fields. They show how the plantation made blackness into disposable labor that was doubled on the bodies of Black women. This sexualized violence was reenacted by some of the mostly white visitors to the exhibit, who would pose in ways that gestured to the sexual violation of the Marvelous Sugar Baby.[156] They created photographs and selfies to look like they were inserting fingers into her vagina or squeezing her nipple, usually accompanying their rapacious gesture with a grin. At one level, this seemed to repeat the pervasiveness of sexual violence toward Black women, one that some white visitors joyfully claimed as their own. But the Marvelous Sugar Baby also halts their desire: she towers over those who cannot actually touch her, and she will not be consumed by them. She is so enormous that she simply cannot be consumed or dominated in this way. Their gestures reflect their own desires, but the gesture itself is impotent, as it cannot do what it aims to perform. Walker explains in an interview that the Marvelous Sugar Baby is a New World mammy figure bent over in supplication, but she is not there to be taken or abused. Nor is she a nonsexual caretaker. She's iconic and monumental, embodying a sexual energy that is not for viewers, no matter how much they may try to "take" her and control her through gestures of sexual violence.[157] The Marvelous Sugar Baby is insistently vulnerable, but she is also overpowering, and she is unconsumable, signaling different bodily relations besides consumption, domination, refining, and profit.

A subtlety is often a signifier of power, and a treasure. What else might the Marvelous Sugar Baby be communicating? What power might she be suggesting? Christina Sharpe argues that Walker sees the subtlety as a gift that elides sugar's horror and does not address the bodily brutality of the sugar plantation; the Marvelous Sugar Baby thus reiterates without redressing the ugly freedom of antiblackness as it continues into the present.[158] I read this gifting gesture differently, not as a conciliatory gesture to embodied pain that repeats antiblack disavowals but as a refashioning project. The Marvelous Sugar Baby is a gift not to masterism but to its destruction. She stands out over the room as a sign of her power, but she does not dominate others.[159] Her power takes shape as a position of openness and supplication, an overwhelming presence that attends to the sickly horrors of the sugar plantation while also asking viewers to envision new forms of freedom that do not stay mired in sugar plantation relations.[160] This invitation to sit with, and smell, the ugliness of freedom does not ignore or bypass the history of sugar but faces it directly, while also pushing in a different direction. This is where the sculpture differs from *Sugar/Bittersweet*, in that it offers alternative figurations to the sugared freedom it both documents and condemns. It suggests that only through direct confrontation with this freedom can alternatives develop that are not predicated on masterism, Lockean possession, or the denigration of the world. The Marvelous Sugar Baby calls for different experiences of freedom, which might be considered unrefined.

Amber Musser argues that the Marvelous Sugar Baby reveals constitutive conditions of lived codependence that are sensorially overwhelming to ponder, even as they shape everyday lived experiences. They are terrifying yet enjoyable conditions and are outside of relations of domination that often make Black women legible in American discourses of freedom only as victims of sexual violence or as perpetrators of sexual manipulation. For Musser, the

Marvelous Sugar Baby instead offers a kind of queer pleasure of vulnerability embedded in social relations that are both dominating and can be imagined otherwise.[161] The Marvelous Sugar Baby embodies a queer Black feminist sexuality that for Musser is not experienced through the typical trope of perpetual sexual victimization, nor does she reflect an opposite reclamation of liberal agency through sexual autonomy and consent. Instead, the Marvelous Sugar Baby escapes that bind with the overpowering figuration of her nakedness and exposed vulva, what Musser calls an "economy of the labial." A labial economy is not a plantation political economy, nor its opposite—which would be predicated on self-mastery rather than mastery, or self-ownership rather than being owned. Instead a labial economy posits relations premised on permeability: "instead of possession, an economy of the labial speaks to mutuality, receptivity, and vulnerability."[162] If being owned, being violated, being dispossessed, being fleeced are the forms of subjectivity offered to the Marvelous Sugar Baby by the ugly freedoms of the sugar plantation, then the Marvelous Sugar Baby confronts them with her own forms of free subjectivity: reciprocal, confrontationally exposed, and dialogic.

Freedom in the labial economy is practiced as an inescapable exposure to others that can be both terrifying and pleasurable, that can build worlds in open and intimate conviviality. It rejects self-mastery in its very construction. As a mammy figure, the Marvelous Sugar Baby is popularly figured to put white needs and white desires ahead of her own, and thus she stands as a monument to exploitation. But as an overwhelmingly tall naked Black woman sphinx whose vulva is open to all viewers, Musser reads her as petitioning audience members to ask what *she* desires, what *she* hungers for, which moves her away from being a forced repository for white desires of doubled labor. The Marvelous Sugar Baby's formidable figuration insists on individual dignity, which is separate from the violence of individualism's isolation and competition. This economy of the labial posits freedom as the pleasure and terror of sensorial permeability and "dialogic selfhood," which relies on the inescapability of interconnection fantasized away in versions of freedom and individual sovereignty.

The Marvelous Sugar Baby is not a universal figure of freedom. Her labial freedom does not position her to become an abstract ideal. Nor is she positioned to be the Black woman who saves white people from their own depredations. The Marvelous Sugar Baby does not redeem those who want to practice violence upon her. In the bottom corner of the sculpture, the Marvelous Sugar Baby's left sphinx paw has its thumb between its first two fingers, a traditional sign of both obscenity and fertility. The paw stands as a subtle but powerful "fuck you" to the conditions that made her as they stretch into the present, while the sphinx's open fertility offers new possibilities for living free. The circulations of the labial economy flow through both ends, through both labial openness and fingered insouciance to those who want to exploit her. In Walker's work, no one ever dominates the Marvelous Sugar Baby, and she will never be mastered, as she no longer exists: The Domino Sugar factory was demolished after the exhibit, along with the Marvelous Sugar Baby, who was its last inhabitant. The only part of the sculpture that still exists is the left paw, the one piece Walker chose to keep as a memento of the work.

As an aesthetic figure, the Marvelous Sugar Baby brings exploitation into a space of "refinement," forcing the audience to see—and smell—their interconnections. The space of refinement is both literal and figurative, not only because the artwork links sugar violence to refined sensibilities, but because the exhibit itself is in a dank sugar refinery turned chic art gallery. It is a refinery that becomes refined. The Marvelous Sugar Baby makes that transformation happen by her presence; as art she refines the refinery. Yet sugar refining is a violent process. It creates enormous pollution, as its factories poison nearby inhabitants in order to turn sugar from brown to white. Refining filters everything from the sugar crystal but shocking, undifferentiated, uniform sweetness. It literally strips nutrients and taste from unrefined sugar, casting off heft and value in order to offer a visual whitening. That is its only purpose: to whiten. It involves stages called "clarifying," "decolorizing," and "standardized sizing," processes done wholly for white optics, not for taste. Yet historically, only when sugar was refined into pure whiteness was it considered fit for consumption in European and United States markets. Refining sugar polluted environments, poisoned neighborhoods, and stripped taste and texture, only to make sugar look white and pure. The bleaching of sugar reflects the bleaching of sugar's bloody production, part of what makes "white and deadly" both a truism and a redundancy.

The Domino sugar factory was once the largest sugar refinery in the entire world.[163] Historically, the industrial practice of sugar refining typically happened on the mainland of metropoles, oceans away from the Caribbean plantations. The Domino factory accepted boatloads of unrefined sugar every day from the Caribbean, which it then whitened for American consumption.[164] American Sugar Refinery Corp (eventually renamed Domino) processed over half of the sugar in the US market after the Civil War, and the company controlled almost 100 percent of the market twenty years later. It became so financially successful that it was one of the original twelve companies composing the Dow Jones Industrial Average. Later, the refinery was the site of huge labor strikes in the 1990s and was eventually shuttered in 2004. By 2014, it was slated for demolition to make way for expensive condos on the waterfront (sprinkled with a few low-rent spaces to satisfy city optics of "affordability"), mirroring the development of the neoliberal landscape of postindustrial luxury that acquires working-class sites of labor to transform them into private leisure spaces for the rich. If anything, the garish levels of consumption gestured to in the exhibit also mark the ugliness of a neoliberal present. Using forty tons of uneaten sugar for art is something only a consumption-obsessed society, indifferent to wealth inequality, could both afford and find unproblematic.

In confronting the ugly freedoms of ownership and dispossession, the Marvelous Sugar Baby invites viewers to imagine the possibility of freedom released from owning and possessing altogether. Rejecting a freedom of mastery, her labial freedom gestures to a freedom of openness, mutuality, and investment in co-constitution. She invites viewers to postulate a freedom not necessarily of flight from dominion, but of commitment to the long-term sustenance of the land rather than exhaustion of the soil and the people who work it. The Marvelous Sugar Baby points to a freedom generated in dialogue with queer Black feminist embodiment, constituted not by abstract claims for likeness, nor by identification, nor by competition, but by many diverse solidarities that move across space and time—and the sweetness, fear, and challenges that come from this experience. It is a freedom that embraces pleasure, but not the pleasures of industrialized, refined, and undifferentiated sweetness, nor the patriarchal pleasures of sexual violence over racialized and gendered bodies. Her labial freedom showcases pleasures of reciprocity, conviviality, and composition alongside others known and unknown that work hard to flourish together amid and against the violence of the world.

This exposed and open freedom can be terrifying, as Hannah Arendt would surely note in her insistence that freedom demands courage. The courage of the Marvelous Sugar Baby is not in public performativity alone, nor only in her insouciant thumb, but in her multisensory openness to the world on relational and labial planes. It is perhaps akin to what Mbembe calls "a democracy of connections," which is the opposite of freedom as disentanglement—a disentanglement from others and from the land often animated by a genocidal destruction of difference.[165] Instead, freedom derived from a democracy of connections embraces the difficulties, pleasures, challenges, and affinities generated out of a commitment to living with many diverse others without exploitation, hierarchy, or supremacy. It can be terrifying, but also world-creating. Indeed, there is something world-creating about the Sugar Baby being built to crumble, as if the sugared edifice that produces ugly freedoms through her doubled labor can also crumble down.

In her book *Wayward Lives*, Saidiya Hartman describes waywardness as a type of freedom, making a way out of no way, practices of living from striking to migration to strolling to mutual aid to loving that involve "the avid longing for a world not ruled by master, man, or police."[166] If the Marvelous Sugar Baby is not exactly wayward in her overwhelming and fixed presence, she shares this avid longing and offers a version of its practice at both ends, in her open labia and her extended thumb, and in her insistence on sensorially overwhelming the sugar plantation's ugly freedom. In the following chapters, I explore each of these forces of power and rule that construct ugly freedoms of master (chapter 2), police (chapter 3), and man (chapter 4). And I examine the second valence of ugly freedoms that emerge out from under their control, showcasing practices of freedom that may otherwise seem unrefined, illegible, or disheartening. There will always be remainders to freedom's practices; no act of freedom is universally desirable or pure, as the history of sugar surely shows. Desires for purity and perfection produce violence and pollution in their wake. Yet histories of freedom and sugar can be confronted, as in *A Subtlety*, to address both forms of ugly freedom: both to attend to the fullness of freedom's ugliness, and to find freedoms otherwise deemed dissolute or shameful. These freedoms help envision what it might look like to reject masterism altogether, to cultivate ways to live alongside diverse others in equality and shared authority over the governing conditions of their inescapably entangled lives.

What other materials and objects can offer a different story of freedom, one in which freedom's practice is neither a sorting mechanism for who is most deserving of its fruits, nor connected to appropriation and hierarchy as disavowed practices, nor even reliant on enslavement or dispossession for its opposing term? What other commodities might directly confront the ugly freedoms of modernity but also imagine free practice separated from mastery or control? This chapter posits one possibility through the history of sugar, but of course there are others. To open to those possibilities is to ask what might freedom's practice look like if it was emancipated from all relations of slavery, domination, dispossession, profit, and property, indeed a freedom that has even overcome "civilization." What will the sweetness of freedom taste like, when it doesn't taste like sugar?

tragedies of emancipation   2

Freedom, Sex, and Theft after Slavery

Not only was I not born a slave, I was not born to hope to become the
equal of the slave-master.

—JAMES BALDWIN, "The Price of the Ticket"

ONLY A YEAR BEFORE MICHAEL BROWN was killed by police officer Darren
Wilson in Ferguson, Missouri, in 2014, the United States had celebrated the
150th anniversary of the Emancipation Proclamation, which offered a telling
snapshot of racial politics before the Black Lives Matter movement exploded
into the nation's political consciousness. Most commemorations painted re-
deeming pictures of the United States as a triumphant moral exemplar for
ending slavery. They celebrated the proclamation's declaring former slaves
"forever free," banning the institution of slavery, and underscoring America's
fundamental commitment to freedom for all. For some commentators, the
proclamation redeemed the nation as it liberated the enslaved, emancipating both at once from their terrible histories. As NAACP president Benjamin
Jealous remarked, the proclamation "did not just liberate blacks from bondage; it liberated America from one of her most glaring contradictions."[1] Steven Spielberg's lauded film *Lincoln* (2013), released to commemorate the anniversary, reflected this sentiment by situating the president and his political

allies as the pioneering actors who brought freedom to enslaved Black people through a combination of moral fortitude and legal savvy. Although most celebrations noted that the nation still had more to accomplish to achieve full justice for Black Americans, by and large emancipation seemed to prove, in Michelle Obama's tribute, "The great American story," which is "the story of continual and breathtaking progress from one generation to the next."[2]

In these celebratory histories, emancipation was an unqualified good that brought freedom to the nation's Black population. Emancipation reflected America's inherent virtue and affirmed its commitment to forging equality out of its unequal past. It is the history of American democracy as a "self-cleaning oven" in Jeanne Theoharis's words, in which racial wrongs are righted and washed away, the constant self-improvement of a fundamentally moral nation committed to equality and diversity.[3] This interpretation of emancipation was not new, but at the 150th anniversary it had reached a new height, ironically, during an era of rising mass incarceration, political disenfranchisement, police brutality, widespread poverty, and defunded social services, all of which disproportionately and intentionally harm African Americans and which were about to break forward into national political discourse. Although the proclamation's celebrations were subtended by an undercurrent of dissent charging that freedom requires not merely the end of legalized bondage but the end of white supremacy, the celebrations generally ignored this dissent to focus on the more celebratory story of "continual and breathtaking progress."

A majority of Americans now recognize that the work of emancipation was as yet incomplete at the time of its 150th anniversary, but the problem is deeper. What if the very history of emancipation, as it is told now, thwarts ongoing struggles for black freedom? It is not merely the case that the work of emancipation is not yet complete, but that US emancipation was never an incontrovertible good; emancipation was a tragic reformulation of racialized unfreedom that continues to the present. Tragedy may seem incompatible with emancipation, as it emphasizes how people are conditioned by ideas and powers not of their choosing, while emancipation wrests control from dominating forces. Tragedy demands the recognition of limits that inhibit one's desires, conflict with one's actions, and truncate one's experience of living in the world, while emancipation envisions a self-determining subject who undoes those limits.[4] David Scott's *Conscripts of Modernity*, however, inscribes tragedy within the very promise of modern emancipation. Scott argues that former colonial subjects, while emancipated from colonial powers, also remain exploited by them, and continually struggle to determine their fate against the overwhelming forces of capital, imperialism, and racism. Emancipation did not establish freedom—a not uncommon argument in Black and postcolonial studies. But a still deeper problem, Scott argues, is that anticolonial discourses of emancipation are themselves built upon the very same modern philosophies and practices that enslaved the colonized and justified their enslavement. Philosophies of emancipation in enlightenment discourses constitutively excluded the enslaved, colonized, and dispossessed from the "universal" subject of freedom, producing a tragic bind in which Black and colonized subjects desire a freedom that has been premised upon their exclusion.

Scott makes this claim by analyzing C. L. R. James's reading of Toussaint Louverture, the late eighteenth-century Haitian leader of the most successful slave revolt in the New World, a revolt that broke open the exclusion of the enslaved from freedom, although the governing system that replaced it entrenched a hierarchical European model of personhood and continued forced labor upon "emancipated" subjects.[5] For Scott, Louverture is the inaugural figure of the tragedy of modern emancipation, as he inadvertently but inescapably recapitulates the racial subordination he aims to countermand. Louverture's predicament is this: "how to use the enlightenment that is his inheritance—and which as a consequence he cannot disavow—to secure and sustain the only image of freedom intelligible to him."[6] Louverture's dilemma continues to the present, in which, for Scott, postcolonial discourses of emancipation recapitulate this tragic bind. To call emancipation a tragedy highlights the failure of national revolutionary projects to overthrow racial domination even when they put a stop to de jure colonial governance. To narrate the end of colonialism in the twentieth century as a decisive break with unfreedom is, for Scott, a "revolutionary romance" of redemption and vindication that disavows the foreclosed future of freedom as it was imagined in the revolutionary era. Tragedy's emphasis on the limits of human action and the ways that oppressive orders are inadvertently reproduced is a more accurate orientation for the post-emancipation era. Enlightenment images of emancipation, produced out of a contrast with slavery and within a dynamic of slave ownership, are inspired by the same forces that create slavery and colonialism. They thus inhibit the freedom struggles they simultaneously galvanize.[7]

Scott's argument is emblematic of an important body of scholarship in Black and postcolonial studies that I call "tragedies of emancipation," which includes seminal work by Saidiya Hartman, Orlando Patterson, W. E. B. Du Bois, and others.[8] For these thinkers, interpreting historic emancipations as tragedies involves attending to the unfreedoms that remain after and through emancipation. They ask not only what emancipation has enabled but what it has wrought, viewing emancipation events less as breaks from the past and more as shifts in the racial logics of exploitation.[9] As Hartman succinctly states, "Emancipation appears less the grand event of liberation than a point of transition between modes of servitude and racial subjection."[10] Tragedy attends to the obstructed struggles against racial oppression and the often insurmountable defeats of this fight that undo even its most ardent advocates. Tragedy, for Raymond Williams, includes "the deferment and corrosion of hope and desire," and thus is better suited to emphasize the defeats of emancipation in which racial terror is a fixture of modern enlightenment, not its antithesis.[11] Modern freedom, for these scholars, is ugly insofar as it is a racial entitlement of whiteness, which marks Black life as the site and condition of unfreedom.

This chapter engages but also shifts the tragedy of emancipation in a US context. It takes as an analytic object the controversial fiction film on emancipation *Manderlay* (Lars von Trier, 2005), in which a Black community chooses to remain enslaved on the Manderlay plantation seventy years after emancipation. There are various ways to read the film, but many critics argue that *Manderlay* is a tasteless spectacle of racism that makes slavery seem preferable to emancipation. *Manderlay*'s Black characters claim that they desire enslavement, that slavery is more survivable than freedom, or at least the freedom that is on offer in the United States. They petition for a new master of the plantation to watch over them and control their labor and lives. As one critic put it, *Manderlay* "denies the historical agency of black Americans" while indulging the conventional racist fantasy of contented slaves.[12] It can be seen as "some sort of white man's fantasy," in the words of another, even recapitulating white desires for plantation mastery examined in chapter 1.[13] The film's narrative of chosen enslavement can certainly be read that way. But it can also be seen to show how possibilities for Black freedom continue to be delimited by the very terms on which freedom is grounded. *Manderlay*'s disorienting past upends the comforting interpretation of emancipation as the founding moment that propelled US racial progress from slavery to freedom. If *Manderlay* emphasizes continuity with the experience of slavery, it does so critically, not approvingly, not to bluntly suggest that past enslavement is coterminous with the present but to highlight the betrayals of America's juridical promise of freedom within ongoing practices of racial domination. It shows how plantation mastery remains a practice of ugly freedom *after* enslavement.

In this sense, *Manderlay* has affinities with the philosophical arguments of Afropessimism, and the film's other reception, besides as a racist film, has been that it is alternately a key visual text of Afropessimism. Afropessimism argues that Black subjectivity is permanently excluded from the category of humanity. As articulated by Frank Wilderson, Calvin Warren, and others, blackness is always equated with enslavement as an ontological category; it is a category of being as social death.[14] Black subjectivity is constitutively barred from inhabiting the subject of politics and only available as an object of violence, which constitutes the organizing antiblack structure of the white social order. Wilderson has placed *Manderlay* on his list of key Afropessimism texts and has argued that "*Manderlay* invites us to think of slavery as a relation of power between those who are ontologically dead, and those who are ontologically alive."[15] In this reading, *Manderlay* reveals how blackness is permanently and ceaselessly coterminous with slavery. *Manderlay* does share kinship with Afropessimism's philosophical commitments, yet whereas Afropessimism sees blackness as an ontological category of social death that is stable and unchanging across and as modernity, on my reading *Manderlay* reveals blackness's coarticulation with enslavement as a political and social dynamic, which makes it subject to change, revolt, and revision. The film's emphasis on political construction rather than constitutive ontology directs focus to the narratives, discourses, and genres that perpetuate the practice of freedom as whiteness, which also means that different practices, histories, and genres can offer different futures.

Manderlay suggests that racialized unfreedom today is partly perpetuated through conventional understandings of the historical event of emancipation. *Manderlay*'s slavery out of time is thus not historical revisionism but a challenge to how the past is narrated in the present and to what effect. It deconstructs, to borrow Walter Johnson's terminology, "the mythic march of freedom."[16] Three aspects of the typical narrative of emancipation are particularly strong contributors to the mythic march of freedom: when the story of emancipation (1) places Black unfreedom in the past, (2) claims uninterrupted progress to the present, or (3) names Lincoln and/or other white actors, including the white body politic, its main protagonists. These readings of emancipation are forms of violence to the Black freedom struggle in the present that also elide how current political structures perpetuate racial exploitation in part by disavowing its continuation. *Manderlay* not only suggests that these mythic visions are dangerous to the present but also demonstrates that, while the past can never be fully re-created and understood, it can be reinterpreted in the present as a challenge and a spur to different

2.1 Intentionally unrealistic mis-en-scène of *Manderlay* (Von Trier, 2005), seen from above.

visions of Black freedom in the future. By not demanding fealty to the historical record or archive, *Manderlay* allows for a wide-ranging exploration of and challenges to Black unfreedom which traverses the fictive, historical, and philosophical. Its deliberately unrealistic mis-en-scène—the entire movie takes place on an empty soundstage with minimal props—forecloses the illusions of realism to foreground the artificiality of its construction (figure 2.1). *Manderlay*'s historical disloyalty is thus not a truth claim or a recovery project but a constructed intervention into contemporary discourses of Black freedom.[17]

Yet *Manderlay*'s tragic vision, so powerful at first viewing, does not actually end in pessimism, resignation, or defeat. In a complex move missed by critics, the film explores how violent racialized imaginaries of freedom might be performatively unmade. *Manderlay* thus contributes to but also reworks tragedies of emancipation, as it depicts actions that move beyond tragedy to imagine the end of racial domination. These actions are not how one might otherwise imagine emancipation, however. They are small-scale, morally ambiguous, and violent performances of racialized freedom that disarticulate freedom from whiteness, counterintuitively, by performing their conflation. In this sense, *Manderlay* addresses ugly freedoms in both valences, as it both showcases the ugliness of freedom practiced as white mastery and depicts unfamiliar freedoms that might otherwise be dismissed as ruinous or negligible.

In an important intervention into slavery studies, Johnson petitions scholars not to fetishize agency in the retelling of life under slavery and its aftermath, in order to more accurately capture Black experiences of enslavement and post-slavery exploitation. A singular focus on agency misses other modes of experience and subjectivity, other forms of pleasure, survival, and daily management of life, to imagine all people through "an anachronistic (and generally unarticulated) assumption that beneath all history there lies a liberal individual subject waiting to be emancipated into the precise conditions" of twenty-first-century life.[18] Yet the response to his argument has sometimes been to eliminate agency altogether as an analytic of history and politics, to pinball from one extreme to the other and now claim that agency is an irrelevant category of action, a fantasy of capacity, or an old-fashioned term fully exhausted by its liberal forms.[19] *Manderlay* suggests that one need not relinquish freedom or agency as desires, actions, and goals of the past or the present. The challenge, rather, is to flesh out the multiple and wide-ranging possibilities of action besides heroic agency or passive domination that extend beyond liberal configurations and may not seem preferable or even desirable within standard analytics of resistance.

The freedom formulated in *Manderlay* is unfamiliar in that it rejects self-mastery, uncoerced choice, and personal pursuits.[20] And it also rejects the belief that fights for Black freedom must be morally righteous or categorically virtuous, claims that stifle freedom struggles by marking them as only worthy when they are normatively sanctioned by existing power structures that delimit freedom's expression. James Baldwin condemned how Black freedom struggles were only legible to white imaginaries when Black actors were envisioned as unthreatening and virtuous victims, and *Manderlay* upholds Baldwin's critical condemnation.[21] The actions it offers may appear to be ugly freedoms in that they trade on racial stereotypes of theft, sex, and ignorance in order to perform an ambiguous emancipation untethered to either the nation-state or the abstractions of universal personhood. They dare audiences to condemn these practices. And in so doing, they project a different type of emancipatory practice resting on a different vision of freedom struggling to be articulated, and for that reason may be easily overlooked, or demonized as self-defeating and shameful.

Manderlay's emancipatory acts respond to Scott's tragedy by both accepting and moving beyond its tragic genre form; while Scott calls for new images and practices of emancipation, he does not suggest what those new imaginaries might look like, in part because he suggests we do not yet have a robust conceptual vocabulary attuned to the possibility of freedom without domination, self-determination without sovereignty, or collective emancipation from white supremacy outside the nation-state. *Manderlay*, I would suggest, offers one rejoinder to Scott's call. It struggles to articulate a different freedom, a confusing freedom that is reflected in *Manderlay*'s own complexities, as on my reading the film depicts not just one analysis but three distinct interpretations of emancipation. In what follows I offer three different readings of the film, as each one offers a different emancipatory form. Each revolves around the emancipation of one character and presents a distinct problem for abolitionist efforts. The first emancipation is de jure emancipation, which neither offers freedom nor ends slavery. It highlights how legal emancipation persists in structuring freedom through white mastery, making freedom continually unavailable for the formerly enslaved and those barred from participation in whiteness. The second emancipation, performed by the main character Grace, a young white woman who emancipates the slaves seventy years after abolition, casts freedom as a gift from free and magnanimous nation to a grateful Black population who first require disciplinary guidance to become responsibly free. This freedom emancipates whiteness from addressing its constitutive antiblack racism. These two versions of emancipation work within the terms of the first ugly freedom: they show how emancipation denies or disavows Black freedom, and thus align with Scott's tragedy of emancipation; here, declarations of freedom articulate new forms of racialized bondage.

The third emancipation is disconcerting, but it moves beyond tragedy to reflect the second meaning of ugly freedom, finding emancipatory actions that would otherwise seem to reflect defeat and despair. When a former enslaved community member, Timothy, steals and gambles away the plantation's money, then has sex with Grace, he helps to do what the first two emancipations could not: bring about the downfall of the Manderlay plantation. On the one hand, his theft could be seen as the culminating failure of emancipation. It could perform how the formerly enslaved cannot yet handle the responsibility of freedom, or merely reinscribe the shopworn trope of Black criminality. But, on the other hand, the theft is a provocative performance of white supremacy *as* theft, which also dismantles reigning presumptions about what freedom entails and who can practice it. Timothy's disconcerting sex with Grace performs the inverse, as an act that often mobilized the violence of white heteropatriarchy throughout US history here thwarts Grace's emancipatory domination. In the end, he neither desires the money he stole nor the woman he had sex with; he is not reclaiming possession of either as proof of his freedom, but is defying possession itself as the ground of freedom. Timothy's acts rend connections between possession, freedom, and whiteness. Indeed, they expose the emancipatory machinations of all of the freed people's acts throughout the film and reveal how the whole film has been a disconcerting emancipation process, which would otherwise seem a self-defeating slide toward ruination. Importantly, this third emancipation is not delimited by enlightenment images of freedom structured within the hallowed claims and whitened content of universal individual personhood. It is confusing precisely because it is not captured by these imaginaries. It reflects, instead, a shared practice that violently upends white freedom even as it may first look like abnegation, subservience, or dereliction. The Manderlay residents have rejected the compulsion to desire the freedom they have been gifted and are seeking instead to define and enact a conception of freedom on their own terms.[22]

This third emancipation eludes and exceeds the filmmaker Lars von Trier's stated intent for *Manderlay* to "kick [America] in the ass" by fronting the racist and antidemocratic foundations of a violent country living in self-satisfied innocence.[23] When he conceived of the film, von Trier only knew "America" through its representations in film and television, and the first two emancipations fit relatively smoothly within this representational economy. They conjure an America incapable of disarticulating freedom from white supremacy and bound by popular histories of emancipation that recapitulate and perpetuate this violence. Von Trier punishes America through Grace's sexual humiliation and the burning of the plantation, as he positions both Manderlay and Grace to stand in for America's white domination. Yet the last emancipation escaped von Trier's control to project a vision of compromised and perplexing emancipatory practices that might otherwise go unnoticed within standard interpretations of freedom and agency. Trading in and trading up on the Black stereotypes and gendered violences von Trier has deployed, the third emancipation slips loose from the auteur's desire to limit alternatives to an endless repetition of racist violence or an affirmation of patriarchy. It points beyond the tragedy of endless domination (racial, economic, and sexual) and beyond the use of revolutionary romance for ending white supremacy—although the freedoms it depicts may bear little resemblance to freedoms envisioned in the past.

The Slavery of Emancipation: Wilhelm's Emancipation

Filmed entirely on a dimly lit, chalk-marked soundstage with minimal props, *Manderlay* opens with a southern plantation that still practices slavery well into in the twentieth century, long after the formal juridical emancipation of American slaves. Grace, a white woman and the daughter of a gangster, stumbles upon the Manderlay plantation just as Timothy, a slave, is about to be whipped. Invoking federal law, she storms into Manderlay with gangster gunmen behind her, grabs the whip from the slave master, and announces to the "Mam" of the house with Hollywood flair, "'Fraid not, lady. Slavery was abolished seventy years ago." The scene mimics conventional melodramatic expectations of rescue, as Grace informs Manderlay's white owners that she will "compel" them to obey her commands. She then unlocks the gates to the plantation and asks Wilhelm, a now-former slave and de facto spokesperson for the newly freed community, to "please let everyone know they can all enjoy the same freedoms as any other citizen of this country." Grace walks out of the gates and expects people to follow. They do not. This is the first of many actions that will confound Grace, who in this first emancipation is an avatar of liberal constitutionalism.[24]

Grace has faith that juridical institutions make people free, and she informs the freed residents that "the constitution can be found at any courthouse." She offers legal advice to Wilhelm on how to bring the plantation owners to trial for slavery and whispers conspiratorially about "a tip for when you sue the family," as if enslavement can be rectified by legal pathways for personal injury that claim all have equal standing before the law. As she lays dying, the Mam of the plantation tells Grace about "Mam's Law," the law of the plantation that the slaves had followed—laws that superseded federal law at the Manderlay plantation. Mam's Law is a terrifying document that demands humiliating actions from the enslaved and categorizes them into racial stereotypes to regulate their behavior accordingly. Grace replies that Mam's Law is now void, replaced by US Law, proclaiming the legal transition from slavery to freedom. But the promise of emancipation to cancel the unfreedoms of Mam's Law is quickly undone when, in the freed people's first engagement with their former masters, the former masters draw up new contracts for their employment. Economic contracts ostensibly confer the freedom to choose one's work and get paid fairly, echoing the liberal premise of free labor *as* freedom, but here they primarily work as a new form of racial control.[25] As the film's narrator notes, the contract is something one signs only if one has no choice, as wages will go right back into the pockets of white owners and instantiate wage slavery. The legal contract offered to Manderlay's Black residents extends Black inequality under a veneer of universal freedom and contractual choices. Like the racial contract explicated by Charles Mills, this contract offers a fictitious egalitarianism that continues Black exploitation through the language of abstract individual personhood; it disavows the subordination it codifies in free choice and paid labor.[26] In response, Grace has her father's gangster lawyer create new contracts that the white masters are compelled to accept at gunpoint. In the new contract, the freed workers are given cooperative ownership of the plantation, and the ex-masters are contracted as their employees but without pay. Grace views this new document as the power of justice and as proof of her capacity to fight for the freed people through legal processes. Domination, however, is not diminished but extended, as the masters now also become slaves under the gun.

From the outset of the film, declarations of emancipation obfuscate rather than support freedom. "I'm afraid," Wilhelm expresses after emancipation. "At Manderlay we took supper at seven. When do people take supper when they're free?" This is not a mundane question, nor does it signify that Wilhelm misunderstands the hallowed nature of freedom. It is a question about the lived possibilities of emancipation, about the real sense of vacuousness and disorder that emancipation confers upon those declared free while still enmeshed in a society structured by racial domination, a society in which the formerly enslaved have no access to power or processes that govern their lives—precisely the unfreedoms Frederick Douglass decries after the Emancipation Proclamation is declared.[27] Wilhelm asks about freedom that is not imagined as an inner state free of coercion but a lived practice of full participation in one's life decisions. Yet Grace interprets Wilhelm's question to be nonsensical and thus a sign that the people she emancipated need her wisdom to make the transition to freedom, and she decides to stay on the plantation to guide their progress. Much of the film covers the trials and tribulations of post-emancipatory life at Manderlay through a loose narrative in which the residents seem to progress in expected ways—with various setbacks—from confusion, ignorance, and mistrust to self-sufficiency, property ownership, and free subjectivity. After a dust storm nearly pulls the plantation into starvation, everyone at Manderlay works together to rescue the cotton crop. Together, ex-slaves and ex-masters, Black and white, lawgivers and law followers, share tasks to harvest a small but high-quality crop of cotton that will provide enough money to support everyone through the season. The plantation survives because all its residents achieve the goal, as the narrator describes it, of "free Americans living together." The crop's success appears to be the realized dream of universal freedom that emancipation confers. In a scene of celebration, Grace pronounces everyone "Graduate Americans," something she alone seems able to determine, and then has sex with Timothy, the Black plantation worker whom she emancipated at the outset of the film, and for whom she has shown an obvious sexual attraction. As the film seems poised to conclude, the narrative toys with viewers' expectations of a conventional ending in which Black residents move inexorably toward freedom and democratic governance and white residents move from racism to inclusion and acceptance—the story of emancipation retold as US history and celebrated on the Emancipation Proclamation's 150th anniversary. It is the story, as Benjamin Jealous explained, wherein the US is liberated from its own contradictions. But the situation changes rapidly, from emancipatory liberation to tragic undoing. During the celebration someone steals all of the money from the cotton crop. A fire starts on the plantation, two people die, and all of the white ex-overseers run away. The plantation has imploded. Grace decides to end her "experiment in freedom," and packs up to leave Manderlay. But Wilhelm informs her that the former slaves have made a democratic decision. They have unanimously voted to continue living on the plantation as slaves, and they want Grace to be their new master, the new Mam of the plantation.

Wilhelm argues that the formerly enslaved people are unable to survive in US society as free people. The world is not ready for them, he says, implying that America cannot accommodate truly free Black people despite the promises of abolition, confirming Angela Davis's argument that "if slavery was declared dead, it was simultaneously reincarnated through new institutions, new practices, new ideologies."[28] Wilhelm suggests, like Davis, that the society the Manderlay residents would be emancipated into would re-bind them through economic practices, segregationist laws, lynching, and other practices of white supremacy, practices that sustain and relocate rather than eradicate racial hierarchy.[29] Emancipation does not offer freedom because the very juridical and cultural grounds of society continue to align freedom with whiteness, and its promises of freedom accommodate, rather than undo, racial oppression. Wilhelm states that the Black residents will "have no chance in the wild," likening the America outside Manderlay's gates to a lawless and bestial place of unrelenting violence. Wilhelm's point is secured as the camera pans out to the front of the plantation where Bart, a Black man who had run from the plantation to freedom at the beginning of the film, is now hanging under a tree. He was lynched as soon as he stepped out as a free man into an emancipated America.[30] Lynching is one of the ugliest practices of ugly freedom, the freedom of white people to reassert mastery and supremacy over Black life, a power that supersedes the law.[31] If whiteness after emancipation congeals as a feeling of entitled sovereignty that must continually be reasserted, then lynching is a practice of white freedom as the power of death over Black life without consequence.

Wilhelm knows this. He argues, "America was not ready to recognize us negroes seventy years ago, and it still ain't. And the way things are going, it won't be in another hundred years from now"—a claim that brings Wilhelm's critique into the present and is reinforced at the end of the film with a concluding montage of photographs documenting racial violence in America into the twenty-first century. If the film is premised upon imagining the continuation of slavery after formal emancipation, the montage places Wilhelm's critique and slavery itself within close proximity to the present, in a gesture that makes visible what Saidiya Hartman has called "the time of slavery," an ongoing time in which slavery conditions the possibility of the present world and manages the governing of blackness so that the racial injustices of the present recapitulate the logic of slavery with minor differences and amendments.[32] Perhaps the law cannot end slavery because it did not establish it, for US American slave laws only legitimated the already existing customs of a social order that constructed the idea of race to justify structures of subordination, inferiority, and unfreedom—just as the *Fundamental Constitutions of Carolina* imported the preexisting practices of racialized slavery established long before in Barbados. Whiteness, here, is a freedom that entails sovereignty over Black life and protection from extralegal state violence, and blackness is exclusion from state protection and subjection to white sovereignty. This is a continuation of the freedom of the Barbadian plantation owner that influences American politics, examined in chapter 1. Legal emancipation does not change this underlying structure, and the residents of Manderlay wager that they will be safer under a system they have a hand in choosing. They use their chosen master to protect them from this system's most violent excesses, and Wilhelm actually calls the choice of slavery "the lesser of two evils." Slavery on Manderlay presents better prospects than freedom in America, articulating the experience Guyora Binder has named "the slavery *of* emancipation."[33]

Wilhelm insists that philosophical discourses of freedom play a role in the tragedy of emancipation. Grace angrily replies to Wilhelm's request for re-enslavement, "Dammit Wilhelm, they're not free! That's what matters," but Wilhelm responds, "I call that a philosophical argument." Wilhelm is right, as David Scott and Charles Mills would note: Grace's vision of freedom is conditioned by enlightened, liberal philosophical discourses that both disavow their racial formation and perpetuate it. This tragedy arises because the slavery of emancipation arises within and alongside the visions of emancipation in foundational philosophies of freedom, especially those of Locke, Mill, and Kant.[34] Their philosophies of freedom combine visions of emancipation from unjust authority with justification of despotism and inequality for "uncivilized" nonwhite peoples; indeed, they make racial exclusion the

2.2 The abstractions of freedom made visible.

condition of their universal visions.[35] Western philosophical visions of individual self-determination can be constructed through racialized slavery and even draw their vision from the experience of slaveholding power.[36] For some, like Locke, the social relations of the plantation create one path for envisioning modern freedom. In canonical treatises, Black freedom is typically cast as both illegible and a threat to the social order; as Nikhil Singh argues, Black subjects' "very existence counts not only as an aggression against freedom but also against life itself, and who therefore can be permanently sequestered, governed without rights, or killed with impunity."[37] Black slavery is the negative through which freedom is envisioned as an ideal.[38]

"How dumb do you think we really are?" Wilhelm asks Grace, for the residents of Manderlay are acutely aware of this constructed unintelligibility and its production of racial violence. The empty, placeless mise-en-scène of the soundstage underscores Wilhelm's critique of the philosophic abstractions in the racial contract, which posit the brightness of universal freedom denied to the Black subjects who provide its contrasting image (figure 2.2). The vacuousness of the filmic setting mirrors the emptiness of claims for legal freedom that disavow their racialized formation. Through the racial contract and the lynch mob, the abstract promise of universal personhood underpinned by racial difference consigns the ex-slaves' lived unfreedom to shadow. *Manderlay*'s static and unchanging mise-en-scène reflects the presumption that slave dynamics are unchanging and static, that proclamations of political emancipation do not actually shift the lived experiences and antiblack underpinnings of racial dynamics on the ground. Reflected in the staging, these dynamics contribute to an Afropessimist reading of the film as illuminating the ontology of antiblackness.

But Wilhelm drops another bombshell that further complicates the role of the legal order both in eradicating slavery and in an Afropessimist reading of the film. He informs Grace that *he* actually wrote Mam's Law. The degrading set of laws that Grace called "the most abominable, contemptible book ever written . . . a recipe for oppression and humiliation from start to finish," which required slaves to perform parades, avoid touching trees, and behave according to racial stereotypes, was actually authored by enslaved people themselves. When slavery formally ended, Wilhelm explains, Manderlay's Black residents felt no relief. "Legislators promised all kinds of things, but we didn't believe them." Mam's Law was a substitute for a legal order that could not enact its own promises of Black freedom. It encoded survival strategies; it made the trees untouchable because the trees provided a windbreak that protected the food crops from debilitating storms. Its mandated daily parade happened in the only shady part of the plantation to provide a social midday respite from hard labor. The personality typecasting in Mam's Law offered strategies for self-preservation within the crushing depredations of white supremacy. Many of the ex-slaves knew this and authorized the laws: they *chose* Mam's Law. They developed their own laws for protection and reprieve from what the narrator calls "the world of no hope that they would surely have to lead in the outside world." Wilhelm specifically states that the only weapons on the plantation before Grace's arrival were a toy gun and a rusty unused rifle. No one was held by force, at least not by the kind of force Grace might have imagined when she first walked into Manderlay. Through Mam's Law, the residents of Manderlay invented a survivable space where they self-organized their daily lives. The terribleness of the laws represents their sense of available options for survival in the United States, and the apparent fact that their survival as a democratic collective was more secure under the pretense of slavery than the juridical revelation of Black freedom, would seem to affirm their decision. If US emancipation was part of a social order shaped by racial domination, what Sylvia Wynter has called the Janus-faced effects of emancipation yoked to mass human degradation, then Manderlay's residents respond to it in a life-sustaining way by inventing their own laws and possibilities for self-governance.[39]

Mam's Law subtly posits that antiblackness is countered—not merely perpetuated—by Mam's Law. The Manderlay residents have crafted a relatively self-governing polity, with laws created and sanctioned by the community it regulates. Mam's Law as a self-governing community reflects the second valence of ugly freedom, as the freed people fight for freedom as shared and mutual participation in the governing conditions of their lives, even though they live in conditions not of their choosing, in an undesired world they are conscripted to live within—and they do this in a way that may be unintelligible or nonsensical to those who live differently. Before Grace and her father came to the plantation, the residents were experimenting with freedom as collective and reflexive self-governance under a regime of racial violence. Their solution for exclusion from the American polity is not inclusion; they are not fighting to be included in American visions of freedom, nor in universal visions of personhood saturated with white supremacist logics. Instead, they remake the terms of political community altogether. Participation in America's universal personhood, they counter, is not their desired inheritance. They are not fighting to claim that American law must recognize them as equals. Instead, they reject the very legal terms on which American freedom is offered to compose their own, even when the perplexing freedoms they proffer through Mam's Law may not seem desirable or inspiring.

Their practice at one level sets up what Fred Moten and Stefano Harney call the undercommons, in which radical refusal is practiced in a range of insurgent practices beneath the radar of the political, a realm in which blackness is excluded from political subjectivity. And yet the problem that *Manderlay* points to is both exclusion and exploitation, not only a rejection from the political per se but also incorporation into the political as its material and reproductive ground, as the exploited center. In this sense, the Manderlay residents do not practice the refusal of the political, but the refiguration of the political. This is an undercommons that remakes and takes over politics, reorganizing the terms upon which political power is generated and sustained. For the Manderlay residents, politics is not the rights and citizenship practices of the liberal subject, but a new form of legal self-making. Linda Zerilli argues that freedom is not about being ungoverned but about how one is governed and what say one has in governance alongside others.[40] Mam's Law is an experiment more akin to this version of freedom. It may seem a disappointing or deflating political freedom, not a hallowed ideal of free agency but rather ambivalent practices of collective reorganization within coercive institutions. And it may be overlooked or disparaged or rejected for that reason.

In this first emancipation, *Manderlay* could be read to suggest that slavery is preferable to American racism or that antebellum slavery is indistinguishable from the current social order. Yet in a more nuanced reading the law-making forms of self-governance practiced by the characters in Mam's Law are not seen as false consciousness, self-abnegating despair, or meaningless irrationality, but instead as a response to the ugliness of US emancipation. It is preferable, even under conditions of extreme duress, to the freedoms offered by legal proclamations of emancipation from systems still deeply invested in antiblackness. In fact, the residents' preference is so threatening to the social order that it can only happen outside sanctioned juridical forms, and through the public prism of enslavement. The world constructed by the community through Mam's Law might seem morally compromised or fatalistic—not exactly the ideals of a self-governing polity romanticized in Tocqueville's New England township—but it is an experiment in freedom that pushes against the boundaries of what seems possible, an ugly freedom in a minor key.

Emancipation as Exoneration: Grace's Emancipation

Manderlay's second emancipation is Grace's act of freeing the slaves from Mam, the old master of the plantation. Here, emancipation is a gift. Grace is the only white character in the film who tries to help the enslaved residents rather than profit from or ignore their plight, and she aims to grant them their rightful freedom.[41] But her vision of emancipation becomes a form of tyranny: she demands indebtedness from the formerly enslaved for her act while also casting them as politically underdeveloped and helpless. In this second form of emancipation, *Manderlay* dramatizes the racial violence done by histories of emancipation that position white people as the central agents of Black freedom.[42] But rather than denying the historic agency of Black Americans, as critics contend, *Manderlay* more subtly shows *how* Black agency is denied within national imaginaries of emancipation. *Manderlay* is, in this sense, a prescient critique of the pantheon of Hollywood films on emancipation, like *Lincoln*, where Black characters are cast as background, dependent for their freedom on the virtuous white leaders who rescue them.[43]

At the outset of the film, Grace sees a terrible wrong done to the enslaved Manderlay residents, and she feels morally compelled to stop it. She argues, against her father, that racial injustice must be her responsibility. When her father tells her to ignore the plantation because however appalling it seems, this out-of-time enslavement is not her problem—thus repudiating shared accountability for social injustice—she retorts: "Do you think the negroes wanted to leave Africa? Wasn't it us who brought them to America? We have done them a great wrong. It's our abuse that has made them what they are." She sees the problem of slavery as one for which white people past and present are accountable, and she feels obligated to help because she recognizes

2.3 Transferring the whip of domination from enslavers to emancipators.

her own structural position of power in this scenario. Unlike her father, and unlike every other white character on the soundstage, she is burdened by the historical weight of racial violence. Yet her burden is also misplaced: she did not personally bring Black people from Africa. She is not individually responsible for the abusive actions of dead white slaveholders, though she is the direct beneficiary of the white supremacy they cultivated. Her argument denies complex claims of accountability to instead position her as the author of Black subjectivity, and its savior. Her statement "our abuse has made them what they are" situates her as a creator of blackness while disregarding Black personhood outside white abuse. This statement paves the way for Grace's educational mission that follows. If she has "made them what they are" in the past, then she also has the capacity to remake them in the present. She envisions her own power through her self-imposed mission to engender free Black subjectivity. When Grace grabs the whip in the first moments of the film, then, the power of domination metaphorically passes from the slave-owners to Grace, from one kind of domination to another (figure 2.3).

Grace hopes that emancipation will shift the subjectivity of the enslaved, from brutalized and disempowered subjects to self-mastering and self-possessed individuals. She wants to see what the narrator calls "the burgeoning change in character that freedom ought to bring," which presumably entails hard work, self-discipline, and dutiful rule-following. But after emancipation the freed people do not behave in the way she expects. The camera pans their actions from Grace's viewpoint, as they gamble, have sex, loaf around, and hit their kids. They enact and affirm the racial stereotypes that structure political discourses and philosophical arguments about preparing the not-yet-civilized for integration into the norms of individual freedom. Grace explains that she expects more of them and attempts to guide the freed people through an educative, disciplinary project meant to assimilate them into the terms of liberal subjectivity. Legal emancipation in the United States took shape through concepts of freedom like property, individual will, and self-possession, as Hartman has argued, all of which fashion Black subjects as permanently obligated to whiteness and seeming to require training from white actors in order to perform values deemed universal.[44] Grace's emancipation enacts this obligation and sustains her erotic investment in Black improvement. Crafted through her sexualization of Timothy's body and her sadistic investments in both Black suffering and in being the person who alleviates it, Grace's emancipation becomes its own form of racial terror.

Grace addresses the legacy of slavery by focusing not on a society structured by the white supremacy that Wilhelm points to, but on the freed people's individual conduct, and presumes that the best way to overcome structures of racial domination is personal character formation.[45] She encourages the residents to cut down the trees on the property to strengthen their rickety shacks and improve their property, what she understands to be a project of individual initiative and personal respectability—but they hesitate, as these are the very trees that Mam's Law had forbidden them from touching. Grace surprised they would still be beholden to that law, and to motivate the behavior she wants to see, Grace employs racism as a shaming tactic, asking, "Isn't it true that even someone poor and colored can still take the time to maintain their home?" When the freed people follow her directions and cut the trees, she views this as proof that she can change their character into self-reliant subjects rather than encumbered followers of Mam's Law; for Grace, dependence on her instruction is individual freedom. Yet she is also uninformed and indifferent to the specific environmental conditions at Manderlay; the lumber improves their shacks, but without trees to shelter the food crops, the plantation becomes vulnerable to the region's devastating sandstorms. The cutting of the trees, actions Grace presumed would fortify self-motivated work and disciplined free subjectivity, soon ruins the plantation's crops and threatens everyone with starvation.

Grace's desire to emancipate Manderlay is inseparable from a desire to see herself as virtuous for doing so. She views her act as giving what Mimi Nguyen calls the gift of freedom, a present of beneficent liberty in which grantees must be ceaselessly grateful and obeisant, in which Grace's capacity to both acknowledge and alleviate their pain is proof of her own potent agency.[46] She wants the goodness of her act to be recognized by those she

2.4 Desiring gratitude for emancipating others: the emancipation of whites.

frees. Grace desires this self-referential virtue and wants to see the "glow" that her actions engender in the freed residents, as the film's narrator notes. While she explicitly denies this desire, her face betrays her; she beams with joy when she thinks the newly emancipated people have come to thank her (figure 2.4). As Jacques Derrida notes about gift-giving more broadly, the relationship between giver and receiver can be a creditor-debtor relationship: "The gift . . . sends itself back the gratifying image of goodness or generosity, of the giving-being who, knowing itself to be such, recognizes itself."[47] Conceived of as a gift, emancipation comes with a burden of debt that recapitulates racial servitude as it gratifies the goodness of the bestower. Grace is anxious to see how Black freedom blossoms through her patronage. Timothy identifies this when he insists, "You do not see us for our humanity," suggesting that the freed people are background objects to the drama of emancipation in which Grace is the main character. Grace attempts to prove him wrong and brings a gift of art supplies to one Black child to show that she recognizes his unique skills, yet she hands the gift to another child because she cannot distinguish between them. Her gift of emancipation develops into what Jared Sexton calls "the emancipation of *whites*," in which white people, through self-described acts of benevolence, are emancipated from their association with antiblack racism, cleansed of their implication in it.[48] The gratitude of the freed people is precisely what will grant Grace the emancipation from complicity in ongoing racism that she desires, what will allow her to feel righteous, unimplicated in racial domination both inside and outside the plantation gates.

While Grace imagines the freed people as grateful recipients of her benevolent act, they thwart her at every turn, not only in their behavior but in

2.5 Democracy under the gun at Manderlay.

their affects. They generally refuse to make Grace feel good for ending their enslavement. Perhaps they see the need to free themselves from the gratitude Grace demands, and they stymie her investment in their racial uplift, almost anticipating her disappointment in their performances of idleness and neglect. When they do not enact the subjectivity of grateful receivers, docile subjects, and virtuous workers, Grace begins to institute lessons on democratic voting and comportment.[49] These are not lessons in coequal and participatory governance but in hierarchical forms of knowledge dissemination that, from the outset, structure her democracy in violent, antidemocratic ways. Her "students" sit below her while she informs them of how to act properly in a democratic space (figure 2.5). Her educational mission assumes the freed people have nothing to teach her about the way democracy should be practiced. Her introductory lesson is in "working together" and resolving problems by voting. The first topic someone brings to a vote is a dispute over who owns "little broken rake." The participants vote based on whom they like more. In the second vote the freed people determine that Sammy, whose laughter annoys others, can laugh only at predetermined times. "That's democracy?" asks Sammy, incredulous and wounded. In the final moments of the increasingly absurd lesson, the students decide to put time itself to a vote.

In this scene, it is important to the story that Grace is not a man, not the typical and expected white male master of the plantation. Grace, and Mam before her, remove the expectation that racist domination is always masculinized, and they re-center white women as active participants in creating and sustaining racial domination, both before and after slavery. As the main protagonist, Grace points to the central role of white women both in structuring slave societies and in generating their own freedom out of Black enslavement, as Stephanie Jones-Rogers and others have examined.[50] Grace's disciplinary, educative power seems to be "soft power," not the masculinized power of beating the dominated into submission through violence, but the stereotypical feminized power of moral, educative, and cultural suasion. Grace's power is, in her own mind, the power of the carrot not of the stick. Her "soft power," however, is clearly backed by violence. The gangsters compel everyone to attend Grace's lessons on democracy, because when the lessons are voluntary, no one shows up. Grace's fantasy of her own world-changing political agency through enlightened democratic pedagogy is sustained by the combined power of her family's accumulated capital and the immediate threat of violence.[51] Grace's gangster dad guarantees a salary to the gunmen, without whom Grace's attempt to enforce freedom by fiat would be untenable. Although the plantation did not have real guns before Grace arrived, it does now.

The hired guns are always in the shadows behind Grace (figure 2.5), imposing her version of liberal democracy and free subjectivity.[52] They lurk behind her in the scene, so she is the only one who doesn't see them at all times. Grace is the only one who can pretend her gift does not involve physical force; it is as if the gunmen are outside her field of vision precisely so that her carefully structured ignorance can prevent only her from feeling their presence control the polity. All of the Black students face the armed men throughout the lesson on democracy. Her enforcement coerces the freed people into dependence on her regulations, a dependence she claims was already there prior to her intervention, and that justifies its continuance. Her freedom to enforce democracy depends on enforced Black subordination. In her gift of emancipation, freedom continues as white access to sovereignty and control over Black bodies, as white capacity to ignore the racialized violence underpinning their freedom.

When Timothy's theft finally explodes Grace's fantasies for establishing freedom at Manderlay, she explicitly enacts the violence of mastery that had been implicitly sustaining her tenure at Manderlay. She subjects Timothy to a vicious whipping, ostensibly for stealing, but certainly also for ruining the trajectory of her freedom project. There is a sexual dimension to her violence, as she had been attracted to Timothy throughout the film, and likely expected that sex with him would fulfill all her desires for the plantation. Timothy was the person most resistant to Grace's disciplinary tactics, and he would explicitly name the white supremacy expressed in her gifting gestures. Perhaps she hoped that having sex with him would let her tame his resistance, help him recognize her virtue, or move him from angry resister to loving and docile subject. Sex with Timothy symbolized, for Grace, her erotic capacity to reproduce freed people as grateful subjects. But their sex forecasts the future; departing from romantic expectations, it is uncomfortably aggressive and violent, leaving Grace tearful and confused. Immediately after their encounter, the plantation implodes. If Grace's ultimate goal for emancipation is her own exoneration from racial domination while retaining the capacity to perpetuate it, she is thoroughly thwarted by Timothy, who refuses to be grateful, rejecting her "gift" of sex and stealing the crop money.

When Grace finds out that the residents want to be re-enslaved, her emancipation project comes fully undone. Grace fantasizes that her agency in single-handedly emancipating enslaved people would prove her heroic virtue while remediating her complicity in white supremacy. Once it crashes down, she lashes outward in violence, then flees. Her whipping exposes the violence that was always present, as she enacts what Hartman calls the "spectacles of mastery" so crucial to white domination, which subtended her power all along.[53] It underpins the larger emancipatory conundrum Grace represents by her self-reflexive articulation of freedom: the desire to be the protagonist of others' emancipation belies a narcissistic investment in one's own redemption—if not the nation's redemption. It leaves the structuring grounds of white supremacy intact and the erotics of white brutality unacknowledged. It is a fantasy of Black emancipation as white exoneration.

By placing Grace as the master of the plantation, the film insists on white women's responsibility in perpetuating racial terror, challenging the claim that as a woman she would be a tempering force upon racial domination, or even unimplicated in it altogether. Grace's erotic attachments to Timothy's body, in one scene masturbating to visions of his body, her eyes lingering over his glistening bare skin in many others, reveals her investments in sexual control and fetishization of his "exotic" flesh, as the narrator describes it. She too turns Black freedom into personal sexual fantasy. Yet by allowing all the white men to escape any responsibility or punishment for perpetuating enslavement, or for their sexual violence so central to centuries of enslavement, and even allowing them to be the sole voices of reason in the film—Grace's father is singularly positioned as the purveyor of truth against Grace's bumbling domination—the film dissimulates the gendered and sexualized nature of racial domination. Roderick Ferguson insists that racism articulates in gender and sexual control, which reveals the limitations of Grace's comeuppance through sexual violence.[54] The camera takes pleasure in Grace's discomfort during sex, in the borderline violence of her coupling with Timothy, in Timothy's clear domination over Grace's body, asking viewers to see this sexual violence as deserved. In so doing it asks viewers to take part in punishing Grace through sexual control, to enjoy her pain, and to interrogate whiteness without interrogating gender and sexuality as enabling both domination and subordination.

By positioning Grace as the only source of racist structures on the post-emancipation plantation, the film does not interrogate patriarchy but instead recapitulates it, even perpetuating heterosexual domination by celebrating the sexualized punishment of its female protagonist. Heterosexual domination is how the film rebuffs Grace's emancipation, seemingly insisting that sexual violence against her is just deserts. The camera gaze's sadistic erotics over Grace's discomfort keep all women in their place and allow the white men of the picture to get off scot free, without any scrutiny. White supremacy has long depended on policing white women's bodies and sexual practices.[55] Von Trier continues this sexual policing, steeped in a masculinist view of power even as he critiques the racist foundations of the US political order. The film's condemnation of white supremacy through Grace shores up misogyny and normative heteromasculinity even as it critiques anti-blackness. It allows patriarchy not merely to escape critique, but also to be the presumptive norm for establishing the Black refusal of white supremacy.

Performing the Freedom of White Supremacy:
Manderlay's Emancipation

Manderlay also depicts a third emancipation, which begins with Timothy's theft of the crop money. The theft at first appears to be an act of wanton destruction that undoes the emancipatory possibilities of Manderlay, and suggests that the newly freed are not yet ready for the responsibilities of freedom. But it also reveals the most capacious emancipatory gestures in the film. On one reading, Timothy's theft is a straightforward crime. Assigned to guard the money collectively earned from the cotton crop, Timothy steals it and then gambles it away. The theft is not a political act; it is simply illegal and immoral, and it reinstates the cultural trope of Black deviance. Because theft is often associated in the United States with Black slavery in particular and blackness in general—Benjamin Franklin's claim that a slave is "by nature a thief" is only the most obvious example—Timothy's act can be seen to fulfill that racist stereotype, to be a self-defeating embrace of Black criminality that blocks the possibility of democratic freedom.[56] Perhaps it even recapitulates John Stuart Mill's claim, tucked into *On Liberty*, that nonwhite subjects require strict autocratic governance until they are disciplined into individual liberty.[57] But Timothy's theft is actually a deft political act, insofar as the theft reestablishes a political community outside dynamics of possession, mastery, and white supremacy. It represents Timothy's effort to "take" emancipation, rather than receive it as a gift from Grace.[58] Bonnie Honig argues that "taking" can be a critical democratic act, in which subordinated actors take and enact political powers rather than waiting for them to be granted by a regime invested in their subordination. And Cathy Cohen argues that deviance can perform a rejection of expectations of Black conformity to social orders, and indeed oppose them.[59] Reading Timothy's action through these perspectives, stealing and taking describe the same action from different viewpoints. In this sense, his theft enacts the second valence of ugly freedom: it conforms to racist stereotypes and is illegal, which may make it seem unworthy of freedom. But it also challenges the very presuppositions of white supremacy by taking freedom, and by dismantling the whitened subjectivity of self-mastery and self-possession as freedom's ground.

This third emancipation destroys Grace's freedom project and leaves the plantation without a master, and in so doing it inaugurates a new kind of emancipation. To interpret theft as an act of political taking and an emergent performance of freedom, we first have to examine the role of money and property in the film. In liberalism property is equated with modern freedom, and in American political economy, when freedom is often defined in a Lockean way through property ownership yet Blacks have historically been both barred from ownership and considered property, the law has protected slavery *as* freedom of property while deeming Black possession ipso facto theft. In response, Timothy's theft aligns with an alternative Black tradition that reinterprets the legality of theft. Lovalerie King argues that enslaved African Americans developed an alternate code of morality in which the real theft became the system of slavery—the wholesale theft of Black bodies and Black labor. They reinterpreted their taking of food and other necessities during slavery as the "reappropriating of what has already been stolen."[60] This continued in the post-emancipatory era as the originary theft persisted without acknowledgment or reparation, and its injustice was compounded by new forms of white theft such as contract labor and chain gangs. Theft in response to this condition is not only a form of garnering sustenance but a break with historical injustice, even an act of freedom. If Locke defines freedom as owning the fruits of one's own labor, then in this scenario reappropriating commodities bought by others with one's own stolen labor power is not a theft of others' property but a form of freedom—it is the pursuit of one's rightful property. From this perspective, thievery can be a

2.6 Racialized freedom: Timothy gains political legibility through criminality.

form of freedom. Stealing labor money, Timothy takes his property as an act of freedom.

Yet Timothy's theft is not precisely this form of taking. After all, he does not steal from the original robber of his labor, Grace as the white plantation master, but from the money earned by the collective laboring power of all the freed people—from those who have already had so much taken from them. In this sense, his theft does something different. In stealing the money earned by other laboring bodies and then spending it as he alone chooses, Timothy performs the freedom of white supremacy. He enacts freedom as the protected right to steal from Blacks and thus performs the ugly freedom of plantation mastery as it continues after emancipation. His theft reveals the underside of individual freedom in an era of racial capitalism. If freedom is found in individual self-interest and sovereign participation in relations of exchange—a political economy that presumes the amorality of financial decisions, harnesses other people's labor for profit, and prioritizes free choice over other values— then taking money is not problematic; it is axiomatic. Money grounds the freedom of the white characters. This freedom rewards the rapacious harnessing of financial opportunity so hostile to community, transmutes bodies into money, and disavows racial exploitation through the language of individual liberty. Timothy's theft claims the economic and political freedom of white supremacy sustained but disavowed in the racial contract.

Timothy's theft enacts individual freedom when performed by white subjects and punished as criminal deviance when performed by Black subjects. His theft is the mirror image of Grace's father, the gangster, who gains his power, wealth, and freedom by stealing from others. When Timothy steals, he gets whipped, but when Grace's father steals, he is granted the status of self-made outlaw who embodies unencumbered individual freedom. Black person-hood becomes politically legible primarily in the context of criminal acts, as Hartman and others detail, so it seems that Timothy claims political subjectivity precisely by embracing the criminal conditions of his legibility (figure 2.6). If theft is the primary act that has made Black agency politically legible in American law since the first slave codes, then Timothy's theft is the single performance of political agency legible to the white actors on the plantation.[61] Timothy's taunting line to Grace just before she whips him, "Remember: you made us," is crucial to this rejoinder. He places the origins of his criminal performance onto the white freedom Grace represents. Grace's claim to have "made them what they are" is part of her whiteness, but Timothy's theft wrests back her power to determine his subjectivity as it reveals that what she has "made" is the cultural inseparability between blackness and criminality as a substitute for Black freedom. His taking of freedom takes political subjectivity as it exposes the presuppositions of the racial contract, which uses abstractions of juridical freedom to obscure Black unfreedom, legally recognizes Black agency only through Black deviance, and legitimates white supremacy under the premise of hierarchies of "readiness" for freedom.[62]

Once again, however, this is not yet the whole picture. Timothy's act is not just an effort to reverse Benjamin Franklin's claim and make thievery equal whiteness. Instead, it fractures the links between whiteness and freedom, blackness and theft—and then practices different types of freedom from this wreckage. Timothy's theft carves out space for a distinct emancipatory vision. First, by performing himself the theft that is the provenance of the propertied white male, Timothy defies the assumption that freedom is only accessible to whiteness. Timothy's act destabilizes liberal presuppositions about who is made to be free and who is not. *He* enacts the individual freedom that is the provenance of white supremacy. He democratizes the entitlements of whiteness. Second, however, while Timothy performs the racialized freedom of white supremacy, in the end this type of freedom is *not* what he is after. He is not "taking" money, nor does he want to "take" the version of freedom experienced by Grace or the gangster, which prioritizes individual self-interest and valorizes theft of collective labor for individual gain. If Timothy only wanted what he had stolen, he would keep the money he acquires, or run away and lead a life of individual self-mastery, perhaps to become an outlaw like Grace's father. Instead, he gambles all of the money away without remorse and then returns to the plantation. He does not ultimately aim to steal others' labor power then claim to be self-mastering.

What can we make of a scenario where Timothy steals money and throws it away, then returns to the community he has stolen from? Timothy does not desire money as some sort of mastering power—to be used over others—as Grace and the slaveowners do. He does not relate to freedom as individual economic self-interest, or as private possession, or as exploitation of others. Nor does not presume that his theft of others' labor means he is self-mastering and self-made, unlike the discourses of white freedom he performs. He refuses to disavow his ties to the community that sustains him, a disavowal that upholds freedom as individual self-mastery. After all, Timothy remains within Manderlay's social fabric after stealing from all of its inhabitants. He is after a different freedom, a freedom disarticulated not only from whiteness, but also from possessive individualism and surplus value. If, as C. B. MacPherson and Cheryl Harris have differently argued, ownership and property are at the heart of liberal freedom and whiteness, then Timothy refuses both of them.[63] He is not after a piece of the pie, but has thrown the pie away.

Timothy thus does not aim to possess money or possess himself. Instead, he defies possession as the very base of freedom.[64] Timothy's theft and subsequent tossing of the stolen money rejects the freedom that money powers in racial capitalism: to own others and possess their labor power as property. Karl Marx posited that the freedom of capitalism is to own property and dispose of it; in throwing away the stolen labor money, the theft throws away this type of freedom—it throws out labor exploitation from the Manderlay community.[65] It rejects the regime of exploitative ownership altogether. Instead, Timothy "takes" nonhierarchical and equalized power relations by eliminating the domination subtending both Grace's emancipation and the legal proclamation of freedom. His theft is in service to the community to which he is a part; it enacts freedom that is a practice of community-making, of mutual assistance and shared power, and a collective freedom from white supremacy—a freedom that could only ever be collective. Timothy steals what seems most prized as freedom under racial capitalism to free Manderlay from it.[66] His criminality is worldmaking.

In a similar vein, Timothy's sex with Grace is also available to a parallel interpretation. In a white supremacist society that, as Michael Rogin argues, has discursively defined Black people's political desire for freedom as Black men's sexual desire for white women, Timothy's sex with Grace seems to enact the clichéd yet powerful white supremacist fear of Black freedom.[67] Yet it is also possible to read his act as thwarting that cliché while undoing Grace's freedom project. His brusque and disconcerting sexual intercourse, seemingly devoid of any desire for Grace, refuses her desire to turn him into a pliant and pleasing sexual subject. If he is grateful, she will feel exonerated from any complicity in perpetuating white dominance. He refuses to be grateful or submissive to her desires, and thus emancipates himself from her desire to use him in the service of her own emancipation. If, as Ferguson argues, Black subjects gain acceptance as good community members and citizens through their willingness to submit to sexual regulation, then Timothy refuses this acceptance. Through their bewildering sex, Timothy disarticulates his political power from Grace's desire. As with the theft, this act is a controversial performance of disavowed racial exploitation that also challenges this exploitation. Just as he is not "taking" money, he is not "taking" Grace. He is instead refusing the roles imposed upon him by the law, by race, by the sexualization of Black freedom, by Grace's fantasy of his pliability, and by categories of Black political legibility altogether. He thwarts her fantasy that her subjection of him is what he too desires.

Timothy dispossesses Grace of her attempted possession of his body. Timothy's goal is not to perpetuate theft and heterosexual dominance as practices of freedom, nor to revise them, but to end them altogether. Grace wants to make Timothy pleasurable for herself, to libidinalize her domination through his submission. Stephen Marshall argues that Black bodies function in a white supremacist society "as a libidinal economy of enjoyment" to provide pleasure and desire for whiteness in their disempowerment, and Timothy's disconcerting sex halts this libidinal circuit.[68] His performances of theft and sex both enact power presumed to be the purview of whiteness, and simultaneously cast off white freedom. In both of these provocative ways Timothy "takes" emancipation rather than receiving it as a gift of white supremacy.

If Timothy's controversial acts can be read as emancipatory, that opens space for other characters' actions to be interpreted in this way too. Take, for example, the seemingly most despairing moment in the film—when Wilhelm petitions for the re-enslavement of the Black community. What if his petition is not a sigh of resignation or a plea for survival, but a well-thought strategy couched in a performance of helplessness? For what would repulse Grace more than to be asked to own up to and accept the role she has only tacitly performed thus far—white master of the plantation? She has, up to this point, convinced herself that she is the benevolent emancipator of Black ex-slaves merely guiding their transition to freedom. When the freed people demand that she become the master and own it, she is forced to face the fact that she already is the master. White supremacy draws sustenance from constructed ignorance of its constitutive violence, and Wilhelm's plea undoes that in an instant. The power of the racial contract lies partly in its disavowal of its production of Black unfreedom, but Wilhelm's request forces Grace to avow what she had previously disavowed.[69] Grace runs away from the plantation, either refusing to accept her complicity in ongoing domination or, perhaps, realizing that the only way she can support real freedom on the plantation is to leave it. Either way, it's possible that the Manderlay community planned on this exact scenario. Timothy steals and performs racialized freedom in a way that derides the freedoms denied him by white supremacy. So, too, Wilhelm insists that Grace perform the freedom of plantation mastery granted to her by the same.

Were all of Manderlay's residents conspiring against Grace's gift all along under the guise of confusion, helplessness, and ignorance?[70] They did not plant for the harvest until Grace realized that no one was doing it, weeks later than it should have happened, though they all knew the correct schedule. They cut down the plantation's trees on Grace's suggestion, though they knew full well that the trees protected their crops from sandstorms. After all, they wrote Mam's Law protecting the trees. They often sat and gossiped rather than perform Grace's vision of self-disciplined free subjectivity. Their inane requests for democratic voting are quite canny in the way they undo Grace's investment in nondemocratic democracy. They perform indecision as a precise technique of what Fred Moten and Stefano Harney see as disruptive practice of the Black undercommons: "We surround democracy's false image in order to unsettle it. Every time it tries to enclose us in a decision, we're undecided."[71] The Manderlay residents' indecision was calibrated to frustrate Grace's gift of freedom with lassitude, befuddlement, and incomprehension. Their idleness was insurgent.

When the Manderlay residents eventually burn the plantation down, they practice the enduring tradition of slave rebellions where setting fire to plantations aimed to eradicate plantation power.[72] The residents draw on that resource to burn down freedom as Grace had enforced it. They burn it down to access new ways of being in place, not to trash the landscape but to destroy the relations of possession that organized it—and to rebuild something supportive on that very spot. In burning down the plantation rather than fleeing it, the residents refuse to relinquish their land, performing a determined commitment to place and community. They do not run away but instead force Grace to run away. They fight for the land as the groundwork for their self-governing polity, a relation that for them is about nurturing life and holding community, not exploitation and possession. Timothy was thus not the only emancipatory actor on the plantation; *all of the residents were acting in concert*. Indeed, Timothy's individual actions would not be successful without the calibrated actions of everyone on the plantation. Removing mastery from the plantation was necessarily an ensemble performance and could not have succeeded without collectivity. To focus on Timothy alone is to miss how his act is only the most visible emancipatory form, to fall prey to the fantasy of individual heroism as a solution for collective unfreedom.

The actions of the freed people are quite risky, in that their seeming illogicality and helplessness may fool not only Grace but also the film's viewers to the extent that they accept the stereotypes they vivify. Their acts of subterfuge, seeming on the surface to perform racial stereotypes of dependence, laziness, and ignorance, may trick the film's white audience as they trick Manderlay's white residents. None of the characters in the film appear particularly virtuous or likeable within conventional Hollywood standards for protagonists, and audience members are not asked to identify with any of the residents. Yet I would suggest that this too is an important political risk, to insist that the freedom of Manderlay's Black residents is not predicated on their virtuous suffering, on their likeability, as if they would have to be morally pure to deserve to be free. This is reflected in the cold and unwelcoming mise-en-scène, which forces a dissociation with the characters and their personal warmth to focus on their actions in themselves. The characters' idleness and moral complexities were not only part of a collective insurrection from white domination. They were also an insurrection from the filmic demands of racial melodrama, which would make their cause righteous only if they played kindly victims.[73]

The title of the film supports this conspiratorial reading of the third emancipation as a counterintuitive and collective insurgency. Manderley is the name of a fictional estate in Daphne du Maurier's novel *Rebecca*, in which another young white woman, invested in her own virtue, is relieved of her cruel optimism. She moves into her older husband's lavish Manderley estate, only to learn that the life he led there was a sham. What looked to outsiders like a proper marriage with his first wife was in fact a mask for socially unsanctioned and shockingly nonnormative sexual practices. Manderlay is also a ruse: what looks like a plantation housing a helpless, dependent, and ignorant Black community that chose to be enslaved seventy years after emancipation actually masks something socially unsanctioned and shockingly nonnormative—a relatively self-governing polity composed of Black people who together shape the laws that govern them. Through Mam's Law, they constructed a world seemingly unimaginable by interpretations of freedom as white domination—and less likely to be accepted than one of constructed subservience. Their polity is a direct undermining of the racial contract, not only in their real egalitarianism but in their refutation of the Millian belief that people would ever need to be disciplined into the proper political subjectivity of freedom. The residents of Manderlay do not need to be civilized into self-determining subjects by those who know better. They construct a living community "separate from the fantasies nestled into rights and respectability" as Jack Halberstam might note.[74] Manderlay is self-constituted as self-governing on its own terms before it is ever "freed" by Grace—a "freedom" that actively cultivated the dependence and exploitation of the polity.

Even Grace has a part to play in this third emancipation. When she leaves Manderlay, she both submits to dismantling the white domination she perpetuated and challenges the patriarchal violence perpetuated on her by the misogynistic gaze of the camera, which left her no options to contribute to ending white domination except to yield to the sexual degradation she supposedly deserved. Von Trier positions masculinized power to be the ground of Manderlay's liberation, punishing America for its racism through Timothy's sexual domination over Grace's body. He yokes Black emancipation to heteropatriarchy. Yet once Grace escapes, she leaves von Trier holding the bag. In von Trier's world, the cruelties of plantation mastery fall mainly on Grace's shoulders as a conniving and self-deluding woman, and he leaves all the white male characters unimplicated—even the initial Mam of the plantation is a woman. When Grace runs away from the plantation, it may seem as if she merely wants to escape her "experiment in freedom" and absolve herself of responsibility for the plantation's implosion. But if Grace's motivation to support emancipation was what brought her to the plantation—against the cynicism of her father and every other white man who informed her that racial domination was not her problem or encouraged her to exploit it—then perhaps she uses the forced recognition of her complicity to help dismantle it in the one way she can. Like the Manderlay residents, Grace remains compromised and unlikeable, unredeemed by a scene of recognition where she would admit her mistakes and soliloquize about her desire to rectify them. She does not perform a virtuous and chastised femininity, which loosens the hold of misogynistic cinematic representational structures. She finds the one way that she can support both Black and feminist freedom at Manderlay; she can leave. When she leaves, her actions are finally guided by the demands of the freed people, rather than by her own diagnosis of how she should engender freedom. And in a double move, she refuses to serve anymore as the repository of male rage, and exits the stage.

The Manderlay residents declared war on forms of emancipation that re-inscribed their oppression in order to create their own world premised on a new emancipatory vision—one stolen from purveyors who construct enlightenment as whiteness and theft. Manderlay's emancipatory theft is a stance against conquest that centers on practices of theft and criminality, akin to what Moten and Harney argue is a central aspect of blackness as fugitive study that involves work "to steal the enlightenment for others."[75] This risky thieving, the stealing of the enlightenment in order to give it to others, wrests white freedom as theft of bodies and theft of land away from those who have harnessed and continue to harness its power, in order to make its emancipatory promises work in a new register of radical mutuality, self-governance, and mutual flourishing. Is this not precisely what Timothy is stealing when he steals the wage labor in order to free the plantation residents from labor exploitation? When the residents burn the entire plantation property down in order to end the reign of white emancipation over their lives? By the end of the film, in the midst of a seemingly burned and failed experiment, the Manderlay residents have offered imaginative and capacious visions of what emancipatory action and nonhierarchical, collaborative freedoms might be.

Emancipatory Acts and Bad Behavior

Manderlay's three emancipations may seem derisory, self-defeating, or ambivalent. At worst, they devolve into theft and arson (Timothy), an extension of white supremacy (Grace), or a desire to be enslaved (Wilhelm). None of these actions seem exemplary or even suitable for the pursuit of freedom, if we envision freedom to be an unproblematic and ideal state or political activity. Freedom understood as a hallowed practice composed of virtuous and uncoerced actions is not to be found except in the self-deceptions of Grace, whose freedom entails a domination she pretends does not exist—much like the terms of universal liberty in various forms of modern liberalism—until she doesn't. Instead, it is precisely the unsettling and compromised qualities of these actions that grant them their power. Each act calls attention to the unglamorous and often illicit possibilities for challenging unfreedom, even when they may seem ambiguous or incomplete.

As such, these emancipations challenge a version of emancipation just as worrisome to David Scott: the belief in a "revolutionary romance" where emancipation is only a large-scale and dramatic practice that successfully frees whole peoples and political systems from the fetters of domination—and that has already happened in the past. In a modern political lexicon, emancipation often implies a grand overthrow that conclusively liberates national peoples from oppression. *Manderlay*'s three emancipations, by contrast, expand beyond this standard interpretation of emancipation and beyond the understanding of emancipation as a past event that, by conferring universal freedom, reveals the nation's moral trajectory. But it is also possible that my reading reinscribes the promise that one can overthrow whole structures in one definitive movement. After all, at the end of the film Grace and all of the white ex-masters leave the plantation, a symbolic exit of white freedom based on plantation mastery. Perhaps this draws from the revolutionary romance after all, "the fantasy of exit or escape from the modern conditions that have contributed definitively (if not comprehensively) to making us who we are."[76] That may be. But reading these compromised gestures as emancipatory acts aims to locate possibilities for the centuries-long task of dismantling white supremacy not only in the ideal behaviors or nationwide movements that are, for Scott, cause for skepticism, but also in disparaged acts, discomfiting performances, and counterintuitive scenarios.

Manderlay attends to the recognition that legal proclamations, national movements, ideal visions, or presumably model behaviors have not done the work they have promised, and that we might look elsewhere, and lower, for more emancipatory possibilities today. This is where these emancipatory acts depart from tragedy, in that their minor actions do not mean real freedom is impossible but that its enactments are more diffuse and also more accessible than revolutionary romance might allow. It is to see possibilities of freedom in acts that might otherwise just look like self-destruction or resignation. Freedom is always ambivalent in its practices and effects, and no form of freedom, no matter how necessary or well intentioned, will be untarnished and without remainders. The emancipatory actions in *Manderlay* emphasize their discomfiting qualities without therefore claiming that emancipation is impossible. As Ira Berlin notes, American slavery was not just made, but was constantly remade.[77] We could say the same about emancipation, a process not just made but constantly remade by the different people who fight for it within and against the conditions they are conscripted to live within. Emancipation is a serial process, not a singular event.

To return to the question that opened this chapter: How could a commemoration of the Emancipation Proclamation emphasize the ongoing racialization of freedom and the harm done by the presumption that past emancipation secured the trajectory of racial progress, while also insisting

that emancipatory acts to generate freedom beyond domination and whiteness are possible in the present, even as they look different than imagined in
the past or in philosophical ideals? Mass actions across the country protesting antiblack racism and widespread police brutality against Black lives can
offer a better commemoration. These protests, which began in Ferguson,
Missouri, in 2014 after the police murder of Black teenager Michael Brown
and spread to local sites across the country, were renewed and reinvigorated
across the nation in 2020 following the police murder of George Floyd. They
simultaneously showed that America has not yet been liberated "from one
of her most glaring contradictions" and also that mobilization for emancipatory actions can happen in the present, even when they appear criminal,
partial, and compromised by dominant imaginaries of freedom's practice.
Glenn Loury argued that the Ferguson protests, and their seeming inability
to stop the racial inequities of the carceral state, show how "the black freedom struggle is in deep trouble today."[78] A *Manderlay*-inspired reading of the
protesters might show that they are in less trouble than Loury fears.

The 2014 protests and subsequent organizing that arose from them set
the stage for the 2020 protests, a significantly larger and more cohesive push
against antiblack police violence and ongoing white supremacy. The massive
summer protests across the country, taking place in every single state in the
United States and in over three thousand sites, were the largest national
protests in US history. They were led by Black Lives Matter activists and included tens of millions of people, making the protests also the most multiracial, multigenerational, and multigendered in US history.[79] They combined
coalitional and agonistic groups articulating a spectrum of transformations
from the end of police violence to full prison abolition, to complete social,
political, and economic transformation toward full equality.[80] Not everyone marching was on the same page or shared the same tactics for achieving freedom, nor did they need to march in lockstep. Their differences were
fiercely debated as a crucial part of, not a barrier to, participation, as part of
articulating what solidarity and mutuality look like on the ground, a compelling vision of democratic freedom to help build, and fight for. It is clear
that the work of Back Lives Matter in the intervening years reshaped public
discourse on mass incarceration, racist policing, and state violence, as well
as the ways that Black freedom struggles experiment with self-governance,
public access, and radical participation. As Minkah Makalani notes, Black
Lives Matter proposals do not reinvest in formal political structures that
devalue Black life, perhaps for the same reasons that Wilhelm explicates, and
instead insist that equalized political power, and equal valuations of all life,

must rely on different structures of governance and accountability.[81] Their call to defund and abolish the police is also a call for investment in more co-operative and critical experiments in self-governing, as well as real economic redistribution, well-funded social support, and shared responsibility for the fate of all members of society.[82]

The protests' challenge to the racial contract was viewed by most state institutions and law enforcement as a form of criminality, regardless of the actions protesters used. While some pundits and critics wanted to arbitrarily separate out peaceful protesters from the few who broke into stores or looted buildings by claiming that peaceful protesters supported a less threatening message of ending police brutality rather than abolishing the police—a call that was deemed automatically violent—the police attacked protesters regardless of their actions or signs. Like Timothy, the protestors gained political legibility through a lens of criminality as "looting." Yet they too continued to insist that practicing freedom might look unrespectable, illicit, or uncondoned—especially from the lens of the state and police, for whom Black freedom so often remains a form of criminality. Protestors were deemed threatening because their actions demonstrated the type of taking upon which the practice of freedom depends, rather than the acceptance of the gift of emancipation most white Americans are trained to think of as the accession to full citizenship that has supposedly already been granted to Black Americans.[83] Whereas looting connotes racialized stereotypes of immorality and illegality, "taking" freedom connotes a refusal to wait any longer for a political system to benevolently gift freedom and mend the damages of the past.

"Taking" freedom refuses the gift of emancipation and performs freedom differently. *Manderlay*'s three emancipations highlight freedoms that fight against antiblack domination and racial injustice without either recapitulating the brutalities of white freedom or asserting the inevitability of defeat. Their emancipatory practices reject individual self-mastery and possession as the end goals of freedom and ask how to "take" collective freedom in ways that may not otherwise look like acts desired in the past or presumed exemplary. Many of these acts may only be able to appear as subversively illegal, and they often risk political legibility to break the links between Black freedom and criminality. Dorian Warren argued, in response to those criticizing Black Lives Matter protesters, "Good behavior . . . won't lead us to the promised land."[84] The residents of Manderlay would likely agree.

thwarting neoliberalism   3

Boredom, Dysfunction,
and Other Visionless Challenges

Not a goddamn thing up in here works like it should.
  SCHOOL SECRETARY, *The Wire*

IN RECENT DECADES, the ideal of freedom has been a central component of the changes in the political economy of capitalism, commonly glossed as *neoliberalism*, that cause skyrocketing levels of economic inequality. These shifts are well known: the deregulation of corporate profitmaking, the privatization of public goods, and the reduction of state support for social services, which together foment freedom as the unconstrained movement of capital and the free association of financial streams. These changes share the postulate that governments should serve the market because the market alone produces freedom.[1] Agency is only seen as free when individuals make self-interested decisions in a private marketplace, while any collective endeavor, indeed political life writ large, is seen as coercive and dominating. Wendy Brown states that neoliberal policies entail "wielding liberty claims" like weapons to dismantle social worlds and democratic practices that stand in the way of capital flows.[2] Although it is commonly assumed that neoliberalism has diminished state power, given its depiction of government as the primary source of unfreedom, it also *intensifies* state power over the most insecure and marginalized segments of society.[3] Surveillance and state violence have become essential aspects of the neoliberal management of escalating social and economic insecurity produced by decimated social safety nets and deregulated profitmaking. Rather than a blanket retreat of state power, neoliberalism intensifies carceral and securitized power over a growing population of impoverished people excluded from capital flows. This is partly why the "land of the free" has the highest rates of incarceration in the world.[4] Neoliberalism guards both the flow of wealth and the bodies of the wealthy from confrontation with the people it exploits and excludes. If, as Anthony Bogues argues, "Freedom is the organizing language for neoliberalism," it is a very specific type of freedom: in neoliberal systems, money, rather than people, must be set free.[5]

Within the United States, these developments have led to a despairing sense that neoliberalism threatens the very survival of the poor and stymies the construction of common, cooperative, and egalitarian social worlds, while granting capital free roam. Although the term *neoliberalism* has been criticized as an overly broad, generic catchall for contemporary social and economic evil, there is as yet no widely shared concept that better marks the specific developments in the history of liberal freedom and capitalism that shift governance to economization, erode public spaces, grant unregulated movement to finance, and spread market values to previously nonmarketized spaces. Although some of its general tendencies—including economic inequality, disregard for poverty, and racial surveillance—have been ongoing for centuries (as traced in chapter 1), many of the most incisive scholars of neoliberalism, including Wendy Brown, Jamie Peck, Philip Mirowski, and Loïc Wacquant, emphasize the precipitousness of neoliberalism's takeover of political, social, and economic spheres, and weakening of fragile forms of survival for people and places denied financial resources.[6]

Yet despite its widespread damages, neoliberalism in underappreciated and important senses is weaker than it often appears. Seen from a macropolitical or global perspective, the power of neoliberalism is devastating, but when viewed from within the intricacies of local structures, cracks and fissures emerge. On close inspection many neoliberal policies are at odds with each other; other policies have no implementation power, are susceptible to attack, or simply cannot produce their intended effects. Furthermore, the worldview of neoliberal freedom as market rationality—which emphasizes individual risk, self-investment, and entrepreneurialism as the sole guideposts for freedom—is often unpersuasive or simply unenforceable. Even at their most extreme points of application, neoliberal measures can be thwarted:

ordinary people reject the terms of market freedom, bureaucracies continue to block "free" capital flows (sometimes intentionally, sometimes inadvertently), and communities fight off the apparatuses of neoliberal security. Like a microscopic view of sand, which reveals not the bland tan color viewed from on high but riotous rainbow hued particles, a microfocus on local cityscapes offers a vibrant, unruly vision of daily negotiations with neoliberal power.

When scholars posit ways to contest neoliberalism, they typically look for macrolevel changes, including revolutionary acts of resistance, popular protest movements, or global regulatory possibilities, actions on the scale of antiglobalization protests, Occupy and Black Lives Matter movements, postnational democratic institutions, socialist political parties, global justice reforms, or corporate sabotage.[7] These important challenges are often well publicized, visually powerful, and most importantly, purposefully organized by a compelling leftist sentiment that offers a collective vision for how to organize the world besides unregulated finance and intensified policing. They often gain inspiration from a vision of freedom as a collective endeavor that demands equal access to public life and governing decisions, provides real support for all members of society to lead a flourishing life, and requires the equality—political, social, and economic equality—of all people. But not all resistance to neoliberalism happens at this wide or inspiring scale. Indeed, not all resistance to neoliberalism has guidance from progressive or revolutionary visions. Instead, these challenges might seem reactionary, dysfunctional, or too outmoded to do real political work. These uneasy, mundane challenges to neoliberalism often simply go unnoticed.

This chapter explores various ways to thwart neoliberal power that lack political vision and that are not particularly galvanizing. It examines both forms of ugly freedom in neoliberalism: both the ugliness of neoliberal freedom in its decimation of nonmarket worlds, and freedoms found in discarded and devalued spaces that can challenge neoliberal power, even if they seem too disappointing or uninspiring to qualify. It considers bureaucratic, dysfunctional, and desultory challenges to neoliberal capitalism as these second forms of ugly freedom. I turn to the acclaimed television serial drama about life in Baltimore, *The Wire* (2002–2008), described by its producer as a series that reveals the effects of "raw, unencumbered capitalism," as an archive of such ugly freedoms.[8] *The Wire* was a watershed moment in the history of television, widely considered one of the best shows in US history because of the supposedly journalistic fidelity with which it tracked the neoliberal transformation of a major American city.[9] The series follows the parallel lives of police officers, drug dealers, local bureaucrats, real estate developers, teachers, politicians, union members, journalists, and denizens of impoverished Black neighborhoods as they navigate various neoliberal policies and norms reshaping their "freedom." From the drug trade to law enforcement, from city hall to city newspapers, from legal to educational institutions, *The Wire* depicts the devastating transformation of the city's institutions and inhabitants by neoliberal practices of governance. And yet contrary to its producer's stated view, the spread of neoliberalism in *The Wire* is anything but "unencumbered." *The Wire* reveals various ways that neoliberal norms are obstructed—not at the broadest levels of inspiring or transnational power but at the lowest, weakest, and most hyperlocal regions of social space, the regions most heavily securitized and exploited.

In the Baltimore of *The Wire*, neoliberal securitizing power is often incompetent, bloated public bureaucracies often obstruct legal and illegal attempts to smooth capital flows, impoverished neighborhoods blunt police micromanagement with unremarkable street pranks, and the moral codes of various actors refuse to cohere into a market rationality that fetishizes neoliberal freedoms of individual risk-taking and unencumbered money. These promising challenges to neoliberal hegemony in *The Wire* are typically overlooked because they are not revolutionary, rousing, or dramatic acts of resistance. They are perhaps not even satisfying, as they are grounded in the forces of bureaucratic inertia, outdated technology, boredom, cheating, personal ambition, and a variety of obstacles to individual freedom. *The Wire*'s production dates from the first decade of the new millennium, so it reveals how these noncathartic challenges to neoliberalism emerge at the same time that the neoliberal takeover of urban life was reaching full force—they were there all along.

Attention to the practices of ugly freedom in the show moves the story of neoliberalism beyond the familiar melodramatic register of powerless victims and omnipotent oppressors, and away from the corrosive impact of neoliberalism toward its failed circuits, ineffective norms, and frayed edges of influence. Ironically, *The Wire*'s intended focus on individual heroes unable to fight against oppressive bureaucracies actually recapitulates a basic belief of neoliberal freedom, that agency only resides in individual agents. Further mirroring the logic of neoliberalism, the series also presents the police as the main solution for creating a peaceable and democratic city, which legitimates structural violence and erases the power of neighborhood organizations, public services, and informal connective tissue. Yet the police, too, fail in their mission. They cannot succeed in making the city's denizens safer, operating to catalyze violence rather than diminish it. *The Wire*'s stymied individuals and police reveal precisely that the political vision of individual heroes and officers batting back crime is a fantasy of agency doomed to fail.[10] By undoing neoliberal visions of freedom as individual self-reliance or police securitization, *The Wire* broadens possible political strategies for thwarting them. It makes room for other conceptions of a flourishing city to develop, grounded in collective, community-focused, and nonpunitive action.

The Wire's provocations address a debate in contemporary critical theory about the lack of alternatives to neoliberal visions. Part of the power of neoliberal capitalism is its insistence that there are no viable alternatives to this way of organizing politics and economics, that the values and practices put forth by neoliberal worldviews are both universally desirable and too dominant to change. Many of the political and economic visions that organized liberal democratic capitalism in the past, including political progress, upward mobility, individual sovereignty, and prosperity for the hardworking, are no longer sustainable in a neoliberal order, yet nothing else has taken their place. Lauren Berlant diagnoses an impasse of vision, more felt than articulated, about how to survive if not flourish within deepening precarity, once the good life inspired by liberal democracy is no longer viable as a desire, even if it was never viable as a concrete material existence.[11] I suspect that contemporary critical theory may have inadvertently contributed somewhat to this impasse, offering ruthless critiques of existing configurations of power but often refusing to posit new future visions for how the world could be organized otherwise. There are good reasons for this, especially in order to not limit the possibility of the future by envisioning it within the confines of present possibilities, but the lack of specific blueprints to organize future possibilities may have contributed to both the strength of neoliberal visions and the sense that they are unchallengeable, and thus deepened the impasse of moving beyond them.[12] To counteract this impasse, scholars are increasingly arguing for, and creating, concrete visions for organizing the world in more just, equal, and convivial ways.[13] I engage this concern over the impasse of vision, but rather than presume that a lack of political vision inhibits political possibility, I use *The Wire* to ask a different question: How do people act without inspiring promises of a free society on the horizon, without investing in the debunked narratives of progress and upward mobility, but also without succumbing to nihilism, capitulation, or defeat? To put it another way: What challenges to neoliberalism can develop without a compelling vision of alternative futures?

The Wire's characters, many of whom are no longer persuaded by liberal capitalism if they ever were—especially as many were not included in those promises in the first place—are also uncompelled by what replaced it:

neoliberal rationality's evisceration of the subject into an isolated entrepreneur investing in his business and himself as the sole focus of his individual agency. They have abandoned the tattered American dream and have also rejected neoliberal rationality, even as their rejection may be unguided by a specific vision for a desirable future, or at least not one explicitly articulated in the show. If, for Berlant, cruel optimism describes people's continued attachments to an unattainable fantasy of the good life that does not serve them and only brings them pain, then many characters in *The Wire* have detached from that optimism.[14] What they have reattached to is not explicitly described, but it is clear that detachment from a fantasy good life does not lead them to paralysis. Their lack of guiding vision does not equate to hopelessness. In their tediousness, their lack of grandeur or idealism, their actions fight for participation in the world beyond mere survival of neoliberal onslaughts, even without well-defined guidance either from more inspiring freedom dreams or from past promises of liberal capitalism.

This chapter presses *The Wire*, then, to answer an overarching question: *What forms of political agency and freedom take shape without galvanizing visions of a better world to guide them?* It focuses on four domains in which the second version of ugly freedoms oppose the ugly freedoms of neoliberalism: one, criminalization and police surveillance of the drug trade in carceral neighborhoods; two, neoliberal rationalities that enforce personal norms of entrepreneurialism, competition, and profit maximization; three, the economization of public agencies through market metrics for growth and efficiency; and four, twinned beliefs that political agency best resides in individuals and that community safety best resides in policing.

Carceral Neighborhoods and Failed Surveillance

Each of *The Wire*'s five seasons tracks different aspects of neoliberal policies and their effects on the city of Baltimore. The show does not emphasize the global or national developments of neoliberalism as much as the changes demanded of local institutions, small neighborhoods, and individuals, in part because it depicts Baltimore as a city somewhat excluded from the racing circulations of globalized finance.[15] *The Wire* is one of the pioneers of the long-form serial televisual form, which is particularly adept at examining the subtle and unfamiliar challenges to neoliberalism that unfold over many seasons.[16] The show demands sustained attention to nuanced and seemingly mundane encounters, rather than only the heightened punches of the sitcom or the commercial-punctured weekly dramas that presume distracted viewing. The long-form serial rewards careful focus on multilayered storylines, rich conversations, and background mise-en-scène that might otherwise be experienced as unimportant filler or overwhelming detail. It works well for highlighting the subtle ugly freedoms that oppose neoliberalism, which could be overlooked or unattended to in other visual storytelling forms.

Season 1 traces the effects of the drug trade and crime on law enforcement agencies and the neighborhoods they monitor, at the same time as it dramatizes the informal but no less organized drug economy on the street. It examines the shifts in policing, security, and penalization as they are increasingly dictated by bureaucratic metrics for efficiency and economic growth. The police focus on monitoring and incarcerating poor Black people participating in illicit economies in order to generate high statistics for solved crime, while they are actively discouraged from examining elites with capital who exploit the poor. Season 2 follows the financial shifts of a postindustrial economy by illustrating waning union power and the concomitant decrease in life opportunities for the working class who labor on Baltimore's docks, even as their jobs enable material goods to circulate more rapidly across the globe. Unions have a unique capacity to tame the inequalities of capitalism through organized and institutionalized collective power, yet neoliberal policies have dismantled workers' collective power in favor of corporate power, and unions are further weakened by a postindustrial economy that relies less on manufacturing—the traditional base of labor organizing. As labor leader Frank Sabotka summarizes the shift, "We used to make shit in this country. Build shit. Not we just put our hand in the next guy's pocket" (season 2, episode 11 [2.11]). Season 3 focuses on the way that governing elites and political institutions push property development, neighborhood securitization, and criminal punishment as primary strategies for addressing the effects of decreasing public revenue on the city's inhabitants. Electoral politics are financialized cash flows from donors who view contributions solely as returns on investments, while the city increasingly defunds the very social services intended to address rising inequality, preferring instead to offer tax breaks to land developers who will turn Baltimore into a tourist destination financed by leisure consumption. Season 4 examines public education, emphasizing the state's public disinvestment in addressing poverty's effects on children besides criminalizing their behavior, as it places money and power in law enforcement rather than strengthening education or social support to students.[17] Season 5 scrutinizes the downsizing of news media as it is reorganized to maximize profits rather than inform the citizenry and hold power accountable. It documents the undoing of critical eyes on public activity, as manufactured drama, clicks, and likes take precedence over investigative reporting on the powerful. Throughout each season, *The Wire* details the uneven neoliberalization of the drug economy, including the increasing consolidation of its money flows, the networks of distribution that shape its local form, and the failure of the War on Drugs to control the trade besides criminalizing poor users and low-level traders.

Toward the end of the twentieth century, after Baltimore experienced decades of deindustrialization, slashed state and federal funding, and white middle-class flight, the city's drug trade became one of the few sources of economic sustenance available to the increasingly impoverished and majority Black population. At the same time, public policies began to more heavily criminalize poverty's consequences, as the police were the primary institution tasked with dealing with the fallout of defunded social services, taking on all responsibilities for rising social problems like poverty, unemployment, drug use, and homelessness.[18] The only government presence in most poor neighborhoods became heavy law enforcement.[19] Ruth Gilmore details how in many deindustrializing cities in the early years of neoliberalism, the institutional response to declining economic possibilities was to redefine social problems by making crime seem like the main problem facing residents, rather than unemployment, poverty, or lack of social support.[20] Much of this was done in the name of freedom, especially freedom from government-produced tyranny of public institutions, which claimed to uphold a particularly American ideal of freedom as individual responsibility against public coercion. And in a double move, drug dealing was seen as the main crime that threatened the public sphere, to the exclusion of other crimes like white-collar theft, public corruption, corporate cannibalism, or violent gendered crimes like domestic and sexual violence.[21] Cities like Baltimore thus addressed rising unemployment and dismantled welfare by criminalizing the nonviolent income-generating activity of selling drugs, and then addressed drug use through incarceration instead of employment support, education, mental health counseling, or housing.[22] Social struggles were addressed through mass imprisonment and mass surveillance of people involved in the drug trade, thus turning impoverished neighborhoods putatively outside the prison walls into extended carceral spaces constantly monitored by police.[23]

The Wire examines the effects of these shifts, both the centrality of the drug trade to informal economies in Baltimore's neighborhoods delimited by the few possibilities available for employment, as well as police efforts to manage increased precarity experienced by poor and minority populations.[24]

The Wire shows how behaviors and everyday strategies for managing intense economic precarity are viewed by the state as suspicious activities that need to be policed.[25] Selling pirated CDs, congregating outside with friends, drinking on an apartment stoop (what one character calls "the poor man's lounge"), or even just walking through the courtyard of public housing, all become justifications for police intervention.[26] If one aspect of incarceration is state-denied access to public life, then neoliberalism furthers this denial as it denies public space as a space worth having. Privatization and incarceration are two parts of an aligned political project of turning neighborhoods, especially decapitalized minority neighborhoods, into spaces where public sociality is viewed only as a site of dangerous criminal behavior or future private investment.[27]

Yet in *The Wire*, police efforts to securitize neighborhoods and public spaces through violence and intense surveillance are often unsuccessful. "The wire" itself, the show's namesake—the technology most prized for its monitoring capacities—does not successfully securitize neighborhoods. The police wire often monitors the wrong targets, proves incapable of getting needed evidence, is hampered by bureaucracy from operating productively, or lies surprisingly vulnerable to physical attack. As Linda Williams notes in her study of the show, the police never acquire the crucial information they need about illicit circulations of drug money, nor does their surveillance help them understand social networks in the way presented to the omniscient television audience.[28] This insufficiency becomes clear in one of the most memorable shots in *The Wire*—and was part of its opening montage throughout its sixty-six episodes.[29] This shot captures the drug trade in the housing projects from the surveillance camera that had been put up to monitor it. The camera was intended to improve direct surveillance by police officers, who can be partial in their observations, who are expensive (paid salary over many weeks or months), and who engage in risky actions to get their evidence. Camera surveillance, by contrast, is less expensive, less risky, impartial in its transmissions, wide-angled in its vision, and capable of efficiently gathering data that can be quickly centralized and viewed by many people. The camera harbors the dream of the neoliberal gaze over precarious spaces and populations: a cheap, unobstructed vision with little risk to those doing the surveillance.[30]

Yet the surveillance camera is also quite weak. Just after it is installed in the first season, Bodie, a savvy young resident and burgeoning dealer, throws a rock at its lens and disables its vision—the lens cracks and the rock shatters the transparent view it was installed to transmit. The camera then dislodges

3.1 Weak surveillance destroyed by a kid hurling a pebble, viewed from the grainy camera feed.

from its view of the courtyard and falls downward. Its lens now observes only the brick wall of the building on which it is installed—reflecting back only itself, its surveillance capacity destroyed in seconds by a kid with a stone (figure 3.1). Like David and Goliath, the allegorical scene of power between Bodie and the police camera reflects the impossible desire for omnipotence that organizes state intervention in a carceral neighborhood. This three-second shot was even mimicked in the final minutes of the final episode of *The Wire*, as a new dealer with a new rock disables the new fancier police surveillance camera in the exact same way.

The very use of a wire signals the police's inability to know and understand the intricacies of the neighborhoods they surveil.[31] Spectators often experience the neighborhood through police surveillance technology: The view is grainy, black and white, lacking audio or visual to capture the fullness of any event. The contrast between the on-the-ground perspective from the people living in neighborhoods to the surveillance camera is always striking. The housing projects that make up many of Baltimore's surveilled poor neighborhoods are often inaccessible to police knowledge; the police cannot even identify or find a picture of the most powerful head of Baltimore's drug trade, Avon Barksdale, for most of the first season. In one scene, when detective Kima Greggs goes undercover in the neighborhood, the kids living nearby flip the street signs around to mislead her. Without official signage Kima is lost and disoriented; she is not of the neighborhood she monitors, and a simple street prank stops her from monitoring the space she is tasked to control.

The very outmodedness of the police technology that monitors the activity of the Baltimore dealers makes their evasion of surveillance significantly easier. Through the show's five seasons, the police equipment is almost always low-level. It is years, even decades out of date, an effect of neoliberal disinvestment in municipal agencies, and easy to evade by its very bulkiness. Police surveillance technology can never keep up with the information it is supposed to gather, and no one can process it insofar as understaffed agencies are years behind on analyzing whatever data they manage to acquire. The city offers low funds to monitor its low-profit neighborhoods. Budgetary concerns about cost often take priority over intended goals of mass surveillance for social control. One neoliberal policy blocks implementation of another. The municipal government thus inadvertently inhibits securitization by disinvesting in its own surveillance.[32] Vulnerable and dated police technology is a surprising mode for thwarting police surveillance, because it is an unintentional tactic that comes from one of neoliberalism's most intense enforcement arms. It is one example of countercurrents to neoliberal securitization occurring within the very fields that administer and generate neoliberal policies.

The dealers intentionally exploit this outmodedness and defunding to resist the securitization of their economic activity. Another effective strategy for eluding surveillance is to use *even lower* technology than the dated police equipment. In season 1, the Barksdale crew communicates using beepers and payphones to elude the police. When the police finally figure out their system, they put a wiretap on the payphone. The crew soon finds out, and they physically rip out the wired payphones to simply stop that mode of communication and surveillance (1.7). This action is a practice of ugly freedom that both evades police monitoring and further decimates the public things their neighbors can access. Payphones are a public service, a utility accessible for those who cannot afford a private or portable phone.[33] By ripping out the phones, the dealers protect their trade but they also rip out a public access point, making it harder for all the public housing residents to keep connected. By season 3 they use cheap "burner" cellphones that they trash after only a few days' worth of calls; eventually they avoid all forms of technology and meet in person to discuss major matters, whether out in the street or in hotel conference rooms. Outmodedness and low-tech solutions enable those collectively on the wrong side of neoliberal capital flows to generate some breathing room from surveillance, even when this also contributes to deepening the lack of access to public resources for people already with few options to support themselves beyond the drug economy. And it works; throughout the show's five seasons, the people targeted by the police are rarely caught.

To focus on outmoded beepers, flipped street signs, broken cameras, and torn payphones is to contextualize evasive actions considered criminal, to point out that part of the problem *The Wire* tracks is the larger structure of the Baltimore cityscape whereby racial and economic inequality, entrenched for centuries, now manifests in public disinvestment and heightened criminalization of survival strategies for the poor. Economic and racial inequality in Baltimore has been long-standing; Baltimore was the first city in the United States to segregate its neighborhoods through the law.[34] Its professional police force, initially created in the antebellum era to manage mostly poor white men, focused on the free Black population as soon as the Civil War ended, instituting racialized policing as an immediate response to and repression of Black freedom.[35] As Khalil Gibran Muhammad shows, the criminalization of Black life in Baltimore and elsewhere emerged in full force alongside the exercise of Black freedom after emancipation, a dynamic examined in chapter 2 that continues into the present.[36] Intentionally marginalized from white and capitalized neighborhoods, Black denizens of Baltimore's poorest neighborhoods are now increasingly penalized for the decrease in their own economic opportunities.[37] Robin Kelley writes of this dynamic, "criminalization is to be subjected to regulation, containment, surveillance and punishment, but deemed unworthy of protection."[38] For the majority of impoverished Black children and young adults in *The Wire*, the city has completely disinvested in their lives, safety, and general flourishing outside predatory policing and incarceration, and for many the drug trade is one area that can offer them economic support and a semblance of order. Other illicit industries and damaging money flows in Baltimore produced by elite levels of economic trade, such as white-collar pillaging of public coffers, remain unsupervised and unpunished, and are even rewarded.

So when the use of police force is justified by the need for securitization, the question that must be asked is whose security is ensured by the criminalization of Baltimore's informal economy and Black underclass. The police have no legitimacy on the East Side of Baltimore, as they for the most part actively thwart neighborhood efforts at survival. Their laws and practices often reflect or enable antiblack violence. Fred Moten argues for an alternative interpretation of criminal activity in this context, to "think criminality not as a violation of the criminal law . . . but as a capacity or propensity to transgress the law as such," especially a law that emanates from white supremacy, the entrenchment of economic inequality, and the refusal to redress poverty.[39] Situating the drug trade in this way is to argue that attacks on the penal surveillance of Baltimore's Black underclass are part of a larger project challenging contemporary manifestations of centuries-long inequities—an attempt to secure one vector of economic activity available to people discarded by neoliberal metrics of investability and targeted for securitization away from flows of wealth.

Yet the evasion of vulnerable security and use of outmoded technology to thwart the police do not generate a substantively more hopeful vision for political, social, economic life outside neoliberal penalty or racial securitization. Nor do these practices promise a more just social order beyond circumvention of police surveillance. Within the larger dynamics of the show, defunded bureaucracies still allow and encourage police violence against Black neighborhoods, as police view fellow residents as enemies, not as equal members of a polity. Outmoded technologies, whether used by the police or the dealers, do not stop the violence of the drug trade or the violence of the institutions tasked with stopping it. They may not reflect the galvanizing freedom dreams of the Black radical imagination. They are reactionary tactics in that they react against neoliberal imperatives without a motivating vision for the future other than countering the present. Yet these actions still challenge carceral and securitizing tactics. Outmodedness and the easy evasion of surveillance level a challenge to the basic premise of neoliberalism: that no other options for organizing society are possible. While not rousing acts of resistance, they still thrust off the increased monitoring of their daily lives, even as their evasions cannot rectify centuries of injustice and racism. Evasion and outmodedness are—by their very accessibility—practices of ugly freedom for challenging neighborhood carcerality. This is especially true for people blocked from accessing circulations of economic or political capital, for those whose lives are primarily viewed through the monitoring equipment of the carceral state. A galvanizing vision of a different world is not needed for this practice, or perhaps it is more precise to say that here, a vision can articulate a "no" as much as a "yes."

Uncompelling Rationalities

Among the most alarming aspects of neoliberalism revealed in *The Wire* is the governing rationality justifying the siphoning of wealth from the impoverished to the elite, in which economic instability is interpreted as personally *desirable* through the language of individual risk-taking and entrepreneurship.[40] Neoliberal rationality describes a set of norms for freedom in which all people should bear alone the risk of economic insecurity and unregulated economic power, rather than dispersing risk across societies, mobilizing public institutions to support the lives of the community, or eliminating insecurity through equal distribution of resources.[41] Michel Foucault names this new mode of subjectivity *homo economicus*, as people are encouraged in various institutional and discursive ways to perform as profit-desiring, cost-benefit-calculating, self-interested financiers in all aspects of their lives.[42] *Homo economicus* develops out of a behaviorist interpretation of individual freedom as self-interested and rational—with "rational" interpreted to mean rationally motivated by incentives, competition, and profit, and distrustful of others. Neoliberal rationality traverses class and racial stratifications to cultivate a subject who is eager to assume risk, adapt to new money-generating ventures, and structure one's life as a series of self-investments to maximize one's own brand. As Brown describes it, neoliberal rationality, as a set of organizing incentives for political subjectivity, "configures human beings exhaustively as market actors."[43]

Yet in *The Wire*, while many institutions take on market rationality, virtually no people do. Few are captivated by its anemic vision of subjectivity. Its uncompelling nature is revealed by the teachers in Tilghman Middle School, a school in the impoverished Westside neighborhood. In a forty-five-second clip of a teachers' meeting that could be easily missed, educators sit in rows as a paid speaker lectures them on what to do when they feel challenged by their job: they are to repeat to themselves "IALAC," which is an acronym that stands for *I Am Lovable and Capable* (figure 3.2). In Baltimore's cash-strapped educational system, money is spent not on material or supportive programs for students but on a private contractor advising seasoned educators with a childlike PowerPoint presentation to repeat an anodyne mantra designed to distract them from their lack of resources, and to compensate for them by drawing further on their own.[44] It suggests that individuals should self-invest by simply reminding themselves that they are capable, and this will make them both feel better about their job challenges and perform them more efficiently. The allure of IALAC to the education system is that it will increase student performance by encouraging teachers to invest in themselves as lovable. A cheap investment, it presumes that with a few affirmative phrases teachers will lift their own morale, with the main goal to improve their students' test scores. It offers a one-dimensional model of rational subjectivity in which saying something about oneself easily engenders personal satisfaction amid deflating and overwhelming job challenges. The lecturer turns this bland phrase into an acronym as a way to make its message even more efficient, but merely turns it into nonsense. IALAC means nothing and is harder to remember than the phrase itself, undoing the very efficiency it is deployed to engender. The scene lays bare the ineffectiveness of neoliberal norms that assume, first, that an acronym encouraging self-love can change the performance statistics of teachers who work with students enmeshed in daily violence, and second, that the burden for educating impoverished students in an underfunded school should fall squarely on teacher self-investment. It assumes that merely choosing to repeat incoherent phrases will increase quantifiable metrics of human capital.

And more importantly, the teachers don't buy it. Few of the teachers find meaning in this exercise to rebrand their affective experience of teaching as the freedom to invest in their own lovability. The reverse shots of the lecture, which pan across a swath of bored, eye-rolling, even actively hostile teachers, are crucial to undoing the norms of IALAC (figure 3.3). Most of the teachers shoot dirty looks, doze, play on their phones, or ignore the speaker altogether. One passes tampons to another in an act of disattention. They together perform boredom, disinterest, and ennui that provide a buffer and a clear rejection of what they are supposedly being taught to desire. Their boredom is likely mixed with exasperation, anger, humiliation, and condescension, but it is also an establishment of a barrier, a refusal to incorporate new directives. Boredom is doing something, by communicating that nothing is happening. Or it communicates that what is happening is so fundamentally uncompelling that it is not worthy of engagement, even when there's nothing else to pay attention to. It is a subtle but profoundly communicated dearth of enthusiasm, and an intended performance of inflexibility.

Boredom here may be even less potent than Bartelby's famous quip "to prefer not to" do what is asked of him in a stultifying job; it is more of a mood and a gesture, conveyed by an eye roll. The eye roll communicates disinterest and blatant disregard to one's interlocutor. It is a performance of nonparticipation hoping to be seen and understood as such. If neoliberal rationality offers a subjective ideal of enthusiasm and flexibility in reaching performance metrics (the "can-do" spirit of performing incentivization), an expectation that one desires to achieve metric success as a mark of freedom and investment worthiness, then this scene is precisely its opposite. The teachers' active performance of disinterest rejects the vapidity of neoliberal rationality. Their refusal to rebrand their psychic lives with a senseless acronym confronts the barrenness of individual responsibilization amid defunded social support. Teachers bask in boredom to reject the cruel location of

3.2 & 3.3 Teachers' boredom and eye rolls reject the cheap self-investment of IALAC.

accountability for student learning in their capacity to choose to find themselves lovable.

And in the very end of the scene, something different starts to happen. The teachers begin to talk back to the speaker, disrupting her presentation and quickly ending it altogether by pointing out its senselessness and inability to address their job conditions. After two teachers in succession insist that the presenter's techniques for classroom management bear no relation to their daily experiences, the whole room erupts in anger. In the last few seconds, the teachers effectively shut down the presentation with their shouting. The eruption was unplanned and uncoordinated, but it is likely that it only happened because of the accumulated small acts of noncompliant disinterest and their contagious affect. Their overt performances of boredom connected teachers and turned them into collaborative resisters, once a few of their peers spoke up. Their revolt could not have happened without a community of people who felt similarly. If teachers had been asked to meet individually with the speaker, for instance, that would likely have squelched any collaborative connection, as they required the affective energy in the room for their action. Their performances of boredom were not an intentional training, yet their collective rejection was built on individuals' simultaneous withdrawals of attention, which perhaps were themselves built on ritualized acts of complaining in teachers' lounges or private conversations. It was certainly not a performance of a Great Refusal, but it was a clear rejection of the institutional imposition of neoliberal rationality.

This does not mean that what subsequently substituted for the school system's inability to compel cheap self-investment was now successful learning, the "Stand and Deliver" promise that individual teachers' can single-handedly invest in poor students of color and solve their problems while making them successful test-takers. Teachers here, no matter how hard they work, struggle to educate students substantively over any length of time. Their rejection of IALAC is not a celebratory revolt; it does not lead to a vast restructuring of the educational system that would overthrow biased standardized testing, prioritize community decision-making, bring well-funded wraparound support services to students, fight for a more just distribution of city resources, and make the classroom a safe and joyful place to learn. Nor do the teachers demonstrate any sense of domination over a vanquished enemy. They seem too stretched and clear-eyed about their difficult job conditions for that kind of false melodrama of victory for the underdogs. But their boredom also signals that they have no problem tossing aside this iteration of neoliberal rationality in favor of a form of self-worth and collaborative solidarity that shuns the desperation of self-investment. It may be small and unsatisfying, perhaps almost negligible from the perspective of large-scale transformation, but it is not nothing.

The weakness of neoliberal rationality is revealed even in characters that first seem to best embody its tenets. Stringer Bell, the "businessman" of the Barksdale drug suppliers, might seem to be the iconic subject of neoliberal rationality. Stringer manifests the neoliberal norm of an aspirational entrepreneur: he has a singular focus on financial acquisition, runs his organization by data analysis, and refers to the drug trade as "business" and to drugs as "product." Stringer talks about "market saturation" and "accumulation" (1.8). He institutes administrative meetings with his crew as a mix of Econ 101 and shareholder conventions, with Stringer as "chair." At one meeting Stringer states, "We're going to handle this shit like businessmen, sell the shit, make the profit and later for that gangsta bullshit" (3.1). He rejects violence—because it interferes with the smooth capital flows essential to rapid profitmaking, and makes their economic activity subject to police surveillance. Stringer aims to turn drug money into legitimate holdings where it is easier to accumulate, so he moves into real estate, the ubiquitous way for dirty money to be laundered clean in Baltimore's local economy. Infusing the drug trade with an entrepreneurial spirit, Stringer shapes himself as the model entrepreneur by mastering the economic texts and management skills necessary to succeed in the corporate workforce: a leather-bound copy of *The Wealth of Nations* has a prominent place in his personal home library, and he attends college economics classes in his free time. From the perspective of someone like Milton Friedman, Stringer proves the maxim that all individuals can succeed in the market and pull themselves up by their own bootstraps if they try hard enough. He manifests the American Dream maxim that freedom is an individual responsibility, and that surrounding life conditions are irrelevant to one's personal ability to succeed and gain social mobility.

But Stringer's monofocus on finance and investment leads him to misread the people and institutions around him, and eventually this mistake contributes to the downfall of his organization and to his own death. Stringer has a poor understanding of the complex dynamics of the drug trade that are irreducible to its monetization. By substituting market rationality for other moral systems, he diminishes his own ability to participate in and understand human relationality in the Baltimore ecosystem. "You bleed green," says his boss, Avon, noting the distinctive vampire effect of *homo economicus*

(3.8). By bleeding green, Stringer replaces blood with cash and thus does not sustain interpersonal relationships or participate in non-marketized social connections. This is what makes him a model entrepreneur but also what kills him. When his assassins come Stringer assumes they want his money and tries to buy them off. Yet as one of his killers, Omar, inveighs, "You still don't get it, do you? This ain't about your money, bro" (3.12). And it isn't. The murder is about retribution, respect, disloyalty, and ethics, but it is also about more than these things—and this "it" is never thoroughly articulated. Omar's statement applies not only to Stringer's death, but to the broader failures of green-blooded neoliberal rationalities to accurately understand either individual behavior or social connections.

Even Omar makes clear that his job as a stick-up boy—someone who robs drug dealers—isn't about the money per se: after someone hands him an unsolicited drug stash presumably worth thousands because they fear him, he states in frustration: "Ain't what you takin'—it's who you takin' it from" (4.3). It isn't the stash, or the cash, that primarily impels Omar's way of generating money, but a more complex web of neighborhood relations and moral "codes" that are always gestured to but never fully explicated. Omar's personal code is never specified or made transparent to viewers, and this protects something. What it protects is also not fully explicated, though we know the code is something Omar feels, lives by, and has a shorthand for describing. All of the characters in his neighborhood understand and respect his code; it is an ethical commitment that is collectively recognized, even if it is never detailed or made legible within a neoliberal worldview, as it has nothing to do with self-interested desires for money or future investment potential. For someone who has so little, who takes from others who don't have much for a living, Omar's untranslatable code means that it also cannot be exchanged or taken.

Many other characters in *The Wire* are uncompelled by the norms of market rationality, and those norms are often simply unenforceable. Characters are generally too complex for spectators to grasp fully what motivates them, but it is often not profit, or self-investment, or financial interest. Some police are motivated to work only by overtime pay and pension pay-outs, some drug dealers are motivated solely by profit, and many politicians are motivated by campaign donations and kickbacks. For many other characters, however, the "profit" gained by their actions is less in monetary currency than in more intricate motivations too subtle to be captured by neoliberal rationality's psychology of self-interest, entrepreneurship, and rational self-investment.

3.4 Lighting a cigarette with a hundred-dollar bill, refusing the fantasy of upward mobility.

Frank Sabotka, the local union leader for the dying stevedores, gets involved in drug smuggling, but his only motivation is to support the people in his union. He makes more than $100,000, but all of it, when it isn't going to support injured workers and their families, goes to paying lobbyists to encourage politicians to support dredging the Baltimore port, which he hopes will bring in more jobs for his stevedores. When the head of the multinational drug trade, named The Greek, the crime boss who is the metonym for borderless global markets, says to Frank, "It's a new world, Frank. You should go out and spend some of the money on something you can touch, a new car, a new coat. It's why we get up in the morning, eh?" Frank looks at him as if he is from another planet, first with shock and then with contempt (2.9). This is not why Frank gets up in the morning, not for things he can touch but for networks of support, friendship, and collective accountability to the workers he is responsible for. It is an entirely different set of organizing norms, and while the show wants to suggest that The Greek's values will soon cannibalize all others, Frank remains unmoved and uncoerced. One evening Frank's wayward son Ziggy wordlessly burns a hundred-dollar bill at a bar to light a cigarette (figure 3.4). His union companions are angry and befuddled at his disregard for hard-earned cash, but his actions can also be interpreted differently. Burning one hundred dollars rejects the fetish of money as the sole lingua franca for motivating individual action, and also casts off the fantasy that hard work will allow him to achieve the American

Dream. He knows the union-supported living wage his father made is unavailable to him now. In torching the cash, Ziggy refuses to be played by the fantasy of upward mobility and a life of postponed returns. He practices a type of ugly freedom, refusing to desire a life organized by the brutal logics of neoliberal capital.

Police detective Lester Freamon, who focuses his work on political corruption and white-collar crime, explains, "I don't get paid like that" when corrupt Senator Davis assumes his motivation for unearthing Davis's illicit activity is financial or to build up his own personal career with the police force (5.9). Lester uses the language of payment to explain his motivations, but it is not a payment that is monetized—and his claim rejects a monetized system that assumes money is the universal language of human relations. Lester is known to refuse payoffs and to "follow the money" of other city elites in order to uncover crime—it is actually what caused him to lose his first position with the police force, as it decreased his "investability" as measured by the police hierarchy that wants to capitalize financial flows, not impede them. Former police major Bunny Colvin is also not persuaded by the norms of neoliberal rationality. He quits a well-paying private security job at a hotel "pulling 52, good bennies, a take home car" because his boss required him to release a wealthy customer who had beaten a sex worker (4.3). "It's clear you ain't cut out for the private sector," says his deacon. Instead, Colvin takes a nonprofit job helping to keep school kids out of the drug economy and provide broader options for their future. The show reveals Colvin's old and new salary to mark his deemphasis on profitmaking for a larger commitment to social care: while describing the terms of the new job, the deacon states, "I'll be amazed if you get 30, an HMO, and a bus pass." Colvin takes it.

Neoliberal rationality may seem to compel Marlo Stanfield, a ruthless and successful drug dealer who takes over the Westside drug market after the Barksdale crew falls apart.[45] Marlo is the show's most extreme version of entrepreneurial subjectivity, more than Stringer Bell, but even he is not fully compelled by its norms. For much of the show, however, it seems that he is: Marlo is all about rational calculation about growth and future investment, the embodiment of the self-interested actor who aims to secure his monetary flow. Marlo organizes the neighborhood drug trade topography like Walmart: he takes over the territory of independent dealers by force, and eventually monopolizes the market. He then sells products that are of poor quality, but which are less expensive and greater in quantity than the existing product. The dealers who are lower on the pecking order make less money than before, but there is more "product" on the street for everyone.

Cost-benefit analyses of product flows and risk management even guide Marlo's decisions about life and death. In a key moment in the final season Marlo kills his mentor, East Side drug kingpin Proposition Joe, in order to gain control over the main drug pipeline to Baltimore that Joe commands. Right before the murder Prop Joe exclaims: "I treated you like a son!" Marlo replies with flat affect, "I wasn't made to play the son. Close your eyes. It won't hurt none" (5.4). Marlo refuses to be bound by kinship ties if they interfere with financial acquisition.

Prop Joe stands for a somewhat different set of economic rationalities. He conducts business by nurturing community ties and is the mastermind behind Baltimore's "New Day" drug co-op, which he creates with the motto "Share and share alike" (3.5). Joe aims for shared support in the drug market among different drug crews to avoid violence from competition and thus evade law enforcement. He is, like Marlo, a profit-maximizer and a murderer, though he understands his role in community fabric differently. As Joe declares, "I'm doing like one of them marriage counselors. Charge by the hour to tell some fool he need to bring some flowers home. Then charge another hour telling the bitch she oughta suck some cock every little once in a while. You know, keep a marriage strong like that" (1.10). Prop Joe makes money in the drug trade *through* his ability to strengthen social ties in his neighborhood and sustain kinship relationships. Yet Marlo, in killing Joe, demonstrates the triumph of neoliberalism's devaluation of kinship and community in favor of an isolated and affectively muted *homo economicus* that values only the vanquishing of competition and financial acquisition. Avon Barksdale, the incarcerated leader of the Barksdale drug crew, watches Marlo take over the co-op and monopolize the city's drug supply and tells him, "You a natural businessman" (5.2). Marlo's divestment in social connections and relentless pursuit of profit are precisely what make him a natural businessman.

Yet the very last episode of the series undoes Marlo's embodiment of neoliberal rationality. The series' finale reveals the uncompelling nature of *homo economicus* even for those who first seem most captivated by its norms. Under indictment, Marlo must resign from the drug trade in order to go free. In his final scene, he dons a suit and enters a reception with the city's wealthiest property developers. He is accommodating himself into a different nodal point in the circulation of capital flows, a white-collar one where money circulates without much regulation or surveillance from law enforcement. Marlo has gained legitimacy as a "natural businessman," the only drug dealer to do so in the show, and this will give him even easier access to capital. His lawyer introduces him to the other entrepreneurs with the caveat

3.5 Even Marlo walks out on neoliberal rationality.

that negotiating with them is a blood sport, and warns him "Guys like that will bleed you" (5.12). The property developers are even more ruthless and bloodthirsty than the murderous drug kingpin. Yet Marlo is not interested in the enormous cash that entrepreneurial real estate can offer him. In the final moments of the scene, and the last time he's in the show, he walks out of the reception. In the end, profit-maximization, return on investment, and smooth cash flows do not seem to be his primary motivation. As with other characters, it is now unclear what has motivated him in the past; we presume that he desired power and control, but we must also assume this desire was not primarily financial. If it were, he would be making deals and learning the skills of senior developers, in the same way he did with senior drug dealers—before killing them. The character who seems to be the logical end point of neoliberal rationality, who spins out the possibilities of entrepreneurship and self-interest to their decimation of kinship, morality, and virtually all social relations, is not captured by the psychology of market entrepreneurialism or by maximizing his investment capital. By the end of the series, even Marlo walks out on neoliberal rationality (figure 3.5).

Perhaps neoliberal rationality has never produced a potent or compelling subjectivity. Foucault, who articulated neoliberal market rationality most elaborately, does not interrogate the desires or pleasures that would catalyze its norms, leaving out an explanation for what would make this rationality inhabitable or persuasive. Neither does Brown in her important book *Undoing the Demos*, which brings Foucault's work on neoliberalism into the present, except for one telling passage, "Any individual who veers into other pursuits risks impoverishment and a loss of esteem and creditworthiness at the least, survival at the extreme."[46] In Brown's description, it is not that people desire the constant entrepreneurial push to give their lives meaning, or take pleasure in thinking of themselves as assets or investable opportunities, or that they come to desire flexibility, self-reliance, or responsibilization as articulations of their freedom. Instead, just as Marx's theory of capitalism never had a fully compelling account of proletarian subjectivity because participating in capitalism was never desirable for the proletariat—people did not want to work in horrible, immiserating jobs for most of their existence, but were forced to for survival—so too with neoliberal rationality, which is after all a recent iteration in the development of capitalism. Participation is less about the seductions of self-investability than about compulsion and forced precarity, "survival at the extreme." Brown centers compulsion as a primary driver of neoliberal rationality, and most people in *The Wire* would agree, even as they often remain uncompelled.

For elites at the top of economic and social power, and for those striving to be there, different factors may be shaping subjectivity, including those that instigate desires for greed and domination, as Lisa Duggan diagnoses in the meanness and cruelty of neoliberal visions for heroic leaders.[47] They may find pleasure in feeling that they are the ones who have come out on top, dominated the competition, taken the risks, and succeeded against the coercive forces of regulation—the feeling that they deserve the enormous riches they acquired and the outsized power they wield. But the majority of people are left out of neoliberal visions of financial investability, and for people who have rarely been part of the promises offered by deregulation and increased risk, it may be easier to reject this anemic vision of free subjectivity. Even as systems of collective social support continue to erode and as local investment in communities decreases, the impulse to reinvest in oneself, dominate competitors, and become flexible may have little traction for those discarded and devalued by metrics of future investability. As this sense of discarding spreads from the most impoverished to the lower and middle classes of advanced industrial economies—people who also come to learn that these new metrics and distribution scales will never benefit them—they may have no desire to willingly embrace the new entrepreneurialism, even if may seem attractive to some.

The Wire, in various ways, reveals how neoliberalism is fundamentally uncompelling as a rationality, that its main mode of power is to capitalize on financial insecurity and desperation, that investability is rarely a gratifying desire in and of itself. For characters in *The Wire*, therefore, the refusal of neoliberal rationality does not devolve into capitulation to powerlessness, depoliticization, or despair. Their subtle acts of freedom entail holding on to community in connected, relational, and less measurable ways of organizing power, even if they are not so much articulated as felt. None of their acts exercise freedom as uncoerced agency by autonomous individuals, nor are they a revolutionary transformation of an unequal society, but they do valuable work. They demonstrate how a communal eye roll, a meeting walkout, or the burning of a hundred-dollar bill can blithely reject neoliberal rationality. They refuse participation in systems that demand enthusiastic individual competition for paltry resources in order to secure domination, even momentarily, over others.

Bureaucratic Machinations

Throughout *The Wire*'s five seasons, various public agencies are transformed into quasi-entrepreneurial entities that operate through neoliberal market metrics for assessing growth and efficiency, rather than by serving their populations. Statistical assessment based on market data is the lingua franca of neoliberalism, according to Foucault; quantitative market-based metrics for assessing growth, profit, cost-cutting, and efficiency are deployed to interpret human behavior and measure institutional performance, oftentimes overtaking the original goals of the institutions.[48] These metrics emphasize financial profit, quality competitiveness, and behavior management, as well as eliminating administrative barriers that get in the way of efficiency and profitability.[49] These metrics burrow deep into the daily workings of public agencies. They become their own forms of governance that encourage individuals and institutions to make choices that promote growth, cutting, and efficiency, and the data they generate enforce competition vis-à-vis other individuals or institutions by ranking winners and losers.[50] Standards for measuring the success of institutions are imbricated with managerial microsurveillance of public agencies—which are positioned as sites of unfreedom, wastefulness, and economic bloat—to make sure they are complying with market metric goals. *The Wire* emphasizes law enforcement bureaucracy in particular as a key site of managerial control via statistical compliance, which aims to improve the efficiency of law enforcement not only by quantifying all aspects of police work but also by compelling arbitrary competition between disparate departments to incentivize both compliance and productivity with fewer resources.

The stated goal of the Baltimore police is to serve and protect the populace and minimize crime, while an unstated goal is to corral and control the effects of increasing economic insecurity produced by the retreat of state support.[51] Yet in *The Wire* statistical metrics of success actually add to the failure of *both* of these law enforcement aims. It suggests that achieving low crime statistics is ironically incompatible with the goal of decreasing crime. In the first season, an underfunded police investigation unit staffed by detectives Jimmy McNulty and Kima Greggs begins to gather information to map the drug networks of the Barksdale crew. McNulty's absence in his home unit of homicide slows the unit's cleared-case statistics, thus decreasing the homicide major Rawls's own performance metrics, so Rawls orders McNulty back (1.6). In an effort to speak to Rawls in the language he values—high performance metrics for cleared cases—McNulty offers files suggesting that his new investigation, once developed, may offer future evidence for three unsolved homicide cases connected to a dealer named D'Angelo, a member of the Barksdale crew. Rawls, at first, is uninterested. Describing himself as "a reasonable fucking guy," Rawls states that his "reasonable" goal is high performance stats, and he needs McNulty to take new cases to relieve the burden on other detectives; "Overworked cops make mistakes, mistakes lower the unit-wide clearance rate, and this can make someone otherwise as reasonable as me. . . ." "Unreasonable," Jimmy responds, understanding well how cleared-case metrics are the language of reason and power in his department, not the slow and careful work of building large cases.

Yet when Rawls finally examines McNulty's files, he uses their scant evidence to subpoena D'Angelo, in what he knows will be a failed effort to indict him. The investigation team clearly does not yet have enough information to convict D'Angelo; he will certainly go free and the case will be destroyed. Yet Rawls's motivation is statistical and individuated. If Rawls merely begins a prosecution, it will count toward his performance metrics as three cleared crimes. As Kima incredulously explains, in a quick summary of Rawls's neoliberal reason, "He's gonna charge murders he can't prove just to get the stats!" (1.6). Short-term statistical measurements encourage Rawls to ruin a big case that might ostensibly decrease citywide crime over the long term. The department's quantification of bureaucratic performance through crime statistics incentivizes the wrong action and works against solving the problems the statistics intend to measure.

By harnessing managerial power through statistical metrics, Rawls works his way up the police hierarchy, ultimately becoming superintendent of the state police by the end of the series. His power operates *through* statistical manipulation. Yet his personal desires for power often work against neoliberal norms and urban policies, even as they help him advance up the career ladder. He often deflects responsibility for murder cases onto less-prepared units in order to maintain his own high record of cleared-case statistics. His tactics, which entail his indifference to solving crimes and his destruction of others' careful cases, are precisely what position him for promotion. Nor are these behaviors unique to Rawls: throughout the series, police officers stall cases, let murderers go free, or are asked to leave cases unsolved. These practices make the city more unstable and create financial risk for Baltimore—all outcomes antagonistic to the city's neoliberal policy goals of security, social control, and capital generation from private developers and tourists. These different practices originate in various institutional sites, including competing law enforcement agencies like the FBI, the state attorney's office, the mayor's office, or the police's own bureaucratic labyrinths. At other times, intra-institutional competition over crime statistics isn't about neoliberal profitmaking or efficiency, but about long-standing resentments, outsized hatreds, or personal vainglory. Law enforcement's own bureaucratic inertia, agency rivalry, and individual desires for nonmonetized power halt neoliberal policies for quantifiable success data. Commonplace careerist desires cross with statistical metrics to unravel neoliberal imperatives for growth and efficiency.

Public institutions, of course, are tasked with sustaining society by supporting the lives of citizens, but they are thwarted by quantitative measurements of growth and cost efficiency that often impede those tasks. In another, less funded public institution, the Baltimore school system, statistical measurements are easily manipulated for non-neoliberal ends. In schools, performance statistics promise to measure the success of teacher effectiveness by compiling data about student performance on standardized tests. The school system is completely defunded by the city and also by state and federal governments. But the municipal political system locates blame for student nonachievement on individual teachers alone, rather than larger structural issues, and aims to solve the problem by measuring teachers' ability to single-handedly improve test scores (the sole metric for student learning) with punitive threats of loss of salary or jobs as consequences for low scores. The numbers take the place of more accurate readings of student learning, decreasing the art of teaching to emphasize the art of producing statistics.

However, everyone in the Baltimore school system, especially teachers and administrators, also knows the inaccuracy and malleability of so-called objective statistics. School employees "juke the stats" in order to make the numbers correlate to upward measurements of growth. Prez, a police officer who becomes a teacher, notes drily at a meeting mandating that teachers refocus their pedagogy solely to standardized testing metrics, "Juking the stats: making robberies into larcenies. Making rapes disappear. You juke the stats and majors become colonels. I've been here before" (4.9). To which another teacher replies, emphasizing the ubiquity of the practice in a biting reappropriation of new age spiritual mindfulness, "Wherever you go, there you are." As the teacher insinuates, nearly every public institution in the city tries to game performance statistics and often in contradictory or incoherent ways. Like Rawls, educators and politicians also falsify, recategorize, and manipulate the numbers in order to secure funding or satisfy bureaucratic measurements of performance and efficiency. In so doing, of course, they upend the very ability to measure progress within their institutions, as the numbers generated are juked, fake. Juking the stats as a practice of ugly freedom develops *directly* out of neoliberal demands for quantifiable measurements of continual growth with fewer resources to assess public institutions. This common practice in its banal small-mindedness is not how one might imagine neoliberal resistance, but it's an ugly freedom in the second use of the term, as it works across institutions to make the idea of constant growth a farce and render efficiency metrics incoherent. It undoes the neoliberal push for expedience from within.

Juking the stats has a kind of vision in that it is a plea to be left alone in one's competence and means of accountability, to accomplish tasks in a more intuitive, qualitative way unbeholden to statistical measurements created by corporate boards or private companies unaccountable to students or educators and unknowledgeable of public institutional functioning. It is a push not only against the numericalization of a craft, but against the sense that a job can only be kept through obeisance to arbitrary numbers. If neoliberal rationality envisions workers incentivized by marks and measures of growth, and thus presumes that statistics serves as an incentive for performance (as would, more subtly, the fear of losing one's job, or the potential decrease in one's self-investability rating for poor performance), then here, metrics of growth have the opposite effect. They incentivize workers of all kinds to juke the stats.

There is one police officer who is tired of juking the stats and doing ineffective work for the War on Drugs—itself a neoliberal policy of punitiveness that treats drug dealing and use as more of a priority than rape or homelessness, and contributes enormously to both mass incarceration and neighborhood carcerality. Major Bunny Colvin creates his own policy for what is called "Hamsterdam": a place where drugs are de facto legal (Amsterdam) but drug trading is confined to certain blocks of the city (hamster cage). Hamsterdam comprises a few "free trade zones" where street dealers and users can meet to exchange money for drugs in an open market. The zones are monitored by the police but without police interference as long as they are run nonviolently, while the police penalize any dealing outside of the zones. The goal of Hamsterdam, from the major's point of view, is to stop the murders that come with the criminalization of dealing. The dealers support it because they can sell their wares without retribution or police interference. Those taking drugs support it as they do not need to fear violence by police or gangs. Hamsterdam is not a challenge to neoliberalism per se; by decriminalizing drugs it can be seen to align with the goal of smooth capital flows in all markets and is referred to many times as a "free-trade" marketplace. Hamsterdam is a title that perfectly captures neoliberalism's dual focus on free markets and incarceration. In fact, the decriminalization of drugs is one of only two policies that Milton Friedman offered for decreasing poverty (the other was school vouchers).[52] In Hamsterdam, as Friedman would note, the state is the "umpire" for "the game" but it does not otherwise interfere with the drug trade.[53] Hamsterdam frees money exchange from state punishment and erases distinctions between licit and illicit sources of cash. Yet Colvin is not motivated to create Hamsterdam by neoliberal imperatives but by neighborhood well-being; he calls his experiment another "great moment of civic compromise" (3.2)—the first being when people socializing with neighbors on street corners put their alcohol in paper bags to prevent arrest for outdoor drinking, and the police agreed to stop harassing them—a compromise that ended incarceration for neighborhood sociality and poor housing.

Hamsterdam would seem to be a palatable neoliberal policy from a purely financial standpoint: it makes cash flows more efficient and less violent by decriminalizing circulations of capital that comes from drugs. It also frees up officers to spend more time monitoring the broader community. Yet when politicians get wind of Hamsterdam, they use it as a campaign smear against the current mayor and shut it down immediately (3.12). Hamsterdam did help the neighborhood in a short period of time—crime was down and streets were safer. At the political hearing on Hamsterdam, however, politicians are most concerned by the way that Hamsterdam jeopardizes federal money for the city's operating budget, and make no mention of the lowered crime and increased safety it produced. Faced with competing neoliberal imperatives—either stable financing sources or increasing the city's investability by keeping crime down—politicians choose the less risky one: guaranteed capital from public coffers over better crime statistics and long-term private investment potential. Questions about the community's needs and desires, or noncoercive and nonpenal ways of supporting city denizens, were never part of the discussion.

Helena Sheehan and Sheamus Sweeney argue that in *The Wire*, "market norms and corporate structures are replicated in every social sector—from the drug organizations and the police force through the schools and the newspapers. All micro-struggles for power are shaped by the macro-dynamics of an all-powerful system."[54] Yet I'm suggesting that rather than depict an "all-powerful system," *The Wire* actually reveals the vulnerabilities of market metrics across social sectors. Various bureaucratic machinations successfully block neoliberal imperatives to defund public institutions, quantify accountability, or hold individuals with little access to structural power solely responsible for structural problems, even when they may not display virtuous or ideal actions. Some neoliberal policies are at cross-purposes with other policies, even if they have the ostensible same goal. Others actually do the opposite of what they are deployed to do or can be redeployed in the service of contrasting aims and effects.[55] Some challenges to neoliberal policies are unintended effects of disinvestment in the public; they may intend one thing but have a side effect that undoes others. As scholars of neoliberal urbanism have noted, people tasked with writing policies and people implementing policies may have different agendas that are incompatible.[56] These operations may not be desirable or provide ideal outcomes, though each thwarts the neoliberalization of the city.

Yet most of these tactics cannot significantly help the institutions they work within to sustain city life more richly or to prevent deeper loss of funding. Juking the stats, for one, does not necessarily improve students' lives, or construct more equitable policies and democratic institutions. Nor does it reshape society toward economic and racial equality. It often looks like a clogged bureaucratic drain slowing neoliberal destructions with detritus. And yet the subtle, minor, daily, and distinctly unheroic actions that go into these forms of blockage show how challenges to neoliberalism can even take shape within the demand for market logics. Linda Williams, in her seminal book on the show, argues that *The Wire* serializes dysfunctional institutional systems and the varying ways people adjudicate them.[57] I am arguing that dysfunction also serves as a counterintuitive and unpredictable force for derailing the neoliberal market management of public institutions.

Thwarted Heroes of Neoliberalism: Individuals and Police

The Wire shows how seemingly undesirable or morally compromised actions, including cheating, burning cash, careerism, inertia, boredom, and institutional bloat, can be unlikely allies in the fight against neoliberalism's view of freedom as decimated publics in the service of personal risk-taking and unimpeded capital flows.[58] This reading of the show is beyond what its creators intended. They aimed to construct a modern tragedy in which strong and righteous individuals who resist unjust power are inexorably crushed by the overwhelming forces of neoliberal capitalism and institutional callousness. As producer David Simon explains,

> *The Wire* is a Greek tragedy in which the postmodern institutions are the Olympian forces . . . that are throwing the lightning bolts and hitting people in the ass for no decent reason. In much of television, and in a good deal of our stage drama, individuals are often portrayed as rising above institutions to achieve catharsis. In this drama, the institutions always prove larger, and those characters with hubris enough to challenge the postmodern construct of American empire are invariably mocked, marginalized, or crushed. Greek tragedy for the new millennium, so to speak.[59]

Many scenes in *The Wire* work in this vein and emphasize how individual heroes are thwarted by the brutal powers of unregulated finance and institutional injustice. Simon and *The Wire*'s many fans understand this to be the show's most damning assessment of contemporary urban politics. Frank Sabotka, the union leader who wants to bolster the decreasing political power and social mobility of the working class, fails. Prop Joe, a leader in the drug economy who tries to deescalate street violence with an equitable co-op, fails. Jimmy McNulty, the detective who tries to solve murders rather than amass proper statistics, fails. Bunny Colvin, the police major who hopes to stop the killing of children in his neighborhood by decriminalizing drug deals, fails. Gus Santos, the newspaper editor who aspires to investigate local corruption rather than publish monetizable feel-good stories, fails. Stringer Bell, the finance officer of the Barksdale drug organization who tries to turn drug money into legitimate capital, fails. Each of these individual efforts fail to improve rigged systems or stop the structural violence that disproportionately harms the most vulnerable and disadvantaged. For many critics this is what makes the series such hard-hitting drama.

Yet focusing on *The Wire*'s masculinized individual heroes destined to fail against overweening power narrows the imaginary of neoliberal opposition. Much like Margaret Thatcher in her insistence that we are not a society but a group of individuated actors, *The Wire* seems to accept the neoliberal decimation of collective association by fronting only individuals as agents of freedom and social change. No one in the show earns their success from public life, only in spite of it. The show thus invests in what it also wants to criticize: a particularly American version of neoliberal subjectivity in which courageous individuals succeed in spite of the institutions that aim to thwart them, so that success can only come in antagonism to public agencies. Its depictions also leave out any possibility of community-based challenges to injustice, whether informal or publicly organized. It thus also inaccurately reflects something enlivening and hopeful about Baltimore. For a show that prides itself on fidelity to the city it represents and stakes its reputation on that fidelity, there is a serious lacuna in *The Wire*: the very real forms of community organization active in Baltimore that have successfully thwarted various neoliberal policies.

Community organizing and neighborhood activism are virtually absent in *The Wire*, but they are prevalent across the city it claims to realistically depict.[60] Various local groups challenge unchecked property development, environmental racism, police brutality, healthcare disparities, and defunded schools in ways more sustaining and less thrilling than models of powerful individual action. Community organizing is an increasingly important counter to a society shaped by private entrepreneurship, police securitization of impoverished minority neighborhoods, and the devaluation of nonmonetized social relations. By ignoring the practice, if not the very possibility, of collective and public action, while focusing solely on individual agency, *The Wire* develops a complex and compromised relationship to neoliberalism: it exposes its terrors, highlights its weaknesses, and recapitulates its key tenets.

Just as *The Wire* focuses on individuals as the only actors capable of challenging injustice, it also focuses on police as the only governing institution capable of addressing Baltimore's violence and instability. The show critiques unchecked police power—it condemns individual officers who are excessively violent and questions the ineffectiveness of the War on Drugs. But it never questions the institution of the police as able to provide for the city's safety nor does it question the basic presumption that routinized force is the best way to enforce the law; as Williams notes, *The Wire* is still at heart a police melodrama. Any excess violence by police officers in the show is depicted as the result of individual proclivities, not as built into the very structure of police power.[61] The police do not protect Baltimore's poor and Black populations; they make those populations more vulnerable.[62] While the series shows how impoverished Black neighborhoods are cast aside by politicians, it does not account for how the ubiquitous presence of the police and the carceralization of poor neighborhoods demobilizes entire neighborhoods from civic participation.[63]

But what if we read *The Wire*'s focus on the tragedy of individual heroism and police power as not only supporting the neoliberal visions of freedom it claims to expose, nor only emphasizing the misery of poverty from a safe distance, but also exposing two important revelations? One, there are no individually heroic solutions to neoliberalism. And two, the police force cannot provide safety and support within neoliberal capitalism. The show's many thwarted heroes and stunted police operations show not that neoliberal policies are tragically unstoppable, *but that individual heroism and police coercion are inadequate strategies to stop them.* Perhaps, even, it is precisely the show's thwarted heroes and unsuccessful policing that inadvertently open space to showcase the less inspiring, but more promising, challenges the characters enact. These low-level acts of ugly freedom likely would have remained unnoticed amid more successful acts of individual heroism or triumphant policing expected from decades of American TV. They show instead that their neighborhoods are sources of sustenance, not just threat, and are necessary parts of the social and political fabric even amid difference and discord. They insist that possibilities for challenging neoliberalism are less dramatic, more communal, less carceral, and more prolific than a model of police power or individual heroism allows.

The pushbacks by everyday Baltimoreans in *The Wire*, which can seem unremarkable, dated, and unsatisfying, might be a kind of exercise for future acts of community revolt, what James C. Scott might call the daily calisthenics that sustain resistance to arbitrary power and Angela Davis calls dress rehearsals for larger acts of worldmaking. Indeed, just six years after *The Wire*'s initial run, the Baltimore Uprising by people across the city took hold. From the perspective of *The Wire*, the mass uprising throughout Baltimore rejecting police brutality and calling for greater public investment in the city could never have happened, as nothing like it is ever shown or even suggested. Yet since then, Baltimore has led the way in children's activism against environmental racism near schools, while active housing groups fight against evictions and decrepit rowhomes, and in 2019 political watchdogs in local journalism unearthed corruption in city hall and put the mayor in jail. By 2021 Baltimore had one of the most progressive criminal justice systems in the country, virtually stopping the prosecution of all low-level and nonviolent offenses while boosting social services, which also lowered crime. The new mayor and state's attorney worked closely with community groups and social justice organizations to pass the policies, which they specifically attributed to their efforts.[64] Even at the time of *The Wire*'s airing, many community grassroots efforts in Baltimore were working to reduce violence and ensure community safety without prisons or police.[65] As with the teachers who revolted against IALAC, unexceptional and seemingly disconcerting acts can lead to larger actions, when they become available, to build a supportive, just, and neighborly lifeworld against the deadening practices of neoliberalism. These are modes of ugly freedom, in that they may appear insignificant, nonspectacular, and sometimes undesirable. But contra neoliberal freedoms, they insist on something more than scraps of circulating capital or individual responsibilization—even when they do not yet concretely articulate what that something more might be.

Widespread securitization, the incarceration of poverty, marketized measurements of social success, defunded publics, and neoliberal rationalities combine to form one of the most powerfully destructive forces of our time. Yet *The Wire*'s depictions of Baltimore city life illustrate how neoliberal governance strategies can be weaker than otherwise presumed. They broaden possibilities for thwarting them beyond expectations for inspired progressive strategies, large-scale and widespread protests, or heroic saviors. What they offer as resistance may seem uninspiring: outdated technology, juking the stats, trashed equipment, eye rolls, careerism, burnt cash, corruption, personal codes, and thwarted agency. These tactics, however minor or perplexing, are expressions of ugly freedom. They challenge neoliberal shifts alongside neoliberal policies and rationalities themselves, which often work against their own aims, thwart their own prerogatives, and operate at cross-purposes. Although some tactics may seem rudderless or banal, *The Wire* shows that challenging everyday neoliberal policies is more accessible than typically presumed. Alone, these tactics do not engender mass movements or compelling visions of a just and equal future worth fighting for. But to discount their work would be to make challenges to neoliberalism seem more distant than necessary, and make non-neoliberal freedoms seem more inaccessible than they are. At the very least, they move beyond the paralyzing claim that neoliberalism is as "unencumbered" as an omnipotent god of Greek tragedy. For not only are the forces of neoliberalism encumbered, but these encumbrances can be mustered within defunded agencies, disregarded local spaces, and neglected neighborhoods. Noncathartic modes of thwarting neoliberal power still successfully fight against attempts to destroy the social, securitize poor neighborhoods, and marketize what remains. Rejection without vision finds vulnerabilities in neoliberalism where none are usually admitted, and thus proliferates possible actions for counteracting them, actions we can even call practices of freedom.

freedom as climate destruction

4

Guts, Dust, and Toxins in an Era of Consumptive Sovereignty

Without collaborations, we all die.
—ANNA TSING, *The Mushroom at the End of the World*

This is . . . about contributing to the rise of a new planet where we
will all be welcome, where we will all be able to enter unconditionally,
where we will all be able to embrace, eyes wide open, the inextricabil-
ity of the world, its entangled nature and its composite character.
—ACHILLE MBEMBE, *Out of the Dark Night*

THE WORLD IS BEING UPENDED by human activities that reshape the planetary environment, including mass carbon emissions, deforestation, pollution, dammed waterways, monoculture agriculture, strip mining, and frantic consumption of both natural resources and synthetic products. These
environmental transformations have already killed and displaced hundreds
of millions of people and are poised to kill billions more living creatures,
from bees to plankton to plants. By some calculations, a dozen animal and
plant species are extinguished every day. Elizabeth Kolbert and others have

provocatively called this destruction the sixth extinction, a mass extinction event propelled by multiple sectors of global society.[1] Many scholars identify industrialized capitalism as the driving force behind the sixth extinction, citing its incessant demand for growth, priority of short-term gain over long-term sustenance, unchecked pollution, and interpretation of all ecosystems and life itself as objects to be exploited for profit.[2] For others, climate destruction begins earlier with the European colonization of the new world, when native peoples and native species were first subject to violent practices of genocide, dispossession, monoculture, enclosure, and a rapacious approach to the planet and its inhabitants as resources for extraction or elimination.[3] There is another, much less noticed factor that traverses both contributing forces: a normative ideal of "freedom" that underpins them. The ideal of freedom as it is often understood in modern Euro-American politics—encompassing a set of definitions that includes control over nature, individual sovereignty, human exceptionalism, uncoerced will, and private ownership—contributes to the mass destruction of the climate.

The Barbadian sugar master of chapter 1 is but one avatar of this climate-changing freedom, for many of the ugly freedoms examined in this book contribute to environmental destruction. Racial capitalism's focus on profit through exploitative labor and mass consumption; neoliberalism's profitization of shared public resources and ceaseless economic growth; patriarchy's control over the reproductive capacities of women and nature; imperialism's focus on non-European land and nonwhite peoples as sites for extraction and management, and especially settler colonialism, as attempts to destroy indigenous stewardship and caretaking relations to land have been central to settler logic from the start.[4] While these ugly freedoms contribute to environmental damage, this book has also identified a series of alternative ugly freedoms alongside these more damaging ones, which thwart this destruction and develop more flourishing relationships to the planet and its inhabitants, even if they may at first seem unvaluable or disturbing. This concluding chapter asks: How do particular iterations of freedom contribute to the violence of climate change, and how can different freedoms, grounded in underappreciated imaginaries of political action and subjectivity, assist in mitigating climate disaster and recomposing a livable world? How can the vast actions required for shared long-term survival and ecological rehabilitation come to seem necessary and pleasurable, and how might different stories of freedom assist in that effort?

Stories about freedom, about people's imbrication in something called nature, and about agency are important for climate politics. As scholarship in indigenous studies and the environmental humanities argue, any large-scale effort to halt global warming will depend upon reworking the stories underpinning destructive relationships to the planet and, I would add, reworking stories about freedom.[5] Within an indigenous studies framework, Heather Davis and Zoe Todd state that these stories must "acknowledge plural human and nonhuman entanglements that shape the present." This is particularly challenging because dominant stories of freedom as individual liberty, self-possession, and private property frame entanglements as shackles, as limits to freedom's practice, producing only paralyzing dependence, determinism, and unfreedom. The positive valences of entanglement are lost within the ideals and practices of freedom contributing to climate destruction. Davis and Todd show how the inheritance of colonial violence includes the destruction of living entanglements and the devaluation of deep ways of relating to the earth in a responsible and interconnected way, which have entailed "a severing of relations between humans and the soil, between plants and animals, between minerals and our bones."[6] How can stories of political freedom emphasize these co-constituting relations of life, and offer counterstories of freedom as nonsovereign, collective, multispecies, and symbiotic between and within creatures and lands, and thus provide one ground for the transformative actions necessary to keep the planet habitable? How do different freedoms divest from individual will, private property, appropriation, and possession as key values, while preserving the possibility of subjects that can act to rejuvenate the world together?

In this chapter, I first explore one example of freedom's imbrication in climate change, a freedom I call consumptive sovereignty that combines different ugly freedoms of neoliberal capitalism, human exceptionalism, settler colonialism, and resource extraction. While chapter 3 examined neoliberal freedoms from the standpoint of those most attacked by its norms, this first part of chapter 4 examines neoliberal freedoms from the perspective of its greatest beneficiaries. I then move to offer three alternate stories of political subjectivity that ground different practices of freedom. They are ugly freedoms in the second valence in which I use the term—freedoms that may seem unvaluable or gross from the perspective of conventional ideals of freedom, but which actually offer more vibrant possibilities for acting in an entangled and interdependent world. The freedoms I explore require connective relations to the world for their exercise. They are connected to place, but unlike popular American settler imaginaries for reconnecting with nature from Henry Thoreau and the Hudson River School onward, they don't require a withdrawal from the social or a visit to an idealized space of untamed wilderness to see the deep imbrications between people and their living world. They are easily accessible to people living in concrete-coated cities, manicured homogeneous suburbs, or otherwise far away from the visions of wilderness or pastoral ruralia constructed by Western colonial discourses of "nature." I examine how prosaic navigations of lackluster space, imperceptible bodily fluctuations, and household garbage bolster connections between the human and more-than-human world, and even challenge that bifurcation. Rather than a majestic singular experience of sublime awe, the visions of free subjectivity I explore are instead ordinary, trivial navigations of social interactions, built environments, small apartments, or polluted waterways. But all reside in the muddle between people and what is cordoned off to the natural world: in the dank register of human guts and fecal matter, in the dirty register of household dust, and in the geochemical registers of preplanetary gases and synthetic toxins, sites rarely explored for their political visions let alone for nurturing the hallowed practice of freedom. Yet they are recalibrated ugly freedoms in that they offer visions of free practice in spaces of waste, shit, and dust. They envision political agency and freedom in dependence with other people, nonhuman lives, and nonliving matter that thrive in varied forms of partnership.

These stories challenge some of the fundamental categories of modern freedom: individual, will, property, and reason. Constitutive relations with other people, living creatures, and inanimate matter are unwilled and unchosen, and often unknown, yet they reveal how a fixation with willing and territorial boundaries impedes political visions for addressing climate change. Many of the boundaries that have organized society—including state lines, private/public distinctions, and even individual borders like skin—are harmful to or irrelevant for solving climate change, as they misunderstand the scope of both individual agency and global connections. If states regulate emissions, which is important, this will not prevent airborne pollution from continuing to cross state boundaries. Private property cannot defend against hurricanes. Individual acts of healthy consumption do not prevent exposure to toxic chemicals. Climate change demands much more: a deep reckoning with foundational living entanglements across lands, species, and environments, entanglements that are both systemic and inescapable. People are akin to, dependent on, and reconstituted by other humans and nonhumans, lands and environments that they may otherwise presume to be the backdrop to their individual freedom. If heroic individualism is not up to the challenges of climate change, the task is to search beyond both heroes and individuals.

This book began by identifying versions of ugly freedom endemic to situations of unfreedom, and this conclusion expands the commons, agents, and collectives that practice freedom. If, as Sylvia Wynter argues, claims for human subjectivity typically elide the socially produced hierarchies within humanity, thus recapitulating the foundational violence that makes "the human" the exclusive category of patriarchal settler whiteness, with its attendant values of "civil," "rational," and "free,"—then rather than expanding agency by rehumanizing denigrated peoples, this chapter instead presses the concept of "human," in its specific liberal variant of "individual," into the nonhuman, the nonautonomous and natural.[7] It emphasizes social relationships between humans, the land, and nonhuman creatures and finds freedoms in imbrication, mutual respect, and caretaking solidarity, qualities Dakota scholar Kim TallBear argues can help repair environmental destruction when indigenous values guide a broad-based decolonizing push in legal, social, and political realms.[8] I connect these claims with what Dana Luciano and Mel Chen term "queer inhumanisms," which emphasize possibilities and pleasures from communing between human and nonhuman matter. Rather than demanding full humanity as a political counter to dehumanization, queer inhumanisms focus on attachments with objects and creatures consigned to the "nonhuman" and inanimate.[9] Aligning with and drawing sustenance from the indigenous values TallBear articulates, it opens to investigations of interdependence with microbes and stardust, the invisible and unseen, the dirty and disgusting, and highlights the possibilities for freedom and caretaking in transmatter relations.[10] If Euro-American traditions of political thought jealously guard freedom as an attribute only of civilized and self-determining individuals with sufficient autonomy to escape the determinism of nature, what would it mean to show the civilized self-determining individual as primarily a nonhuman assemblage of microbes, detritus from other humans, toxins, stars, and dust constituted in webs of dependence? What freedoms might emerge from this vision, and what forms of freedom recede as no longer viable?

If so many dreams and practices of freedom are linked to ecological despoliation and making others expendable, then this final chapter contributes to shifting stories of freedom and political subjectivity in which multiliving entanglements lead to different visions of collective action. I am inspired in this in part by the new materialisms, which sees agency as an assemblage of natural and material actants beyond the exclusively human, but I foreground classical political concerns of freedom and collective action in my analysis.[11] My intent is not to invent new forms of collective agency to combat climate change—as if that were even possible—but instead to locate already existing forms of collective political agency in unacknowledged places, with guidance from a mix of indigenous studies, queer theory, and feminist science studies. Indigenous studies in particular shows how the "new" of new materialisms is actually a long-standing indigenous recognition, as TallBear argues, "that nonhumans are agential beings engaged in social relations that profoundly shape human lives."[12] Part of the ongoing work of settler colonialism is both the continuous disruption of those social relations and the forgetting of them (or the relocation of them in the premodern past) to privilege a "modern" freedom as the self-possessed individual who dominates over nature—including over people, creatures, and matter consigned to that denigrated category.[13] Different stories of subjectivity and freedom that already permeate daily life, but are consigned to the unremarkable, backward, or gross, can contribute to a more connected and equalized polity oriented to mitigating global climate disaster rather than to the damaging logics of property expansion, economic growth, and excess consumption.[14]

I focus on ugly freedoms cultivated through the human microbiome, in shed skin and feces, and in the accumulation of stardust and toxic pollution across bodies. Microbiotic collective subjects challenge individual will and agency, skin shedders challenge the presumed sovereignty of individuated bodies, while toxic and geochemical connectedness challenges private property, individuated responsibility, and personal choice. Together, they offer porous, fluid, multiple, and deeply dependent political subjectivities where poisons seep in, DNA sheds out, agency is conditioned by a combination of microbes, non-self cells, and geochemical substances, and borders are both shedding into others and carefully protected by nonhumans. All of these conditions become the fertile groundwork of freedoms practiced in fundamental interconnections that work through, not against, the natural world, and that are always engaged in collective actions. If modern freedom stands in the way of fighting for the future of the planet, then how can freedom not merely be limited, but reimagined, to support that fight?

Freedom as Consumptive Sovereignty

One recent environmental disaster reveals how mainstream US visions of freedom contribute to ongoing climate violence. From 2015 to 2017 California experienced the most severe drought in its history, and the state government attempted to address the crisis through voluntary water restrictions. These restrictions angered many of the state's wealthy residents, especially in the southern California enclave of Rancho Santa Fe. Some refused to curb their use of water and viewed their refusal to follow the restrictions as an enactment of freedom.[15] They argued that they purchased the freedom to use water as they want and that this personal choice is an integral element of their individual liberty. For one resident the state's voluntary restrictions directly limited his sovereign decision-making about economic prosperity: "California used to be a land of opportunity and freedom. It's slowly becoming the land of one group telling everybody else how they think everybody should live their lives." The average resident of Rancho Santa Fe's multiacre estates consumes *five times* as much water as the average Californian, disproportionately contributing to lowered water tables and the desertification besieging California. Yet the Rancho property owners argue that they need more water than other Californians because they have more property, and it must stay moisturized. They "should not be forced to live on property with brown lawns, golf on brown courses, or apologize for wanting their gardens to be beautiful," says one, using the language of coercion and social conformity to explain the stakes of water restrictions. Another resident refused any responsibility for redressing the drought, arguing that twenty houses could fit comfortably on her estate; since she and her husband, the land's only residents, use less water than twenty families would, they did not contribute to the drought. One similarly protested that they were "overly penalized" simply because they owned more land than others, presuming that wealth and resource use are irrelevant for measuring accountability for climate change. When the state responded to Rancho Santa Fe's continued water use during the drought by imposing mandatory restrictions, the residents used *even more water* as a way to insist on freedom as the right to private, unlimited consumption of nature. One resident decried, in an echo of gun advocates' insistence on the individual freedom to purchase their own object of desire, "They will have to pry my hose from my cold dead hands." This resident sat on the municipal water board. Another called mandatory restrictions an act of "war." As one resident conclusively stated, "we're not all equal when it comes to water."

The Rancho Santa Fe residents may seem excessively selfish, motivated solely by irresponsibility and greed, but much more is at stake here than personal psychology. A focus on psychology obscures the larger and shared worldview that influences their actions. A popular and widely valued story of freedom underpins all of their claims and grants them political legibility. Water use, to the residents of Rancho Santa Fe, is a form of freedom that entails individual choice to consume natural resources that one pays for. Freedom is the agency to extract valuable goods from the commons without concern for others; ability to pay, not collective good, determines free action. In this version of freedom, territorial borders demarcate the practice of freedom: sovereign boundaries, both of the self and of property—private and self-determining spaces that one has authority over—fix freedom's limit.[16] Freedom is enclosed within an individual self and personal property, barricaded from others in an assertion of separation. Responsibility extends out to the four acres of one's private property but not beyond, which appears separable from the low lakes and parched hills immediately adjacent.

This story of freedom as individual choice, private property, and self-determined use of natural resources at will, along with the right to opt out of collective concerns, congeals liberal concepts central to Euro-American thought and practice that specifically link individual freedom to control over nature through ownership. The Rancho residents are not outliers but striking enactments of a notion of freedom shared by many in wealthy nations like the United States. This conception interprets freedom as individual sovereignty, as the capacity for self-mastery and the condition of having final authority over one's decisions—and thus being unbound by the will or desires of others. It abhors dependence on others as domination. This freedom entails freedom *from* others, from their demands, needs, and sustenance.[17] It includes freedom as capitalism and free markets, in which freedom is an economic practice of uncoerced selling and purchasing. Agency entails the ability to profit from anything and everything, while unforced financial calculations determine personal choices. It includes freedom as private property, in which individuals have final authority to use and dispose of their property as they see fit, what Jodi Dean calls liberalism's mutual constitution of individual and owner.[18] To possess, for John Locke, is to appropriate from the common for individual use, a process that is always unequal and that condemns other ways of relating to shared land as illegitimate or nonmodern. This freedom also includes rational will and human exceptionalism, as Immanuel Kant described it, in which only humans have the capacity for freedom because they are reasoning and intelligent creatures; part of being human is the self-extrication from nature's determinism. Freedom is the exclusive human capacity to master nature and harness its powers, to stand apart from and above the natural.[19] As a consequence of human exceptionalism, all of nonhuman nature appears differentiated from and subservient to the human. Freedom, in explicit contrast to nature, is the ability for self-rule through reason.

This stew of human exceptionalism, private property, reason, and individualism entails settler freedom of white entitlement over indigenous land, and a view of environments and living creatures, including nonwhite people, as resources to exploit and as things that can be owned. As W. E. B. Du Bois interpreted these modes of freedom, "whiteness is the ownership of the earth for ever and ever."[20] Such freedoms denigrate indigenous relations to land, creatures, and other humans characterized by reciprocity and nonhierarchy.[21] They share many foundational assumptions of the Barbadian sugar plantation master's freedom examined in chapter 1, in which individual autonomy and independence are found, first, in the sugar plantation's emphasis on profiting from (stolen) land and (enslaved) labor, and second, in the claim that government has no jurisdiction over private property—including land and people. These freedoms view ownership of private property as almost the opposite of land stewardship, as freedom takes shape through domination of the land, through the capacity to parcel, raze, remake, and extract from them.[22] These freedoms similarly devalue relations premised upon listening and support rather than control and coercion, on what Potawatomi scientist Robin Wall Kimmerer names indigenous practices of cohabitative living and equal flourishing rather than conquest by the master.[23] As Locke states in a claim that the Rancho residents echo over three hundred years later, "Tis plain, that Men have agreed to disproportionate and unequal possession of the earth."[24]

The final addition to this vision of freedom is a neoliberal insistence that any regulative mode of state power is only ever coercive unfreedom. Restricting water use is unintelligible as a collective practice to rehabilitate the shared ecosystems that sustain life. Restrictions are only understood as an infringement of individual freedom enforced by irrational social conformity and government usurpation. Freedom is the exercise of individual power without concern for public consequences, indeed with the insistence that public consequences are irrelevant to one's exercise of power. Assertions of domination over the public are the very practice of freedom.[25] It is a similar freedom that led so many Americans to refuse to follow government health measures during the COVID-19 pandemic. People refused to wear masks because they believed that mask mandates were government coercion, blocking their individual freedom to make uncoerced choices, rather than a necessary form of community cooperation, public health, and mutual care for the lives of others. For this freedom, to be mandated by the government to consider others is always an experience of domination.

These amalgamated freedoms in Rancho Santa Fe can be characterized as *consumptive sovereignty*, as they offer the freedom to conquer nature by consuming the objects one desires, to bend the world to one's will by devouring resources however one chooses. More than just a practice of American consumer citizenship in which mass consumption is encouraged and rewarded, consumptive sovereignty ties high consumption to the exercise of freedom, to sovereign control over oneself and one's property, and to domination over objects, people, and resources as an expression of agentic subjectivity.[26] In freedom as consumptive sovereignty, individuals owe nature nothing, but it owes them everything, and exists to endlessly satisfy their wants.[27] Consumptive sovereignty powers current forms of extractive capital and partakes in a freedom that, as Max Horkheimer and Theodor Adorno define it, bespeaks a desire "to dominate nature boundlessly, to turn the cosmos into an endless hunting ground."[28] Wendell Berry contends that American freedom often means "'free' to be as conspicuously greedy and wasteful as the most corrupt kings and queens."[29] Freedom is envisioned as the sovereignty handed from royalty to individual sovereigns and practiced as conspicuous waste, recalling both the regal spectacles of sugared subtleties and the planter power to decimate biodiversity in chapter 1. Spectacles of unbound consumption *prove* one's sovereignty.

Certainly those who invest in consumptive sovereignty have sufficient resources and power to imagine themselves as separable from and above others. The wealth of the Rancho Santa Fe residents, for one, fuels their sense of autonomy from the social order and sustains their belief that private property marks both their individual sovereignty and the limits of their responsibility. It powers their sense that they have the right and capacity to opt out of collective problems.[30] But it extends outward too. Subjects of consumptive sovereignty find pleasure in consumption, in part because it confirms their personal freedom as a mark of economic independence and a triumph over contingency. It is also, importantly, a privileged *release* from the ceaseless reinvestment demanded by neoliberal rationality. The freedom of consumptive sovereignty defines a political subjectivity much like the *homo economicus* of neoliberalism, analyzed in chapter 3 and interpreted by Michel Foucault and Wendy Brown. These subjectivities posit rational individuals who strive to be entrepreneurially resourceful and controlling, value the individual freedom of the economic sphere, and construct a life across political, social, private, and economic realms using market metrics of free choice and cost-benefit analysis.[31] Homo economicus, however, focuses on investment rather than consumption as a practice of freedom, attending to a risky future by investing in hope for greater returns in a distant world to come. By contrast, the subject of consumptive sovereignty *consumes* in order to minimize the delayed satisfactions inherent to neoliberal investment, instead devouring resources and claiming control over their use. Many scholarly accounts of contemporary neoliberalism, including Foucault's, presume that consumption has become less important than financialization for understanding the current global political economy—that neoliberal economies value financial speculation over material goods. Yet consumption has skyrocketed in the last few decades to propel economic trade and climate crises; consumptive sovereignty, rather than homo economicus, accounts for that increase. Freedom in consumptive sovereignty is experienced as a distinctly pleasurable exercise of immediate satisfaction, as voracious control over quickly devoured resources, the privilege of which is otherwise so often denied or deferred in neoliberal regimes. Freedom as consumptive sovereignty rejects the logic of postponed returns.

But this freedom is consumptive in another sense as well, for in this model the consumer will eventually be consumed by their practice of consumption. Like the disease of consumption, consumptive sovereignty eats away at its host. Consumptive sovereignty is an act of self-consumption, as its vision to liberate individuals by installing them as masters over things they consume makes the world they live in uninhabitable. It is a subjectivity that leads to worldly destruction, to the frantic extraction and consumption of irreplaceable and life-sustaining ecosystems. The desire to conquer nature refuses to acknowledge that individuals *are* nature and forgets that resource depletion is also a slow act of self-destruction. The wealthiest members of society, like the Rancho residents, often aim to shield themselves from the effects of their own consumptive climate violence by building secret bunkers or floating homes—by burning through all the resources their money can buy while refusing to see how they are tied to the world they consume. They perceive power and freedom in delusional self-buttressing from world destruction that they contribute to disproportionately. Yet as the example of Rancho Santa Fe highlights, the practice of individual freedom as consumptive sovereignty inexorably leads to the wasting away of much life, to incinerated landscapes, extinct species, desiccated habitats, toxic dust storms, climate refugees, and increasingly precarious populations with unequal access to resources necessary for life.

The changes needed to slow climate destruction are well known: decarbonization, heavy regulation of emissions across the globe, decolonization of political, economic, and ecological systems, agroecology and caretaking processes for land stewardship, transnational democratic takeover of entrenched political and economic regimes that prioritize economic growth over life on the planet, decreased consumption, the end of environmental racism, narrowing of global trade, renewable energy use, and a conclusive end to a for-profit growth economy. All of these changes are possible now. They do not require new forms of technology or unprecedented feats of engineering, only collective action. Yet within consumptive sovereignty, every one of these changes is framed as a form of unfreedom and oppression, precisely because they challenge investments in individual sovereignty, the pursuit of profit and property, and self-willed consumption. Rather than viewing climate change as a shared experience that affects people and ecosystems unequally and unjustly across economic, geographic, and racial lines, consumptive freedom and its sovereign borders block sustainable alliances and solidarities to mitigate climate disaster. Its emphasis on individualism, conquest of nature, consumption, and private property makes it difficult to imagine proactive and effective responses to climate change besides personal voluntary acts like recycling, donating to rescue efforts, or purchasing carbon offsets in a free market.

It might be easy to condemn the selfish disregard for others exemplified by the residents of Rancho Santa Fe and to presume that those of us who care about environmental degradation are unimplicated in their consumptive freedom—that people who recycle, use renewable resources, faithfully follow water restrictions, and even participate in climate blockades do not adhere to similar practices. Yet the Rancho residents exemplify common practices of freedom marking many people's daily negotiations, in the United States and the Global North, with consumptive sovereignty, albeit in heightened form. Every time we drive to work when we could take public transportation or bike, when we order products from Amazon, when we forget to turn off the air conditioning, or even when we buy a new item of clothing, we damage the environment with thoughtless patterns of consumption; we prioritize individual choice and personal ease over public needs and the flourishing of shared ecosystems. In some sense, although differentially, we are all Rancho Santa Fe.

Yet changing individual consumption practices will not remake infrastructures of energy use and distribution, create transnational movements for decarbonization, or repair damaged legacies of land dispossession.[32] To focus on individual consumption is to remain within the terms of consumptive sovereignty's focus on boundaries of individual agency and enclosed property for interpreting freedom. Within consumptive sovereignty, to consume less means to have less freedom, so that restricted consumption can only be understood as a burden. Yet limiting consumption need not be a fundamental loss. Lowered consumption, collaborative stewardship over land, and shared dependence on others are not actually unfreedom, but the very preconditions of freedom. It is dangerous and self-destructive to view efforts to halt climate change as a limit on freedom. Instead, climate change presents the clearest reason to disarticulate consumption from freedom altogether.

Alternative enactments of freedom that include equal participation in and access to composing, sharing, and regenerating a world in concert with others, across dependence and difference, for the mutual work of climate resurgence, are possible. They emphasize, rather than negate, collective actions, relations of cooperation, and nonsovereign partnerships as practices of free action.[33] Broad challenges to climate change become possible when the very subject of freedom stops being envisioned as a special human entity distinct from and superior to the natural world, or from the multiple species and matter that compose its agency.[34] Freedoms emerging from transpersonal and transspecies collectives (rather than individual consumers and self-determining owners) can prioritize the work of making livable futures. The three alternatives I examine below offer political subjectivities of freedom that are multi-human and multispecies, rooted in the land but not property. All destabilize freedom as mastery, willing, and human exceptionalism. In them, individuals are nested ecosystems that rely on openness and are co-constituted with others, human and nonhuman, living and nonliving. Their freedom is always already in concert with myriad others who are in, and of, any rendering of a self, and who are necessary for any worldly action.[35] They do not offer a recipe for collective action but insist that freedom premised on (and generating pleasure through) collaboration, as well as responsibility for one another and the land, depends upon the ability "to cultivate with each other in every way imaginable epochs to come that can replenish refuge," in Donna Haraway's formulation.[36] For them, "nature" is not a constraint on freedom or an object to conquer via consumption, but the condition of any free act.

Three Political Subjects of Freedom

OUR MICROBES, OURSELVES

The first political subject of freedom that challenges the consumptive sovereign engages the microbiome. The human microbiome refers to the trillions of nonhuman microorganisms living inside and around the human body, forming distinct ecosystems in the gut, as well as in the nose, brain, armpit, anus, and labia. Microbiota cover the entirety of the skin like a thick "shag carpet," in the words of one scientist.[37] They are central to the life and functioning of the human body, where they play important roles in developing bodies, detoxifying poisons that could otherwise damage internal organs, and buffering against disease. They help digest food, fight infections, and protect skin, and also influence personal actions and desires, inflecting decisions from what to eat, to how to feel, to how to interact with the world.[38] Recent research has shown that microbiota help to determine when their hosts are hungry or cranky, and help them to pursue nourishment and pleasure. They contribute to feelings and emotional states, to affective experiences of euphoria and lethargy, peacefulness and frustration.[39] Microbiota help compose the body and cultivate its agency.

Many actions previously attributed to autonomous willing, including adaptation to new environments and responses to challenging situations, are assisted by microbiota. Even self-preservation, the foundational desire that justifies all action according to Thomas Hobbes, cannot happen without microbiota.[40] On the epidermis, microbiota protect bodies from elements and predators. The fleshly boundaries of the human are literally maintained by invisible and nonhuman microbes unknown to their hosts. Individual protection is a collective effort uncontrolled by any single force.[41] There are also striking similarities of microbiotic colonies across different peoples' bodily regions; the microbiota in my elbow creases are more similar to those in your elbow creases than to the microbiota on other parts of my body, such as my teeth or foot arch. Microbiota also literally make up the human, as foreign nonhuman microbes outnumber human cells in the body by a factor of nine to one. Most of the genes in the human body are from different beings. From a numerical perspective, the human is primarily nonhuman. Microbiologist Gregory Schneider suggests that the human is most precisely described as "a collection of nested habitats."[42] What have been presumed to be bounded and self-determining processes of decision-making, self-interest, and survival are only possible because of vast microbial collaborations. Some microbiologists call the human body a "partnership," using the same language indigenous studies scholars have long used to describe living relationships among people, animals, plants, and the land.[43] Their partnerships in living allow humans to adapt, grow, flourish, even think.

Importantly, the composition of microbiota constantly fluctuates in response to cultural, political, and economic practices. Their population in the guts or on the hands changes depending on cultural and historical norms of eating and caring for the body, on corporate-technological inventions for processing food or putting chemicals in soap, and on public health policy decisions about what medications to regulate and how to treat wastewater for reuse. Antibiotics dramatically alter the composition of the microbiome, as does the type of cleanser used to wash skin and hair. Water treatment also shifts the microbiome, depending on what type of chlorine and other chemicals are put into or filtered out of municipal water sources. Eating patterns—processed or natural, cheese, yeast, sugar, fermentation—all change microbiota. So does pet ownership, as it makes human microbiomes more diverse; people and pets often cross-pollinate microbiota. Birthing practices affect the microbiome of the new baby. Many of these are political, societal, or economic decisions made outside individual control by long-standing religious and cultural practices, pharmaceutical labs, municipal agencies, corporate profitmakers, hospital certification boards, or the FDA and USDA, even if the final end point seems to be individual choice. Microbiota condition aspects of the subject, while political and economic forces condition aspects of microbiota, in circular patterns with no singular moment of choice-making or origin of willing. The actants that contribute to "individual" action from this perspective must include digestive capacity, nonhuman and foreign microbes, political forces, corporate interests, and cultural inheritances that all come to bear on agency.[44]

The human microbiome reveals the individual subject to be a fluctuating, multispecies plurality constituted in part by trillions of nonhuman microbiota that form an ever-shifting composite of matter constantly responding to environmental stimuli, which are also economically, politically, and culturally conditioned. Free action, from a microbiomic perspective, is already a collective action, an amalgamation of actants working in concert as a "subject." A focus on microbiota suggests that feelings and ideas are shaped with input from trillions of critters beyond autonomous will, even as they may be experienced as personal and self-generating. Different microbiota dispose hosts to particular affective states, while microbiota depend on food intake that in turn cultivates gut ecosystems. Even though there are certainly individuated ways of incorporating microbiomes into understandings of agency, such as individuals taking probiotics or filtering their water to enhance microbiomic capacity, microbiota are still unpredictable, unmasterable, and complex collective ecosystems. In some sense, the cyclic and fluctuating composition of microbiota make the origin moment for individual agency less important, and instead return focus to the expansive relational context for collective action.

This reading of microbiomic assemblages draws sustenance from Haraway's work on the Chthulucene, a term describing our present that Haraway prefers to Anthropocene for its focus on ongoing multispecies practices that generate ecosystems.[45] The Chthulucene emphasizes agency in processes of composing and decomposing, rather than disconnected practices of will, boundary, and sovereignty, recognizing that "we require each other in unexpected collaborations and combinations, in hot compost piles. We become with each other or not at all."[46] It attends to the earthy, mucky cooperation of creatures who are absolutely dependent on and vulnerable to one another, nourishing each other in life and in death. Haraway describes this action as "teaming up to make each other capable of something new in the world of multispecies relationships." Her interpretation is preceded by indigenous feminist work on the heterogeneous agencies that have always circulated in relations between humans and the more-than-human, as Mohawk and Anishinaabe scholar Vanessa Watts elaborates: "Non-human beings choose how they reside, interact and develop relationships with other non-humans. So, all elements of nature possess agency, and this agency is not limited to innate action or causal relationships. . . . Non-human beings are active members of society. Not only are they active, they also directly influence how humans organize themselves into that society."[47] Watts emphasizes the agency of nonhuman beings in the construction of mutual shared worlds. This interpretation finds affinity in Hannah Arendt's vision of freedom as acting in concert with others to bring something new into the world, though Watts expands the realm of agency to insistently include beings of all kinds upon which living is constituted, and she moves the realm of action far beyond the constructed boundaries of a public sphere.[48] Neither Watts nor Haraway theorize freedom explicitly in their arguments, yet their attention to new and inventive processes involved in the mutual composition of society, of thriving and recuperating a flourishing living-scape as an ethico-political practice, offers vibrant ways of imagining freedom that directly contrasts the fantasy of sovereign actors heroically taming nature to individually determine the course of their existence.

Taking the microbiome into account for political subjectivity divests freedom of self-mastery, since actions interpreted as individual will and desire are here often powered by imperceptible and unknown forces. It is virtually impossible to pinpoint the site of final authority for individual actions when gut microbiota feast on brain chemicals to shape their hosts' moods and desires, when these same microbiota depend on cultural traditions, chemical inventions, and municipal investments, many of which have no single decision-making site or reflect long-standing practices.[49] This is not to say that the microbiome reveals that subjectivity is without agency or that invisible microforces are the real power behind the individual throne. But it is to say, as biologists Scott Gilbert, Jan Sapp, and Alfred Tauber assert, "we have never been individuals."[50] They emphasize the co-constitutive nature of all action that the concept of "the individual" disavows but Watts highlights; the microbiome posits a radically collective agency composed of people and nonhumans that together make decisions, which are not wholly determined by microbiota but are certainly incited and enhanced by them. As Watts might argue in her emphasis on nonhuman social agency, microbiomic agency does not weaken the possibility of an active subject but insists that sources of active agency could never be grounded solely in something like an individual will, reason, personal sovereignty, or self-mastery. From a microbiomic perspective, an action is always already a collective composite.

There are always bacterial and antibacterial forces in the body that cause harm, that challenge other microbes for dominance, that vie for the best position with which to inflect desires and actions of the acting subject. The microbiome can produce violent biotic attacks, including infections that can ultimately destroy the human and all the creatures who survive with and as the human. Bacteria attack, colonize, destroy. Collective action, viewed through the microbiome, is not consensus action. The microbiome is a site of contestation at all times, which can lead to warfare if microbiota lack the diversity or capacity to protect against destroyers. Yet for the vast majority of bacteria, establishing and maintaining a healthy microbiome is to sustain shared lives, and the struggle against bacteria who can destroy it is the struggle for a collective place to flourish. The best indicator of microbiomic health and longevity is its diversity of species. To focus on the microbiome is to emphasize the unruly and unaccountable forces that sustain shared existence, and also to emphasize how survival depends on diversity, on different qualities and capacities working together for the project of mutual thriving.

Multispecies agonism is not a constraint on agency but is the grounding action of any free act, if we understand freedom to be active and shared composition of a world. A microbiomic subject opens the possibility of a political subject for whom "the collective desire for collectivity," as Dean describes communist affect, is part of its bodily constitution.[51] Rather than consumptive sovereignty's fear of collective action as only unfree and coercive, a vision of political agency informed by gut microbiota necessarily moves from individual decisions to collective actions made by heterogeneous and multispecies collectives working together in many-layered partnerships. Unlike the social relations presumed in neoliberalism, settler colonialism, and consumptive sovereignty, which emphasize competitive fights over resources, microbiota offer an array of different relations, which include but are certainly not limited to competition and warfare. They primarily involve mutuality, participation, cooperation, co-constitution, agonism, antagonism, and even dissolution when relations become unsustainable. Participation in robust collective action as a practice of freedom seems less threatening and more necessary when the self is already an agonistic collective with no singular site of final control. Microbiota offer a story of "individuals" whose actions are fundamentally dependent on trillions of others, and that this condition of interconnection need not provoke only terror or fear or disgust. Indeed, it is the spongy, fertile ground of freedom. Agency is always multifarious and in concert—though not always in agreement—with millions of unknown others and practices and processes, not only limited to other humans near and far, but also the microbes and critters that inter-constitute them. As Anna Tsing remarks of interspecies action, "Without collaborations, we all die."[52] Microbiotic subjectivity dramatically expands who and what participates in the collaborations of collective action, dissipates the insistence that collective decisions always entail unfreedom, and acknowledges those that have been comrades and collaborators all along.

SHEDDING CANNIBALS

The second political subject that challenges the sovereign individual to offer different grounds for freedom is a shedding subject, in which bodies are always shedding and seeping into the world and leaving themselves behind.[53] Each person sheds a full pound of skin cells a year, about ten billion particles a day per person.[54] Much of it coats the surfaces of home, work, and public places, becoming dust. It is breathed into and eaten by other humans and animals. The very boundary between self and other constantly sloughs into others and is taken into them.[55] Every time people shake hands, they shed bodily boundaries onto one another. They may then ingest one another's skin and absorb it into their body or pass it onto a door handle where someone else they've never met will pick up that "boundary" and ingest it. Personal DNA, found in skin as well as saliva, blood, urine, vaginal secretions, and semen, is constantly emitted from bodies and taken up by others, whether into other bodies, into the land, or into water. The boundaries between people intermingle, as they constantly extrude their intimate materiality. We literally eat each other's boundaries on a daily basis.

For a shedding subject, the boundaries of the individual are mobile, scattered, and absorbed into the world. Of course, shed boundaries are not limited to the human body. Insects, birds, and companions shed into human bodies and eat individuals' DNA all the time. Some of the creatures in the "shag carpet" of skin microbiota are dentrivores, feeding off our skin as we shed it.[56] The fecal matter of many living creatures is found in others' bodies at one time or another. Shit coats public things, workspaces, and the floors of one's home, and often finds its way into mouths. Places presumed "private," whether four acres of land or a small shared mattress on a floor, are saturated with bodily extrusions of other creatures, known and unknown, dead and alive. Individuals are constantly disintegrating, as they ceaselessly influx into others and into the world.[57] Shedding exposes personal sovereignty as border fallacy.

This vision of a shedding subject, constantly eating the skin and feces of others, crosses common cultural taboos and is affectively coded as repulsive because it seems filthy. Yet as queer theorist Gayatri Gopinath provocatively states, "Bodily detritus is ultimately generative."[58] Usually filth is placed in the realm of "other," the less human, or the nonhuman, as filth and disgust can be pressed to represent the borderline status of people who are not accorded a stable identity in a sovereign self, especially those who have been historically colonized and enslaved.[59] Yet for Gopinath there is a productivity to an aesthetics of filth. Filth offers a point of affinity that can be used to imagine new forms of relationality, an affinity that is not about universal sameness but about shared experiences of intimacy with and among detritus.[60] For William Cohen, filth usually generates disidentification, signifying "that is not me"—but here filth is a point of communing among disparate creatures, as eating others' dust, shit, secretions, and skin implies constant and unavoidable intimacy through and across bodily shedding.[61]

Often, challenges to the racial and colonial ascription of "filthy" subjects take shape by showing how marginalized subjects are not filthy at all, but are clean. Yet as Gopinath might argue, rather than placing people in the realm of the pure—to show that what was coded as bad is really good—it is worthwhile to stay in the filth, where all partake in eating one another's bodily detritus and sharing their own. There can be pleasure and gratitude in commingling with others in this way, a delight that arises in these fleeting and unexpected connections. Indeed, there is something erotic about these intimate connections to others' shedding bodies. Luciano and Chen point to the unexpected affinities and "tactile erotics" of communing with and among nonliving matter, matter sometimes relegated to the disgusting or unvaluable. Their vision of queer inhumanism helps to emphasize both intimate attachments between human and nonliving matter like shed skin, and processes of absorbing inanimate matter into the self, amalgamating with it. Affiliations through the sharing of bodily sheddings do not erase differences of power and identity under a false claim to sameness, but can reveal how differences are constructed in relation to the norms of a sovereign subject whose purity and impermeable boundaries are constructed through a fantasy of bodily mastery over self and others.

The commingling of disintegrating bodies is part of living, a creaturely proximity not based on sameness or on willed consensus but on shared ingesting. A kind of innocuous and anodyne cannibalism is inevitably part of the everyday. The concept of cannibalism in modern Western discourses established hierarchies of peoples allied with colonialism and extractive capitalism to separate free from savage, white from Black, civilized from uncivilized.[62] Cannibalism marks its practitioner as barbaric, undomesticated, irrational, unable to control its passions or reflect on its actions. Yet the skin cannibalism here, of fleeting and unchosen shared skin and feces, undoes those claims. These acts are typically nondestructive and point to constant intermixing of boundaries that circulate across environments. Everyone partakes in activities imagined to be cordoned off into the realm of the uncivilized and savage. Skin cannibalism is a different type of consumption than that practiced by the consuming sovereign or by the constructed figure of the uncivilized cannibal. It dissolves rather than instantiates hierarchical separations. Eating others' shed skin and shit is peaceable, ubiquitous, and even somewhat life supporting, as growing bodies would burst if they weren't constantly shedding old skin. The worldmaking of the skin's living body depends on this shedding.

The shedding of cells might seem to happen only at the level of external, unintentional, excreted matter, but there are also forms of bodily shedding that happen inside bodies. Microchimerism describes a process when cells from one human body become part of another human body. Microchimerism happens during pregnancy when fetal cells, even from terminated pregnancies, circulate in the host body years later. These cells can be found in the host body's blood, organs, and brain; the "foreign" cells become part of that body and are fused into it. Some of these microchimeric cells, called "non-self cells," just seem to float around and coexist in the body, but others actively seem to help heal the body and keep it healthy.[63] With microchimerism, bodies are reconstructed, supported, and maintained by human non-self cells living and fusing together. Many people have "non-self" cells from parents, children, fetuses, organ donors, and blood donors in their bodies. The relationship is generally not one of competition and antagonism, though it can be with some transplants; with microchimerism the relationship is primarily one of support and contribution. And researchers insist that these supposedly different DNA "non-self" cells become bodies—they become part of a "self." "Non-self" cells are thus a misnomer in that they help to constitute the body that brings them into being.[64] Microchimerism challenges understandings of a self as homogenous with itself, familiar, and self-reliant.

Shedding and microchimerical subjectivity proffer agencies that do not control others, master oneself, and dominate nature but instead extrude into others and extend into the world as the world sheds and extends back, as assemblages called subjects gently and intimately consume each other's boundaries, and cells from different bodies prop one another up to assist in the project of flourishing. The promise of sovereign borders, in bodies as well as in national politics, is that the bordered self is separate, enclosed, and self-protective, unentangled with others unless that entanglement is chosen and controlled, because controlled boundaries are crucial for survival and integrity. Yet if the microbiome challenges autonomous willing and self-controlled agency, as in the first story, then in this second story shedding and edible boundaries challenge sovereign boundaries in a self. Parts of other humans and nonhuman creatures are in us and are us, sometimes assisting in growth, adaptation, and survival without anyone's express control or choice in the matter. A body offers less a border than what, following Gloria Anzaldúa, one might call a "borderland," an indecipherable in-between space that combines identities, bodies, and practices of various entities.[65] Edible boundaries and microchimerism dissolve "freedom from others" as the groundwork for freedom's action, to show how action always entails processes of being with and as others. They do not show a total dissolution of a self nor do they claim that all living creatures are really the exact same. They show that diversity and transcorporeal affiliation are part of any creature experienced as a "self," a self whose boundaries are fluid, extrusive, edible, and dissipating into the world at all times.

GEOCHEMICAL AND TOXIC SUBJECTS

A third subject that displaces the individual shaped by the human/nature binary is a preplanetary and geochemical subject, in which subjectivity is shaped in multiple scales. For this subject, not only living but also nonliving matter become part of an acting body. Subjects are vitalized by rocks that come from outer space.[66] The minerals powering practices of freedom predate the creation of the earth. One exemplary story of geochemical, transmatter subjectivity can be found in a children's book called *Older Than the Stars*, which, while for a young audience, offers powerful implications for challenging sovereign subjectivity in various iterations.[67] *Older Than the Stars* shows its readers how their bodily matter is older than the stars, how the carbon atoms that constitute their bodies predate the formation of the sun and solar system. The iron minerals in their blood, iron they need for living, comes from supernovas that are billions of years old. This supernova sediment gives them vitality and agency, while the lack of it leaves them enervated. The oxygen they breathe to nourish their cells is the exact same oxygen that circulated in the bloodstream of dinosaurs. Subject constitution in other words, both in matter and in temporality, exceeds the individual and is deeply connected to networks of nonhuman worlds so old they preexist the earth.

This preplanetary, geochemical subject offers a radically nonsovereign and interpenetrating story of the individual if not the world.[68] It reenchants mundane bodily processes as it envisions a cosmic body, where vitality and nourishment come from nonliving substances older than stars. It connects with what TallBear names an indigenous standpoint that emphasizes how social and cultural relations with nonhumans make up peoples' emergence as peoples, in which life is more than things that are organismically defined.[69] People are constituted not only by other living systems, as the microbiome shows, but also, as TallBear emphasizes, by "nonliving" rocks and matter that are part of social relationality. The acting subject of freedom is part virus, part Milky Way, part rock. This dramatically expands the temporality of bodily life by broadening existence to acknowledge sustaining partnerships created with cosmic worlds before and after death, even star death. It thus also implies an expansive and relational context for all action and decision-making.[70] Connected transcorporeal matter with planets, stars, algae, and minerals challenges the premises both of sovereign integrity and of nature as an inert site of extraction and domination separate from and unequal to individual bodies. It offers rapid shifts of scale from the planetary, to the local, to the microscopic, showing the interconnections of vast scalar relations in space and time that contribute to action.

Shared geochemical atoms are not limited to rocky, cosmic enchantments. They also include human-made synthetic poisons in many commonplace household products. We all—animal, flora, and land—contain atoms from toxic perfluorochemicals, DuPont's chemical compound known as "Teflon" now coursing through most people's bodies on earth. Perfluorochemicals (PFCs) cause fetal damage, cancer, organ failure, and ecosystem destruction.[71] They alter brain functioning, tangle digestion, and are indicted in various diseases that affect physical and mental capacities. These chemicals not only poison life but alter it by affecting emotional states, bodily capacities, microbiotic composition, and energy levels. PFCs are just some of the thousands of shared poisons and heavy metals coursing through the bloodstreams of humans, living species, and nonliving systems. Millions of metric tons of toxic waste from extractive capitalism and the production of goods are released into land, air, and water every year.[72] Mel Chen argues that chemical toxicity is an animating force, as it shapes subjectivity and longevity, contributing to everything from affective states of aggression, sluggishness, and depression to disease and bodily mobility. This is different from stars' enchanting potency, as it is a noxious contribution to subjectivity, even as it brings new connections and agencies to life.[73]

The increasing toxicity of ecosystems across the globe is part of what connects geochemical bodies to one another and/as the commons. As Chen says, "lead deterritorializes."[74] Its toxic circulations do not obey sovereign borders or enclosed property, and it connects disparate places and peoples to one another through its effects. Toxicity is not only about chemical particles but about structures of power shaped by political and economic systems, material distribution, and historical networks across race, gender, class, nation, and land.[75] The lead crisis in Flint, Michigan, where lead pipes for distributing water poisoned poor and Black neighborhoods after city managers used a cost-cutting technique for water management, was both a specific crisis of racial neoliberalism in Flint and also a common crisis afflicting communities across the world.[76] The dangerously high levels of lead in in Flint's water are found in municipalities across the US and the globe. As Robin D. G. Kelley has argued, "The world is Flint."[77] Flint is part of a global crisis of toxicity, even when toxicity is unevenly distributed; Rancho Santa Fe, for one, has no known lead crisis at this time. And yet claims for private property, so important to the freedom of the Rancho Santa Fe residents, cannot prevent the saturation of the land from airborne chemicals originating hundreds of miles away or from rivers poisoned upstream. While the Rancho residents may have the capital or political clout to replace their own lead pipes, the lead that remains in the soil or in constantly circulating air particulate does not magically disappear. The toxins from a distant chemical plant, lead from aging water pipes, and the dust from the drought-parched earth outside one's door may become the self and share mineral affinities regardless of juridical claims for protecting private property or upholding individual rights. Boundaries are often chimerical when it comes to the circulations of poisons and the destruction of climates. How can one be master of one's own self and private sphere when unchosen toxins and unknown preplanetary gases enter into them at all times, when they share atoms with the land outside their borders from the same supernovic lineage and from the same chemical plant? And why would mastery even be a horizon of desire in these conditions?

Alexis Shotwell calls this condition "toxic connectedness."[78] People are connected by the stuff of land, water, and air, including toxic synthetic compounds, regardless of whether they want to be. Few would choose toxicity, or perhaps will dependence on supernovic iron, yet these relations affect all bodies regardless of will or choice, even when toxicity is differentially allocated based on economic, political, racial, and citizenship privilege. To note these shared elements in a "toxic connectedness" is not to erase or flatten differences between bodies but to emphasize both that geochemical affiliations are inevitable and that toxicity is never evenly distributed. It is always worse for people whose lives have had less value in colonial and capitalist hierarchies of worth. For one, the people, animals, and lands close to DuPont's chemical facilities, whether in Virginia or in India, are saturated at significantly higher rates with toxic chemicals; they die more frequently of cancer and other toxin-induced diseases. Lead poisoning is often least remediated in poor urban neighborhoods with majority minority populations. Indigenous lands, bodies, and waters are some of the most polluted in North America, as native reservations are often used as covert dumping grounds for the waste produced by nearby settler towns.[79] Impoverished people of color around the world have higher levels of chemicals coursing through their bloodstreams, as factories and poison dumps often happen in the land and air closest to their homes. They have incinerators built by their schools, their land taken for fracking, pipelines built across their ancestral and life-supporting rivers, oil drilled on their farmland, and chemical plants built in their neighborhoods. The people living close to toxic waste sites often become climate and anti-corporate activists because their lives, and the lives of their family and neighbors, are directly threatened by the chemicals dumped on their lands. They are conscripted into climate activism in an attempt to save their health, lands, and way of life. And yet a focus on the toxic connectedness between people, especially when toxic distribution is uneven, can add to the building blocks for collective action and solidarity around becoming toxic.[80] If "the world is Flint," can this claim increase possibilities for collective action to fight against global Flintification?

Thinking freedom through toxic connectedness can ground a trans-material political solidarity between humans and between humans and nonhuman orders, even when toxicity differs in magnitudes. Toxicity propels multiple affiliations with bodily nonnormativity that extend beyond the exclusively human and the constructed hierarchies within it—and the dangers and pleasures of efflorescent partnerships that trespass established boundaries. The pesticides notoriously producing birth defects in Ecuador are also found in Washington, DC, and the chromium 6 that infamously poisoned the town of Hinckley, California, is also in the drinking water of two hundred million homes across North America; toxic connectedness can particularly mobilize those who do not yet feel that their lives are imminently under threat but are still connected to danger. It is akin to what Neel Ahuja calls the role of queer-inhumanist critique to emphasize "lateral forms of affective entanglement that link geographical and temporally distant bodies through ecological and economic processes of extermination."[81] Can the toxic chromium 6 in so many bodies and lands challenge investments in private "property" and expand visions of common worlds, as well as amplify the many lives that all are responsible to and for? Can the toxins that circulate in ecosystems redistribute responsibility and agency for combatting poisoned bodies and bodies politic, rather than dumping responsibility solely onto the people and creatures conscripted into direct disaster?

Environmental harm cannot be rectified by individual behavior, by fantasies of heroic self-mastery, by continued mass consumption of resources, or by sovereignty over personal property, but it can be remediated by militant collective action invested in rehabilitating ecosystems and decarbonizing the economy, grounded in nonsovereign solidarity and radical mutuality between diverse and dispersed bodies connected by air, water, microbes, toxins, and other bodies. In the context of indigenous studies, Navajo scholar Mishuana Goeman calls for deep community responsibility "to each other's and the land and water's well-being," a call for responsibility that could be central to all solidarities around toxicity and climate degradation.[82] To be responsible in this solidaristic way does not reproduce racial, settler, and gendered hierarchies of power and epistemology. It fights for real equality of land knowledge and reconstructs relations based on mutual caretaking and partnership. All poisons deterritorialize, which can spur widespread and collective efforts toward climate resistance organized by solidarity, reciprocity, shared stewardship, and care for the well-being of the land and others, rather than competition, hierarchy, frantic consumption, and sovereign buffers.

Stories about people made of plants, other people, dinosaurs, rocks, the sun, heavy metals, and PFCs matter for the different politics and visions of freedom they offer for constructing a more habitable world. They offer an understanding of agency in which 90 percent of bodily matter is "foreign" and this matter shapes desires; in which individual choices are already a microbial effect of the commons; in which parched land and toxic waste dumps circulate in bodies; in which actions imagined as individuated reverberate across the land; and in which bodily boundaries are intimately shed into the mouths of others one may never know. As TallBear, Watts, Tsing, Goeman, and others insist, no living creature can navigate existence without fundamental dependence on other humans, nonhumans, and nonliving matter. These dependencies are generally not willed or chosen. And crucially, they operate outside some key terms of modern freedom.

None of this posits the impossibility of freedom, however. It is, rather, that these amalgamating and fluid subjects practice freedom in different terms, ways that rely on dirt, guts, porous bodies, and toxic systems for their solidaristic commitments. Embracing these ugly freedoms entails an expansion of collaboration and responsibility for myriad others and the land, which also comes with expansive solidarity across space, chemicals, flora, and creatures, as agency for any action is widely distributed rather than narrowly individuated, and thus proliferates more possibilities for freedom as worldly co-composition. In this sense, they might also offer a *release* from the burden of consumptive sovereignty and its incitement to mastery over self, others, and nature, from the sense that freedom only resides in the capacity to do things on one's own or dominate over others. The multispecies and transmatter freedom they postulate instead is not concerned with whether other humans and nonhumans share an identity. Nor is the issue anthropomorphism, whether animals or microbiota are really like people. The issue is that they are inseparable for the project of life, and that this is a pleasure, a danger, and a necessary building block for inventive, collaborative actions of shared worldmaking and expansive organizing against climate destruction. In opposition to individual, property, will, and consumptive sovereignty, freedom as collaborative acts of world-tending depends on relational entanglements for its power.

Dust to Dust

I conclude with the generativity of shared filth, which can help to envision freedom as the practice of deep collaboration in worlding and inventive, militant caretaking for a flourishing world. I focus on the art of Dalia Baassiri, an emerging artist in Lebanon, who combines the three political subjects above to depict ugly freedoms based on transmatter and multispecies interconnectivity within a toxic landscape. By focusing on Baassiri, I take Lisa Lowe's provocations from chapter 1 to focus on aesthetic objects that tell encompassing stories of modernity's past violence and intimacies, while also moving the story to a more speculative and future-oriented register. Baassiri's work does not depict either a story of impending climate apocalypse or a satisfying solution to climate change but instead examines the inescapable enmeshment

4.1 Dalia Baassiri's *Dust Wander*, an artwork in *The Dust Series* (2017).

of the world—human, nonhuman, nonliving—of beings inseparable from other humans past and present as the necessary groundwork for any political action.[83] It tells a story of liveliness through the most inert, deathly, and undesirable of substances: dust. Using dust, Baassiri recomposes landscapes one might presuppose are otherwise "natural" and thus separate from or a backdrop to human action. Baassiri's *The Dust Series* (2016–17) depicts oceans, mountains, and birds using dust as a medium (figure 4.1). The works are subtle, greyscale, and perhaps seemingly bland or uninspiring at first glance. There are no figurative likenesses of people in Baassiri's work, yet people are all over the canvas. For dust is significantly composed of sloughed off human skin. But not only that; dust includes dead microbiota from one's own body and the bodies of others, living dust mites that feed off dead skin, animal hair, fecal matter, toxins and pollution from the environment, house particles, preplanetary minerals, and—of course—dirt. The canvas plays with the fantasy that nature is distinct from humanity and thus offers a different form of freedom than that practiced by the Rancho Santa Fe residents. If consumptive sovereignty is premised on freedom as the desire to dominate nature, eradicate detritus (including people forced into that category), and consume anything that demonstrates power and individual sovereignty, Baassiri shows the difficult yet pleasurable freedoms generated out of embeddedness in the filth.

Baassiri works with the dust found in her apartment, showing how her home space is in fact never delimited by the barricade of private property. Instead, the world has always been in Baassiri's home, as the shed skin of her own body commingles with life, death, and histories near and far. The dust includes shed skin and feces contributed by each person and animal who has come in her home, as well as the constant goings-on of neighbors, the particles of car exhaust pervasive in her crowded neighborhood of Hamra, chemical drywall produced in China, the Lebanese government's trash crisis that burns waste into cancer-causing particulate, the insects that compose and decompose in her corners, gunpowder residues from the Lebanese Civil War, bomb residues from the Israeli invasion and Syrian occupation, the cosmic stardust that settles into minute particles of iron oxide on her windowsill, dust mites and dentrivores, and nuclear fallout from bombs tested by the US military thousands of miles away in the Pacific Ocean sixty years ago, right after Lebanon declared independence from French colonization. The dust in Baassiri's home is the stuff of ineradicable political, social, economic, and intimate relations otherwise ignored or repressed. As Gopinath states, shared waste and the detritus of the everyday showcase "the inhabiting of multiple times and places."[84] Dust, seemingly disgusting, lackluster, or the material sediment of dismal lifelessness, is also the vibrant and dangerous material of co-occupancy, of interlocking fate across territories and lifespans. Dust is also humbling, showing the intermixing of life typically cordoned off to waste, a waste that includes the disintegrating self. *The Dust Series* reminds viewers both of the grounds by which they inevitably make worlds with others and also of their fate, to once again become dust in the cycle of living and dying.

Dust is generally considered a hindrance that people try to eradicate in a desire to direct and tidy one's space—a vision of freedom as control over property as well as the removal of things that seem dirty or unwanted. To dust is to exterminate the material sediment of undesirable waste and monotonous ugliness. It bespeaks a desire to be free of things one does not will or determine—and to escape from things that condition a self. It is to be free from unchosen things, to uphold a fantasy of sovereignty and power. In Baassiri's work, by contrast, dust is inescapable. It contains the unavoidable filth of pollution, mass violence, colonialism, intimate love, prior occupation, companion species, political corruption, and neighborly friendliness, but also a world in which these connections are fronted. Dust here draws on the unremarkable and filthy to heighten affiliations across the widest of scales. Pasts and presents commingle on the canvas, bound to the ordinary everyday and to the wildness of a future not yet determined by the past.

Dust connects peoples and histories on its worlding canvas but in ways not predicated on genetics or blood. It depicts the intimacies described in Luciano and Chen's queerness of trans-material attachments. Baassiri views her work as a feminist commentary on the housework expected of women in maintaining a home and being confined to it. Yet I would suggest that it is also a queer project that, in the spirit of Luciano and Chen's argument, explores alternate orientations to the world by examining affiliations that may be suggestively pleasurable, even sensual, in the unchosen commingling of different matter. This intimacy moves over vast scales of nonliving matter, from distant stars to obliterating bombs to household poison. Jill Casid asks "the queering question of how dying, decay, and decomposition may be used as material media to agitate for livable life," and Baassiri's work offers one answer.[85] It renders visible the banal and violent yet effervescent material ground of a freedom that fights for a livable future within the sediments of people, animals, synthetics, and histories communing with one another. Few things are more desultory and mundane than dust, yet few things contain more sediments of a world, and thus can be reengaged for a different world-making path that cultivates, rather than destroys, shared life as a practice of freedom. The Dust Series puts on the canvas collaborative acts of worlding as the basis for freedoms that depend on entanglements for their power.

This is not merely a commemorative picture of shared interconnection, however. Many forms of interconstitution in Baassiri's work are brutally violent, including bomb fallout, colonial inheritances, and burned garbage. And if you look closely, the medium by which Baassiri collects dust and shapes her images is dust wipes (figure 4.2). These natural landscapes are created entirely by the tools made to eradicate dust from one's private sphere. Dust wipes materialize a fantasy of sovereign control over nature in which the wipe can make its user sovereign over private property by wiping off the residues of everything unchosen—multispecies bodies, the muck and poison and the material of political decisions, the matter decomposing on the canvas. The dust wipe offers a promise to opt out of collective enmeshment. It aims to eliminate unwilled connections, enacting a fantasy of sovereign self-determination over discarded bodies, dangerous events, and abnegated histories.

4.2 Close up of *Dust Wander* from *The Dust Series:* birds made of dust and dust wipes.

This wiping is also surprisingly dangerous, as the wipe itself is toxic and is not biodegradable. Its use pollutes the seascape and poisons the flora it depicts and will remain in the land for thousands of years. It will also poison Baassiri as she uses it. It will kill the microbial shag carpet on her hands and in her lungs, and will later be introjected into the people and creatures she encounters who will ingest her sloughed-off toxic skin. Like self-consuming acts of consumptive sovereignty, the cleanliness and eradicating power that the wipe promises come at the cost of life itself. *The Dust Series* depicts environments trashed by fantasies of conquest and mastery; by the presumption that people are not interconnected to one another, neither to the dead nor to the not-yet-living, nor to the land that nourishes them, nor to the nonhuman worlds that compose them; and by people willfully forgetting that they will eventually decompose and turn to dust no matter how much they invest in freedom as the capacity to wipe death away and master nature.

The Dust Series documents relations that are alive and ongoing, even amid toxicity, even after death, as the ground for any act considered a practice of freedom. Freedom, as participation in the collective composition of a filthy world, starts in the thick of complicity and bound responsibility for climate violence, as well as for global inequalities of race and resources and their effects. Complicity in climate change is certainly differentiated depending on levels of consumption and privilege, on whether one resides in Rancho Santa Fe or Hamra, Beirut; Miami Beach or Flint, Michigan; Dubai or Agbogblashie, Accra, on whether one comfortably makes ends meet or struggles for basic resources, on racialized disparities of access to healthcare and clean water, but many are imbricated in different ways. Any climate action generated within relations of equality and broad social complicity—and shared though uneven responsibility for climate destruction—would certainly shift what seems possible right now. To equally incorporate into mass climate actions the people conscripted to the front lines of climate change with the people with access to many resources, both natives and settlers, land extractivists and land protectors, as well as microbiota, poisons, geological actants, and droughts, means that this new "we" that one is fighting for, and the relationships to place that anchor care, will of necessity shift in unpredictable ways, altering the diagnoses of antagonists and the stakes of action. If the trajectory of truly free action cannot be predicted in advance, and this is part of its possibility and its danger, then these broader and often uncomfortably intimate alliances will certainly unsettle many of the more privileged people who experience climate change less intensely. The actions demanded might be radically different from what they imagine, and ask more of them than they want to give.

Yet discomfort with radical equality need not just lead to reinstating hierarchy. The alternative is solidaristic action like those that rose up in the #NoDAPL and Mni Wiconi (Water Is Life) protests against the theft of sacred land and water for the Keystone XL oil pipeline, and led to new energy, momentum, respect, and mutuality across peoples and places. As Nick Estes shows, NoDAPL protests were guided by indigenous epistemologies and modes of organizing for protecting water. They brought together humans and nonhuman allies in creative acts for land protection and resurgence, where "action" is distributed across land, bodies, species, flora, space, and time. Participation in the protest, grounded in relations akin to Goeman's articulation of land care, developed unexpected solidarities among participants, whether between US military veterans and indigenous activists, or between flowing rivers and camp cooks, or between different tribal nations' on-the-ground negotiators, or between those guarding Standing Rock and their many supporters across the globe.[86] The #NoDAPL protest generated one of the most powerful environmental actions in recent history, precisely because it both relied on and cultivated broad alliances for expressing freedom as the collaborative fight for the flourishing of life over profit, guided by the shared caretaking of land over the conquest of nature.

All truly participatory, egalitarian, and free action unsettles its participants, as they are compelled to engage with new people, new experiences, different agents, and challenging ideas. It makes tactile what Soren Larsen and Jay Johnson have called challenging coexistence work "calling humans and nonhumans to their inevitable, ongoing entanglement" that brings dissimilar ways of worlding together, even when it feels forbidding.[87] It involves destroying constructed hierarchies that get in the way of collaborative action, and therefore is the exact opposite of the relations supported by the Rancho Santa Fe residents, predicated on hierarchical violence, isolation, consumption, and boundaries. Alliances can begin in place and community, even and especially when that place is saturated with dust, toxic fallout, mass consumption, colonial residues, and inequality. Developing successful climate alliances raises difficult questions: What visions will be part of a majority, and what visions will not—who will lose and at what cost? Will all life share equal value, or will new hierarchies ensue? What are the effects of bringing together the widest of scales into the everyday, from the cosmic to the microbiotic, and how will that shift what counts as political action? How do people invested in their own exceptionalism learn to consociate with people and creatures they previously ignored or oppressed? All of these questions are important, and their difficulty should not be used to inhibit serious efforts to think, act, and form alliances against and beyond consumptive versions of sovereign freedom that power contemporary imaginaries, especially within more privileged sectors of the globe.

These freedoms offer unwilled affiliations and unchosen connections as the groundwork for participating in collaborative acts of flourishing. They are practiced in reciprocal relations with different people, animals, microbes, contaminants, trees, exhaust, rivers, and dust, as all are imbricated in political agency. They loosen demands to recognize subjects as fully human to instead build on possibilities for action with and among the nonliving, inanimate, and inhuman. They also recognize how collaborative action to challenge environmental catastrophe is already ongoing, and can be significantly strengthened when solidarities are intensively cultivated for the collective fight to rehabilitate a damaged planet. They call for a solidarity not necessarily of love, but of partnership, shared concern, and the pleasures of arduous alliances in the filth of the world, of dependencies and reciprocities that cannot be willed away but can be developed, negotiated, or intensified to fight for the sustainability of the world.

The freedoms emphasized here insist that all people, and all creatures, share waterways and food and circulating air that flows out of one and into another, and also that lives are interconnected by vast exploitations and disavowed dependencies. Aggressively eradicating exploitations, while building on mutuality and equality in all forms, they can orient collective political action for truly just and equal climate mitigation. These connective freedoms are rooted to land, not to relations to place based on privacy or contract but, as TallBear would emphasize, on co-constitution and mutual caretaking. These connections redefine unfreedom—from the unruliness of the commons to the hierarchies of domination, from nature's determinism to the sixth extinction, from other individuals to the very ideal of individual mastery, and from dusty filth to the fantasy that sovereign boundaries will protect anyone as the world gets ever hotter. In fashioning radical solidarity, they make a bid for a world without hierarchies and exploitations, a world of conviviality amid our shared filth, and envision the difficult pleasures of collaborative tending as an ongoing, worldmaking process of freedom.

notes

INTRODUCTION. UGLY FREEDOMS

1   Paul Kramer offers historical analysis in *Blood of Government*, 140–43. As he argues, the song shows how in the context of US empire, "torture and liberation would be expressions of each other" (141). See also Immerwahr, *How to Hide an Empire*, 100–101. Singh argues that the Filipino war was a crucial site for war-making as race-making in the United States. See Singh, *Race and America's Long War*, xii.

2   On ways in which the brutality of the war in the Philippines has been disavowed in multiple valences, see Rodriguez, *Suspended Apocalypse*.

3   Foner, *Story of American Freedom*, xiii.

4   Audra Simpson notes that George Washington was referred to as "Town Destroyer" in Mohawk, since his practices during the revolutionary war were so historically destructive. "Savage States."

5   Rana, *Two Faces of American Freedom*; Morgan, *American Slavery, American Freedom*, 375–87.

6   Calhoun, "Speech," 18.

7   Calhoun, "Slavery a Positive Good."

8   Mimi Nguyen has called this "the gift of freedom," in which US wars that claim to free other countries both enlarge American empire and demand ceaseless indebtedness from those "granted" freedom. *Gift of Freedom.*

9   For greater elaboration on this dynamic see Anker, *Orgies of Feeling.*

10 Hartman, *Scenes of Subjection*.

11 Henderson, *Ugliness*; Eco, *On Ugliness*; Rosenkranz, *Aesthetics of Ugliness*.

12 For excellent analyses of the importance of political aesthetics, see Beltrán, "Mestiza Poetics"; Frank, "Living Image of the People"; Panagia, *Political Life of Sensation*; Shulman, "A Flight from the Real"; Schoolman, *Democratic Enlightenment*.

13 Those most important for this book include work by C. L. R. James, Frantz Fanon, Sylvia Wynter, Charles Mills, Orlando Patterson, Wendy Brown, Saidiya Hartman, Lisa Lowe, Uday Mehta, David Scott, Jodi Dean, Kim Tall-Bear, Leanne Betasamosake Simpson, Fred Moten, W. E. B. Du Bois, James Baldwin, Aziz Rana, the Combahee River Collective, Lisa Duggan, Donna Haraway, Walter Johnson, Nikhil Singh, Gary Wilder, Eric Williams, and Linda Zerilli.

14 Schweik, *Ugly Laws*.

15 Eco, *On Ugliness*, 12.

16 Harpham, *On the Grotesque*, 7–9.

17 Henderson, *Ugliness*, 29.

18 On mutuality and separation, see Gilroy, *Postcolonial Melancholia*.

19 In some 2020 uses, for example, American politicians described the theft of public money by predatory for-profit educational institutions as "Freedom Scholarships" and organized the burning of mail-in voting ballots as a "Dumpster of Liberty Lighting Ceremony"; these uses, while a form of social media branding, also indicate how freedom can entail siphoning money from the poor to the wealthy, as well as the rejection of one's own authorization of leadership. "Education Freedom Scholarships"; "Dumpster of Liberty Lighting Ceremony."

20 Desmond, *Evicted*.

21 I write about this in greater depth in "Mobile Sovereigns."

22 Singh, *Race and America's Long War*, 27. Singh examines how policing at home and imperial wars abroad are connected by shared practices of racism, and I would add that they also reflect shared practices of freedom.

23 Reddy, *Freedom with Violence*. See also Fanon, *Wretched of the Earth*.

24 Alexander Weheliye insists—without the embrace of freedom but with a deep focus on the spaces that would otherwise seem devoid of it—on "the importance of miniscule movements, glimmers of hope, scraps of food, the interrupted dreams of freedom found in those spaces deemed devoid of full human life." *Habeas Viscus*, 12.

25 Aristotle, *Poetics*.

26 As opposed to the major tradition in aesthetics, in which ugliness is rarely examined—including in Kantian, Hegelian, and Platonic aesthetics.

27 Adorno, *Aesthetic Theory*, 49.

28 On conviviality as an everyday practice of joyful interaction across difference, see Gilroy, *Postcolonial Melancholia*; Mamdani, *Neither Settler nor Native*.

29 Hochman, *Ugliness of Moses Mendelssohn*, 9.

30 Compelling examinations on the links between difference and democracy include Norton, *On the Muslim Question*; and Beltrán, *The Trouble with Unity*.

See Wingrove, *Rousseau's Republican Romance* on democracy's bodily comportments. On the opposite dynamic, which involves salacious pleasure in encounters with racial and economic difference by the white and wealthy, see Heap, *Slumming*.

31 Panagia, *Rancière's Sentiments*; Rancière, *Politics of Aesthetics*.

32 Sianne Ngai, *Ugly Feelings*.

33 Baldwin, "Everybody's Protest Novel."

34 Hartman, *Wayward Lives*, 104.

35 Hartman, *Wayward Lives*, 59, 61. See also Hancock, *Politics of Disgust*.

36 "Ugly, adj. adv. and n." in *Oxford English Dictionary Online*.

37 Jason Frank notes how conservative political theorists including Edmund Burke find democracy's undoing of established hierarchies disgusting, that the reconfiguration of authority and power is so unsettling for Burke that it is felt as disgust and bad taste. Frank, "Democracy and Disgust."

38 On blackness and animality see Jackson, *Becoming Human*. On medieval monstrosity see Eco, *On Ugliness*.

39 Tocqueville, *Democracy in America*.

40 On the problems with settling for the small and weak as the only politics on offer, see Dean, *Crowds and Party*, 25.

41 Coulthard, "Place Against Empire"; Leanne Betasamosake Simpson, *As We Have Always Done*; TallBear, "Caretaking Relations, Not American Dreaming." See also Audra Simpson, *Mohawk Interruptus*; Estes, *Our History Is the Future*.

42 Horkheimer and Adorno, *Dialectic of Enlightenment*.

43 At one moment and with one set of concerns, freedom might mean collective activity oriented to what Joel Olson has called the abolition of white democracy. At another it might mean participation in acts of land resurgence inspired by indigenous systems where the "actor" is distributed across nations, bodies, species, flora, space, and time—as in the #NoDAPL protests of native people protesting alongside allies, both human and nonhuman, against the theft of sacred land for an oil pipeline. Or it might mean both at once in a moment where climate change most violently upends the lives of impoverished people of color across the globe. Olson, *Abolition of White Democracy*.

44 Foucault insisted that freedom is not a perfect condition to which one aspires, or a property one has or does not have, but is instead a practice and a capacity and a relationship. It is not limited to resistance but also includes experiments with new forms of subjectivity, alliances, and actions. Foucault, *History of Sexuality*. On tending and intending, see Wolin, *The Presence of the Past*.

45 Arendt, "Freedom and Politics: A Lecture," 28.

46 Isaiah Berlin, "Two Concepts of Liberty," 204.

47 For Berlin absence of power is the only true condition for freedom. Negative freedom does not require politics for its realization, as participation in larger projects or collective activity for a better world only lead to despotism. Any shared endeavor will enforce conformity and grant others authority over oneself. Yet freedom in liberalism has never entailed merely the negative right to be free of power, but it also makes freedom the medium and instrument to

take charge of political power. The production of negative freedom and its space of privacy relies on organizing governments, laws, peoples, and power in disciplinary ways to actively carve and maintain the space of freedom from power.

48 Mill, *On Liberty*, 13. For an argument to recoup Mill's liberalism for a more anticolonial politics, see Marwah, *Liberalism, Diversity and Domination.*

49 Mehta, *Liberalism and Empire*; Pitts, *Turn to Empire.*

50 Mbembe, *Out of the Dark Night*, 72. On the idea of a "right to maim" as indicative of the liberal state (which is also a form of ugly freedom) see Puar, *Right to Maim.*

51 Some of the most formative works include Skinner, *Liberty before Liberalism*; and Pettit, *Republicanism*. For a more progressive deployment of republicanism see Gourevich, *From Slavery to the Cooperative Commonwealth.*

52 On nondomination and democracy see Markell, "Insufficiency of Non-Domination." On Black republicanism, see Rogers, "Difference, Domination, and Republicanism." See also Costa, "Is Neo-Republicanism Bad for Women?"

53 Arendt, "What is Freedom?" and *Human Condition.*

54 Arendt envisions the subject of freedom, using the words describing Achilles in the *Iliad*, as "the doer of great deeds and the speaker of great words." *Human Condition*, 11. See also Arendt, *On Violence* and "Reflections on Little Rock."

55 The late Dustin Howes argued that much of the Western canon of freedom sees violence as necessary to instantiate or protect freedom, and he normatively argues for freedom as nonviolent action to bring a just world into being, including actions like general strikes, sabotage, and noncooperation. I wish we could have had more time to talk over these ideas before his untimely death. *Freedom without Violence.*

56 There are two freedoms articulated in the document, one centered on abolishing tyranny, and the other on the act of shared worldmaking through governance. Dustin Howes argues that this contributes to a phenomenon starting in the eighteenth century in which war is only justified when it is in defense of liberty. *Freedom without Violence*, 65.

57 In Marx's vision of freedom, equal participation in the political does not address the conditions of material inequality sanctioned by social and economic powers of capital already in place before political participation begins, so human emancipation therefore requires the revolutionary overthrow of capitalism. "On the Jewish Question."

58 Marx, *Grundrisse*, 464.

59 Colonized societies must thus be liberated from what Fanon calls "the Mediterranean values, the triumph of the individual, of enlightenment, and Beauty," and decolonial liberation will turn these violent ideals "into pale, lifeless trinkets . . . a jumble of dead words." *Wretched of the Earth*, 11.

60 Fanon, *Toward the African Revolution*, 49.

61 On freedom originating with those who are first denied it, see Patterson, *Freedom.*

62 This is particularly notable, as within modern political thought access to the supposed elevated realm of freedom is often barred for the poor, women, and people of color, those doing the drudgework who have been categorized as a problem for freedom throughout the history of Western thought. See Hirschmann, *Subject of Liberty*; Pateman and Mills, *Contract and Domination*; Patterson, *Freedom*.

63 Gary Wilder analyzes nonsovereign anticolonial freedom practices in *Freedom Time*.

64 Political theory's investment in tracing the correct philosophical lineage of any iteration of freedom, as well as the presumption that scholarly critique has to come from a particular lineage or camp—the discipline's efforts to separate and cordon off different versions of freedom in order to isolate and identify ideals in their pure or canonical form as they emerge in different historical moments and individual arguments—can often be intellectually productive. But when applied to lived experience it can also work to prevent political analysis of complex practices of freedom as they are exercised and articulated. To make claims for freedom as if they must derive from one tradition or another misses how freedom is reconfigured and practiced today in most political, cultural, and economic spaces and diminishes the ways that political commitments can draw from a range of seemingly disparate ideas.

65 Butler, *Notes Toward a Performative Theory of Assembly*, 136.

66 On purity, see Shotwell, *Against Purity*.

67 James C. Scott, *Weapons of the Weak*.

68 On the value of public things, see Honig, *Public Things*.

69 On the doggie paddle as a form of everyday survival, see Berlant, "Slow Death," in *Cruel Optimism*, 117.

70 Berlant, *Cruel Optimism*; Berlant, *Female Complaint*; Brown, *Politics Out of History*; Brown, *Walled States*.

71 Brown diagnoses reactionary formations developing in the wake of these lost visions, including *ressentiment*, moralizing righteousness, border walls, and attachments to violent state power, even within putatively emancipatory projects. Berlant diagnoses an impasse, more felt than articulated, within ordinary lived experience about how to survive if not flourish at the moment of deepening precarity, once the good life inspired by liberal capitalism is no longer operable as a desire (even if it was never viable as a lived possibility.) For both, the lack of compelling guiding visions for how to create and live in a significantly more free and equal world damages political and social futures. I would suggest that this impasse is itself partly a product of neoliberalism. Neoliberal rationality offers no vision beyond ceaseless risk-taking for economic growth; as capitalism in its liberal-democratic-American-Dream variant lays dying there *is* no vision in mainstream political imaginaries to organize social dreams because neoliberalism simply doesn't offer one. See Brown, *States of Injury*; Brown, "Resisting Left Melancholy"; Brown, *Walled States*; Berlant, *Cruel Optimism*.

72 I think here in particular of the important work by David Scott, which I examine in chapter 2.

73 Bonilla, *Non-Sovereign Futures*.

74 Lightfoot, *Troubling Freedom*, 5. On new modes of freedom that may seem insignificant, see also Kazanjian, *Brink of Freedom*.

75 Kennan Ferguson, "Beholden: From Freedom to Debt"; Povinelli, *Economies of Abandonment*; Sharpe, *In the Wake*; Calvin Warren, *Ontological Terror*; David Scott, *Omens of Adversity*. Evan Kindley asks, "Was 'freedom' always empty after all, an ideological fantasy we are ultimately better off without?" "The End of Freedom," 57.

76 See Gourevich and Robin, "Freedom Now"; Robin, *Reactionary Mind*.

77 As Walter Johnson has importantly argued, scholarship that focuses solely on agency in the study of enslavement, and equates agency with an expression of autonomous individuality, is not only historically inaccurate but also ignores the multifarious ways people lived, survived, and loved during enslavement. Yet Johnson's provocations have led some scholars to err in the opposite direction, to refuse to value agency at all, as they collapse all forms of agency into liberal individualism and ignore the possibility that most forms of agency are not invested in this model of subjectivity. W. Johnson, "Agency," 26. See also chapter 2.

78 On the pleasures of diversity for democracy, see Norton, *On the Muslim Question*. On the ambivalence of authoritarian resistance, see Wedeen, *Authoritarian Apprehensions*.

79 See Arendt, "Freedom and Politics": "We first become aware of freedom or its opposite in our intercourse with others, not in intercourse with ourselves" (29). See also Zerilli for an elaboration of freedom as action in *Feminism and the Abyss of Freedom*.

80 Wilderson and Dean, "Frank B. Wilderson III in conversation with Aria Dean."

81 Roberts, *Freedom as Marronage*.

CHAPTER ONE. WHITE AND DEADLY

1 Lowe, *Intimacies of Four Continents*, 175, and "Colonial Pasts and Conditional Futures."

2 For Lisa Lowe, archives of slave ledgers tell an important story of numbers, agricultural practices, or trading routes, but like any singular source cannot tell the full story. Historical political theory tells important stories of freedom, but as many of us acknowledge it is often a story of freedom told by the colonizers, settlers, and enslavers, even as these theorists often grapple with the terrible histories in which they are entwined. Yet there is an archive problem of trying to tell the history of freedom from the perspective of the enslaved and indentured. As Saidiya Hartman and many others have argued, the absence of enslaved people from the archives means that the story of freedom must be told in spaces of absence. While my project is not engaging that precise problematic, I am similarly interested in how maligned or seemingly irrelevant "texts" tell different stories of freedom, or present alternative perspectives on ingrained stories. Lowe, *Intimacies of Four Continents*; Hartman,

"Venus in Two Acts." See also Helton, Leroy, and Mischler, "Question of Recovery"; Fuentes, *Dispossessed Lives.*

3 Lowe analyzes Campos-Pons in "Colonial Pasts and Conditional Futures."

4 Campos-Pons, "Interview on 'Sugar/Bittersweet' at Smith College of Art."

5 These different global projects are not driven solely by freedom—for most, the pursuit of freedom is not their primary motivating force—but freedom as a multifarious concept and practice is capacious enough to have supported and legitimated each of them. They reveal that legal emancipation does not grant freedom, universal personhood extends only to a small fraction of the world population, and modern commodity production is generated out of settler colonial practices of dispossession.

6 Fuente, "On Sugar, Slavery, and the Pursuit of (Cuban) Happiness." See also Goffe, "Sugarworks."

7 Mbembe, *Necropolitics*, 17.

8 James's claim is a central argument of Caribbean thought. James, *Black Jacobins.* See also Kamugisha, *Beyond Coloniality;* Hooker, *Theorizing Race in the Americas.*

9 Newman, *New World of Labor*; Beckles, *History of Barbados.*

10 Beckles, *First Black Slave Society.*

11 Sheridan, *Sugar and Slavery*, 124–34.

12 For a thorough history of freedom in Europe and North America, which also leaves out a global history of the concept, see De Dijn, *Freedom.*

13 Betty Wood, *Origins of American Slavery*, 60.

14 Alyosha Goldstein argues, "As the liberal capacity to possess, whiteness in this sense is made by perpetual taking and justified by tears at the prospect of not having." "Possessive Investment," 1083. On whiteness as access to participatory democracy see Beltrán, *Cruelty as Citizenship.*

15 Walvin, *Sugar*, 11–12.

16 Darra Goldstein, *Oxford Companion to Sugar and Sweets*, 690–91. According to Henry VIII's logs, it took an extraordinary amount of labor—by seven chefs over four days—to make the dungeon, which included a sugared "manor" with a pond filled with swans.

17 Eric Williams, *From Columbus to Castro*; Richard Dunn, *Sugar and Slaves*; Mintz, *Sweetness and Power.*

18 Eric Williams, *From Columbus to Castro*, 25, Mintz, *Sweetness and Power*, 22.

19 Walvin, *Sugar*, 34.

20 Galloway, *Sugar Cane Industry*, 65.

21 English settlers attempted to plant sugarcane in the North American colony of Jamestown as early as 1619, but the land could not sustain cane, so sugar planters focused on tropical regions. Mintz, *Sweetness and Power*, 37.

22 Sheridan, *Sugar and Slavery*, 107–18.

23 Menard, *Sweet Negotiations*, 13–14.

24 Sheridan, *Sugar and Slavery*, 234–60; Beckles, *History of Barbados.*

25 Sheridan, *Sugar and Slavery*, 21–22.

26 Mintz, *Sweetness and Power*, esp. 53–61.

27 Curtin, *Rise and Fall of the Plantation Complex*, 197.

28 Ashworth, *Short History of International Economy since 1850*, 28–29; Dunn, *Sugar and Slaves*, 188–223.

29 As Eric Williams summarized the general trend, "The commercial capitalism of the eighteenth century developed the wealth of Europe by means of slavery and monopoly." *Capitalism and Slavery*, 210.

30 Mintz, *Sweetness and Power*, 44–61.

31 Richard Dunn, *Sugar and Slaves*, 224.

32 James, *Black Jacobins*, 391–92.

33 Tsing, *Mushroom at the End of the World*, 39.

34 Richard Dunn, *Sugar and Slaves*, 223.

35 Gómez-Barris, *Extractive Zone*, xvii.

36 Haraway, *Staying with the Trouble*, 206n5.

37 Coulthard, "Place Against Empire," 80; Kimmerer, *Braiding Sweetgrass*; Leanne Simpson, *As We Have Always Done*.

38 Du Bois, "Souls of White Folk," 24. On Du Bois's argument that whiteness is dominion, see Myers, "Beyond the Psychological Wage."

39 Ralph Davis, *Rise of the Atlantic Economies*, 251, cited in Mintz, *Sweetness and Power*, 47; also see Mintz, *Sweetness and Power*, 14–16. On sugar's shift of palate see Tompkins, "Sweetness, Capacity, Energy."

40 On the local specificity, autonomy from the Crown, and hybridity of propriptary constitutions, see Hsueh, *Hybrid Constitutions*.

41 Laurent Dubois and Richard Lee Turits argue that "planters throughout the Caribbean developed a rich political and juridical tradition that brought together demands for the same political rights as other subjects within their empires with an insistent defense of their own right to hold slaves." *Freedom Roots*, 78.

42 Goveia, *West Indian Slave Laws*.

43 Rugemer, *Slave Law*; Horne, *Apocalypse of Settler Colonialism*.

44 Wynter, "Unsettling the Coloniality," 266.

45 Jennifer Rae Greeson argues that the idea of freedom as self-possession first emerged out of slavery, as it required an understanding of humans as possessible objects, which only happened with the emergence of Atlantic slave capitalism. For Cheryl Harris and Aileen Moreton-Robinson, both possession and self-possession were, from the start, formed out of the contrast with possession and ownership of bodies. Greeson, "Prehistory of Possessive Individualism." Harris, "Whiteness as Property"; Moreton-Robinson, *White Possessive*.

46 Johnson, *River of Dark Dreams*, 24.

47 Mbembe, *Necropolitics*, 80.

48 See Rana, *Two Faces of American Freedom*, 47, 90–93.

49 Free Labor movements grew in England as slave labor was practiced in the colonies, both part of the same overarching political and economic system. Mintz, "Plantations and the Rise of a New World Economy."

50 Beckles, *History of Barbados*, 8.

51 Menard, *Sweet Negotiations*; Sheridan, *Sugar and Slavery*, 395–96.

52 Richard Dunn, *Sugar and Slaves*, 85.

53 The House contained a representative body of the biggest landholding planters, chosen by popular elections, who established a measure of local autonomy from the English Crown. They created their own system of laws, even as
they were overseen by a governor who had power to dissolve the assembly at
will. See Goveia, *West Indian Slave Laws*; Beckles, *History of Barbados*.

54 Puckrein, *Little England*, 34.

55 Puckrein, *Little England*, 32.

56 Puckrein, *Little England*, 37.

57 Robertson, *Denmark Vesey*, 12; Newman, *New World of Labor*.

58 Beckles, *First Black Slave Society*. See also Menard, *Sweet Negotiations*, 1.

59 Beckles, *First Black Slave Society*, 13–15, 19; Richard Dunn, *Sugar and Slaves*, 64–65.

60 Robertson, *Denmark Vesey*, 12–23.

61 Beckles, *History of Barbados*, 44.

62 Ligon, *True and Exact History*, 72, 75, 94–96, 102.

63 Schwartz, "A Commonwealth within Itself," 158–200.

64 Amussen, *Caribbean Exchanges*, 83.

65 Richard Dunn, *Sugar and Slaves*, 59–67.

66 Beckles, *First Black Slave Society*, Part 1.

67 Puckrein, *Little England*, 12, 13.

68 Puckrein, *Little England*, 25.

69 Beckles, *First Black Slave Society*, 5.

70 Robertson, *Denmark Vesey*, 12–23.

71 Richard Dunn, *Sugar and Slaves*, 77.

72 Rugemer, *Slave Law*; Beckles, *First Black Slave Society*, 19–21.

73 Richard Dunn, *Sugar and Slaves*, 85.

74 Beckles and Downes, "Economics of Transition." See also Richard Dunn,
Sugar and Slaves, 72. For an account of the rebellion, see Ligon, *True and Exact
History*, 44–47.

75 Monahan, *Creolizing Subject*, Chapter 2.

76 Rugemer, "The Development of Mastery and Race," 431.

77 Rugemer, *Slave Law*, 11–34. Bradley Nicholson has argued that the Barbados
slave code had antecedents in English laws for controlling servants and colonized Irish people. Nicholson, "Legal Borrowing."

78 Wynter, "Unsettling the Coloniality."

79 Goveia, *West Indian Slave Laws*, 22. For an encompassing history of Black surveillance, see Browne, *Dark Matters*.

80 Rugemer, *Slave Law*, 31–34.

81 Goveia, *West Indian Slave Laws*, 19–28.

82 Jennifer Morgan, *Laboring Women*, 95.

83 Weinbaum, *Afterlife of Reproductive Slavery*, 7.

84 Norrece Jones, "Rape in Black and White." See also Vermeulen, "Thomas
Thistlewood's Libidinal Linnean Project."

85 Fuentes, *Dispossessed Lives*, 5–8.

86 See also Cecily Jones, *Engendering Whiteness*.

87 Richard Dunn, *Sugar and Slaves*, 240–45.

88 Even as racial enslavement and native dispossession are different processes that cannot be conflated, their developments are connected through sugar. On the importance of this distinction, see Byrd, *Transit of Empire*.

89 Armitage, "John Locke, Carolina, and the Two Treatises of Government"; Arneil, *John Locke and America*; Bernasconi and Mann, "Contradictions of Racism"; Dilts, "To Kill a Thief"; Farr, "Locke, Natural Law, and New World Slavery"; Fitzmaurice, *Sovereignty, Property, and Empire*; Sheth, *Toward a Political Philosophy of Race*; Tully, *Approach to Political Philosophy*. For the influence of these claims in the later British Empire, see Bell, *Reordering the World*; and Morefield, *Empires without Imperialism*.

90 Rana, *Two Faces of American Freedom*, 7.

91 Glausser, "Three Approaches," 200–201; Parekh, "Decolonizing Liberalism."

92 On Locke's expertise, see Irving, *Natural Science*, 109–32.

93 Arneil, *John Locke and America*, 90–91.

94 Tully, *Approach to Political Philosophy*, 137–77.

95 For Hagar Kotef, Lockean theories of expropriation produced the appearance of indigenous "landlessness." *Movement and the Ordering of Freedom*, 103.

96 Locke, *Second Treatise*, Sec. 37.

97 For Armitage, Locke sees all people as having the capacity for rationality, but civilizational practices prevent them from accessing it. Different practices and norms, or better access to proper tools and commodities, would enable that capacity. This may actually bring him closer to the disciplinary liberalism of J. S. Mill. Armitage, "John Locke, Theorist of Empire?"

98 Locke, *Second Treatise*, Sec. 102. Popes and temporal sovereigns often agreed about the expropriation of indigenous lands, though for different reasons. See Pagden, *Lords of All the World*. Barbara Arneil argues, "The doctrine of natural rights allows that anyone may lay claim to the soil of America if he adopts a settled agrarian style of life, joins the rest of mankind in the use of money and commerce, establishes laws of liberty and property, and adopts the primary principle of God, and secondary principles of arts and sciences as the basis of knowledge. The difficulty is that in meeting all the requirements of Locke's property owner, the Amerindian must in all significant ways become European." Arneil, *John Locke and America*, 166. See also Ince, *Colonial Capitalism*.

99 Barker, "For Whom Sovereignty Matters," 7. See also Taiaiake Alfred's argument on how the strategic use of sovereignty for indigenous reclamation is still tied to the violence and dominion of Lockean relations to land. "Sovereignty."

100 Tuck, *Rights of War and Peace*, 175.

101 Locke, *Second Treatise*, Sec. 40.

102 Ralph Davis, *Rise of the Atlantic Economies*, 250–52.

103 Amussen, *Caribbean Exchanges*, 9.

104 Parker, *Sugar Barons*, 126.

105 Glausser, "Three Approaches to Locke and the Slave Trade," 204.

106 As Secretary for the Council of Trade and Plantations, Locke knew intimately the colonists' arguments that colonization by plantation agriculture
was only possible with enslaved labor. Locke argues that labor is ownership
but also argues that the labor of enslaved people and servants is considered
to be the labor of the owner who bought them and owns the land, rather
than the more expected suggestion that would emanate from his argument—
that the laborers doing the work are the ones who would own the land.
Bernasconi and Mann, "Contradictions of Racism," 90.

107 Locke, *First Treatise*, Sec. 131.

108 In this way Locke demonstrates what Hagar Kotef calls a theory of the dis-
possessor. See Kotef, *Colonizing Self.*

109 Farr, "Locke, Natural Law, and New World Slavery."

110 Locke, *First Treatise*, Sec. 130.

111 Locke, *Second Treatise*, Sec. 35.

112 Beer, *Old Colonial System*, 179–80; Newman, *New World of Slavery*, 251–53.

113 Quote by H. R. Foxbourne, *The Life of John Locke, London, 1876*, quoted in
Arneil, *John Locke and America*, 89. See also Bernasconi and Mann, "Contradictions of Racism," 91.

114 "*Fundamental Constitutions of Carolina: March 1, 1669.*"

115 Armitage, "John Locke, Carolina, and the Two Treatises of Government," 607.
See also Hinshelwood, "Carolinian Context of John Locke's Theory of Slavery."

116 Beckles, *History of Barbados*, 31; Beer, *Old Colonial System*, 15, 179–80.

117 Peter Colleton's father, John Colleton, was one of the original plantation
owners on the island who made his fortune in sugarcane, and John was also
an original lord proprietor of Carolina. When John died, Peter took over
both his father's Carolina proprietorship and his Barbados plantation, which
was one of the largest slaveholding sugar plantations on Barbados. Colleton served for twenty years on the council that ruled Barbados, eventually
becoming its president. Newman, *New World of Labor*, 252.

118 Colleton knew that Barbados faced a growing problem: because planters had
cleared all the land for sugar monoculture and land was only in the hands of
a few planters, the island lost the capacity to provide necessities for its population. The planters were unwilling to diversify their agriculture because
profits were so large from sugar; they gave up self-sufficiency and looked to
other colonies, hoping to turn them into provision-makers for Barbados. At
the same time, many English settlers coming to Barbados could not get land,
as all of it was already consolidated in large plantations. They too wanted
somewhere to establish their own plantations, and Carolina became a place
to go if one could not own land in Barbados. Carolina was thus colonized in
large part to be a provision-maker for Barbados, and to extend its plantation
practices in a new agricultural space. Newman, *New World of Labor*, 253.

119 Peter Wood, *Black Majority*, Chapter 1.

120 Gordon, *Creolizing Political Theory*; Simon, *Ideology of Creole Revolution.*

121 Morgan details: "Like their counterparts in Barbados, Carolina slaveowners
found that newly enslaved Africans were the primary means of immediately

increasing their own wealth and the size of their slaveholdings." Jennifer Morgan, *Laboring Women*, 128.

122 Parker, *Sugar Barons*.

123 Locke scholar William Uzgalis suggests that the elder Colleton, John, was responsible for adding the section on slavery and uses this claim to dismiss Locke's personal investment in the section. However, John Colleton died three years before the Constitution was created, so it would have had to have been his son Peter Colleton who made the addition. Besides that error, I would agree that one Colleton, Peter, was one of the influencers for this section, as the Colletons were exporting Barbadian practices to Carolina. However, it is certainly possible that Peter Colleton originated the phrase *and* that Locke supported it; the first does not divest Locke of responsibility for legalizing absolute power over enslaved people. It is likely that they were coauthors who together had a hand in shaping the document and signed off on it before instantiating it in the colony. Uzgalis, "An Inconsistency Not to Be Excused," 98n2. See also Henry A. M. Smith, "Colleton Family in South Carolina."

124 Robertson, *Denmark Vesey*, 13–14.

125 Thomas Wilson, *Ashley Cooper Plan*, 46.

126 Armitage, "John Locke, Theorist of Empire?" 88. Locke continued to be involved in promoting the success of Carolina. In one letter in 1671, Colleton asked Locke to create promotional material to help bring people to the struggling Carolina settlement. He asked Locke to write "in the nature of a description such as might invite people without seeming to come from us [the proprietors]" in order to "conduce our speedy settlement." Although there is no conclusive evidence linking Locke to published promotional material for Carolina, next to Colleton's letter Locke made notes on "Writers of Carolina" that listed material and subjects on the infant colony. Locke, "Letter 254," 355–56.

127 Bernasconi and Mann, "Contradictions of Racism."

128 "*Fundamental Constitutions of Carolina: March 1, 1669*," Sec. 109–11.

129 In this sense it aligns in part with what Vicki Hsueh has called the hybridity of the Carolina Constitution, which takes shape in dialogue with ancient, feudal, and modern forms of governance, both native dispossession and accommodation, as well as protoliberal and republican versions of rule. I am emphasizing more dispossession than accommodation here, while holding together enslavement with liberal practices of property and republican practices of self-rule. Hsueh, *Hybrid Constitutions*, 55–82. See also Scherer, *Beyond Church and State*.

130 Achille Mbembe interview with David Theo Goldberg, "The Reason of Unreason." See also Mbembe, *Necropolitics*, 162.

131 As Peter Hoffer argues, "without slavery, Carolina never would have been profitable enough to merit colonization." Hoffer, *Cry Liberty*, 37.

132 Menard, *Sweet Negotiations*, 6.

133 Singh, "Pervasive Power of the Settler Mindset."

134 Incoming settlers from Barbados wanted to create their own rules in Carolina—in large part because they wanted to enslave Native Americans and profit from an indigenous slave trade, a practice the Crown frowned upon for its propensity to cause costly wars. These new Barbadian settlers, called the Goose Creek Men, wanted to steal indigenous land by conquest, not by trade as the proprietors preferred, and to enslave them. The Goose Creek Men argued for their greater participation in governance so that they could legalize indigenous enslavement. Once again calls for self-rule aligned with desires to enslave other humans, steal their land, and derive profit from it. Part of the Lords Proprietors' continued efforts in the colony were not only to benefit the initial proprietors but to stop incoming Barbadian settlers from enslaving local Native Americans. By some accounts, the vaunted religious tolerance practiced in Carolina was mobilized to bring in more white settlers from other European regions to counter the machinations of settlers like the Goose Creek Men. See Sirmans, *Colonial South Carolina*.

135 On the ongoing importance of agriculture to dispossession, see Goldstein, "Ground Not Given."

136 Nichols, *Theft as Property*.

137 Beckles, *First Black Slave Society*, 4, 11.

138 On this power in Haiti, see Kevin Olson, *Imagined Sovereignties*, 112.

139 Edmund Morgan, *American Freedom, American Slavery*.

140 There were many slave revolts on sugar plantations, including three major island-wide revolts in Barbados before emancipation in 1834 (finally establishing independence in 1966), and many on Jamaica, as well as the world-changing Haitian revolution, which was the first large-scale slave self-emancipation enacted by Afro-Caribbean people enslaved on French sugar plantations. On the role of sugar in abolitionist movements see Sheller, *Consuming the Caribbean*; Glickman "'Buy for the Sake of the Slave.'"

141 Follett, *Sugar Masters*; Gourevich, *From Slavery to the Cooperative Commonwealth*, 1–6. Sugar barons fought hard against this activism, however, and by the early twentieth century they squashed many newfound worker freedoms and formed the backbone of new white supremacy movements. Abbott, *Sugar*, 296–99.

142 April Merleaux argues that sugar was one of the central parts of the US wars for Cuba, Puerto Rico, the Philippines, and Hawai'i, in which islands lands were taken over by individuals and corporations for sugar production. The islands were compelled to follow US rule but remain subordinate to the nation, as the Fourteenth Amendment and citizenship policies did not apply to the new territorial possessions. Sugar became a central feature of British and American kitchens for people of all classes by the early twentieth century. Merleaux, *Sugar and Civilization*.

143 "Sugar Farming's Toll on the Environment."

144 For more on freedom's sartorial and social forms, see Anker, "White and Deadly," 190–92. On sugar's sensorial fecundity, see Tompkins, "Sweetness, Capacity, Energy."

145 Yudkin, *Pure, White and Deadly*.
146 Quoted in Follett, "Legacies of Enslavement," 53.
147 Roberts, *Freedom as Marronage*.
148 Roberts, *Freedom as Marronage*, 13.
149 Gonzales, *Maroon Nation*.
150 Rooney, "A Sonorous Subtlety."
151 Tompkins, *Racial Indigestion*, 98.
152 Ortiz, *Cuban Counterpoint*, 58.
153 Loichot, "Kara Walker's Blood Sugar."
154 Hartman, *Wayward Lives*, 27.
155 On this point, see Roberta Smith, "Sugar? Sure, But Salted with Meaning."
156 On audience member's actions, see Loichot, "Kara Walker's Blood Sugar";
     and Powers, "Why I Yelled."
157 Forster, "Kara Walker."
158 Sharpe, *In the Wake*, 98–99.
159 She is in a position both "subordinate and overpowering" as Mark Reinhardt
     describes her. Reinhardt, "Vision's Unseen."
160 I am deeply grateful to Lida Maxwell and Andrew Dilts for their brilliant
     provocations in helping me to make this argument. See Maxwell, "Pleasures
     of Freedom"; Dilts, "Ugliness of Freedom's Practices."
161 Musser, "Queering Sugar"; Musser, *Sensual Excess*, Ch. 1.
162 Musser, *Sensual Excess*, 28.
163 Municipal Art Society of New York, "Save Brooklyn's Industrial Heritage."
164 FundingUniverse, "Domino Sugar Corporation History."
165 Achille Mbembe interview with David Theo Goldberg, "The Reason of
     Unreason."
166 Hartman, *Wayward Lives*, 227.

CHAPTER TWO. TRAGEDIES OF EMANCIPATION

1   Jealous, "Freedom," 55.
2   Obama, "Remarks by the First Lady."
3   Theoharis, *More Beautiful and More Terrible History*, xxi.
4   See work by Patchen Markell, Steven Johnston, Bonnie Honig, George Shul-
    man, Simon Stow, William Connolly. Johnston writes, "Tragedy thus deflates
    the will to power as a will to control to which humans are susceptible." *Truth
    about Patriotism*, 209.
5   See, among others, Ciccariello-Maher, "'So Much the Worse for Whites.'"
6   David Scott, *Conscripts of Modernity*, 174.
7   Patterson, "Unholy Trinity"; Lowe, *Intimacies of Four Continents*, 15.
8   Hartman, *Scenes of Subjection*; Patterson, *Slavery and Social Death*; Du Bois,
    Black Reconstruction. For a study of emancipatory tragedy facing free Blacks
    in the antebellum era, see Calvin Warren, *Ontological Terror*.
9   See Helton et al., "Question of Recovery," Introduction.
10 Hartman, *Scenes of Subjection*, 6.

11 Raymond Williams, *Modern Tragedy*, 13; Gilroy, *Black Atlantic*, 56.

12 Younge, "Liberty? No, Thanks."

13 *Der Spiegel*, "Spiegel Interview with Lars von Trier."

14 Wilderson, *Red, White, and Black*; Calvin Warren, *Ontological Terror*. See also Sexton, *Amalgamation Schemes*.

15 Wilderson and Armah, "Lady with the Whip."

16 Walter Johnson, "Slavery, Reparations, and the Mythic March."

17 On recovery projects, see Helton et al., "Question of Recovery."

18 Walter Johnson, "Agency: A Ghost Story."

19 For a thoughtful example of moving beyond agency for interpreting Black aesthetics without eliminating its possibility, instead focusing on the elusiveness of personhood, see Freeburg, *Counterlife*.

20 Ramgotra, "Republic and Empire."

21 Baldwin, "Everybody's Protest Novel."

22 For a sharp analysis of freedoms that may seem confusing or superfluous, with a focus on nineteenth-century Liberia, see Kazanjian, *Brink of Freedom*.

23 *Der Spiegel*, "Spiegel Interview with Lars von Trier."

24 Vincent Lloyd argues that Grace's liberal stance is connected to the political-theological realm of purity and "grace" in her expectations for the work of Law. I agree with some of his analysis of theological expectations for juridical power, though I find that Wilhelm's law complicates the view that the film supports a critique of one conception for how "Law" works. Lloyd, *Problem with Grace*.

25 Glenn, *Unequal Freedom*; Roediger, *Wages of Whiteness*; Du Bois, *Black Reconstruction*.

26 Charles Mills uses the term *racial contract* to name how the social contract of liberal theory proclaims universal individual freedom but excludes blacks while enabling their political and economic exploitation. *Racial Contract*.

27 Douglass, "Present and Future."

28 Angela Davis, *Meaning of Freedom*, 140.

29 Gilroy, *Black Atlantic*, 49.

30 Nikhil Singh writes with bracing clarity, "Lynching in particular was defined as the reassertion of the sovereign rights and capacities of white citizens." *Race and America's Long War*, 51. Fred Moten argues, "Lynching is the disciplinary outrage of whiteness, which is to say, of dispersed, degraded, defeated, and, nevertheless, dominant, modernized sovereignty." *Stolen Life*, 134.

31 Lynching in post-emancipation America was a key practice for reestablishing white supremacy. It continued the work of the slave codes that put white men beyond the reach of the law while granting them full control over black bodies. Lynching was the sovereign practice of whiteness in a new era, the power to declare who shall live and who shall die without legal structures. See Wells, "Lynch Law in America"; and Goveia, *West Indian Slave Laws*, 31.

32 Hartman, "Time of Slavery"; see also Lowe, *Intimacy of Four Continents*, 60.

33 Binder, "Slavery of Emancipation," 2066.

34 There is a wealth of important scholarship in political theory grappling with the foundational colonial and racist ideas found in early theorists of modern freedom, especially John Locke, John Stuart Mill, and Immanuel Kant, arguably the most central thinkers for Euro-American theories of freedom that continue to inform our present. In the 1780s, Kant famously argued for the self-reflexive subject who wills his own action as the model of individual freedom, while also penning the first modern theory of racial hierarchy, which categorized the moral worth of persons by phenotype and denied Africans and indigenous Americans the capacity for free subjectivity. In the 1840s J. S. Mill's canonical text *On Liberty* famously argued that every individual was sovereign "over himself, over his body and mind." Five sentences later he argued for despotism over people who must be disciplined into individual freedom. This presumably included Indian, Chinese, and other non-European people under British colonial rule, who required obedience to a dictator until they were mature enough to handle the responsibilities of individual liberty and limited government. I discuss Locke in chapter 1 and Mill briefly in the introduction. Mill, *On Liberty*, 13. Mehta, *Liberalism and Empire*; Pitts, *Turn to Empire*; Eze, "Color of Reason"; Mills, "Kant's Untermenschen."

35 Philosophical constructions of freedom have long been understood contra slavery, at least since Aristotle. But in Euro-American modernity this understanding of freedom becomes saturated with racial categories, such that freedom and self-making seem available through whiteness. See chapter 1.

36 See also Edmund Morgan, *American Slavery, American Freedom*.

37 Singh, *Race and America's Long War*, 93.

38 Patterson, *Freedom*.

39 Wynter, "Unsettling the Coloniality of Being/Truth/Power/Freedom," 270.

40 Zerilli, "Critique as a Political Practice of Freedom."

41 As thinkers from Karl Marx to Frantz Fanon to Jacques Derrida have insisted, emancipation is not something that can be gifted to others. It must be acquired by the unfree, otherwise it still circulates in a transactional economy of obligation to those who bestowed it. See Nguyen, *Gift of Freedom*.

42 Among decades of sources on the work of Black people who fought for emancipation in fields, courts, and social movements see John Hope Franklin, *Runaway Slaves*; Quarles, *Black Abolitionists*; Roediger, *Seizing Freedom*; Hahn, *Nation under Our Feet*; Stephanie M. H. Camp, *Closer to Freedom*; David Williams, *I Freed Myself*. Early work on this topic included Du Bois's prescient argument for the black general strike in *Black Reconstruction*.

43 The nationwide controversy over the film *Selma* (dir. Ava DuVernay, 2014) is another example of how heated debates over the agency of Black freedom play out in Hollywood cinema. *Selma* positions the communal efforts of the members of the Southern Christian Leadership Conference, guided but not controlled by Martin Luther King, as the primary agents of change pushing for passage of a Voting Rights Act. Some critics, most notably former cabinet member Joseph Califano in a *Washington Post* op-ed, argued that Lyndon Johnson was given short shrift in the film, that he was not an ambivalent supporter of civil rights

who required the instigation of grassroots social movements to support the VRA, but its spearhead. This debate is, at its core, about who gets to be the primary agent of Black freedom, and perhaps critics like Califano are uncomfortable with the history told in *Selma*, in which freedom is not gifted from white elites but taken by black community members and organizers. I see *Manderlay* as offering a critique of the types of history that aim to delegitimize the history told in *Selma*, or that place the Voting Rights Act in a narrative of racial progress supervised by open-minded white actors. Califano, "Movie 'Selma' Has a Glaring Flaw."

44 Hartman, *Scenes of Subjection*, 116–20.

45 Hartman, *Scenes of Subjection*, 133. Nicholas Mirzoeff argues that overseeing is a central practice of whiteness in *Right to Look*, 50–51.

46 Patterson suggests that emancipation was always understood as a gift from the master. *Slavery and Social Death*, 209–19.

47 Derrida, *Given Time*, 23.

48 Sexton, *Amalgamation Schemes*, 105.

49 Guyora Binder writes, "When emancipation is conceived as governance, education, assimilation, or rehabilitation of a socially or psychically disabled slave, slavery has not perished." "Slavery of Emancipation," 2075.

50 Jones-Rogers, *They Were Her Property*.

51 Grace is a "beneficiary" in Bruce Robbins's sense of the term, aiming to "help" the poor while refusing to acknowledge her causal relationship to others' poverty. Robbins, *Beneficiary*.

52 Mill, *On Liberty*. See also Mehta, *Liberalism and Empire*; Anker, "Liberalism of Horror."

53 Hartman, *Scenes of Subjection*, 8.

54 Ferguson, *Aberrations in Black*. On the creativity of Black sociality beyond violence, see Nyong'o, *Afro-Fabulations*.

55 On this point, see Belew, *Bring the War Home*; Feimster, *Southern Horrors*.

56 Benjamin Franklin, "Observations Concerning the Increase of Mankind, 1751," no. 12.

57 Mill states, "We may leave out of consideration those backward states of society in which the race itself is in its nonage. . . . Despotism is a legitimate mode of government in dealing with barbarians, provided the end be their improvement, and the means justified by actually effecting that end. Liberty, as a principle, has no application to any state of things anterior to the time when mankind have become capable of being improved by free and equal discussion. Until then, there is nothing for them but implicit obedience to an Akbar or a Charlemagne, if they are so fortunate as to find one." Mill, *On Liberty*, 14; and also Mill, "Civilization."

58 Honig, *Democracy and the Foreigner*.

59 Cathy Cohen, "Deviance as Resistance."

60 King, *Race, Theft, and Ethics*, 10.

61 Mohammed, *Condemnation of Blackness*. Natasha Lightfoot describes how Black practices of freedom often enter the political record as "punishable offenses." *Troubling Freedom*, 232.

62 Cathy Cohen, "Deviance as Resistance"; Stanley, *From Bondage to Contract*.

63 MacPherson, *Political Theory of Possessive Individualism*; Harris, "Whiteness as Property."

64 On the challenge to possession that does not presume prior ownership, a challenge that refuses to accept possession retroactively imputed by dispossession, see Kazanjian, *Brink of Freedom*.

65 Marx, "On the Jewish Question."

66 Saidiya Hartman writes, "Owning things, land, and people had never secured their place in the world. They didn't need others beneath their feet to establish their value. . . . If the past taught them anything, it was that the attempt to own life destroyed it, brutalized the earth, and ran roughshod over everything in god's creation for a dollar." *Wayward Lives*, 270–71.

67 Rogin, *Ronald Reagan*; Anker, "Cinematic Dream Life of American Politics."

68 Marshall, "Political Life of Fungibility."

69 If, as Hartman suggests, Black subjects struggle to express the ambivalences of freedom to white audiences "without being woefully misunderstood as a longing for the good old days of slavery," then in this vein Wilhelm and the ex-slaves know they will only be misunderstood and play on that misunderstanding to fight for a freedom that is less violent than the one they live under. *Scenes of Subjection*, 137.

70 On conspiratorial readings, see Martel, *Textual Conspiracies*; Honig, *Antigone, Interrupted*.

71 Moten and Harney, *Undercommons*, 19.

72 "Fire was so common in slave rebellions as to be symbolic of them." Hoffer, *Cry Liberty*, 86.

73 Linda Williams, *Playing the Race Card*.

74 Halberstam, "Introduction," 12.

75 Moten and Harney, *Undercommons*, 40.

76 David Scott, *Conscripts of Modernity*, 190.

77 Berlin, "American Slavery in History and Memory," 14.

78 Loury, "Ferguson Won't Change Anything."

79 Woodly-Davis, *Reckoning*.

80 I make an extended argument that connects to this paragraph in Anker, "Tale of Two Protests."

81 Makalani, "Black Lives Matter," 531–32.

82 See McLeod, "Law, Critique, and the Undercommons," 263.

83 For a critique of the related problem of respectability in relation to Black Lives Matter, see among others Michelle Smith, "Affect and Respectability Politics."

84 Dorian Warren, "Response to Ferguson."

CHAPTER THREE. THWARTING NEOLIBERALISM

1 Market logic now "monopolizes the language of freedom," as Eric MacGilvray notes. *Invention of Market Freedom*, 3. On neoliberal visions see, among others, Friedman, *Capitalism and Freedom*; Hayek, *Road to Serfdom* and *Constitution of*

Liberty; Foucault, *Birth of Biopolitics*; Duggan, *Twilight of Equality*; Harvey, *Brief History of Neoliberalism*.

2 Brown, *In the Ruins of Neoliberalism*, 37.

3 Wacquant, *Punishing the Poor*. As Wacquant has argued, neoliberalism involves the intense securitization of "the nether regions of social space" that would otherwise seem to inhibit or resist its capital flows (58).

4 Alexander, *New Jim Crow*; Gilmore, *Golden Gulag*.

5 This subtle reworking of freedom is part of what makes neoliberalism a shift in the development of liberal capitalism. In this shift, free enterprise is the hallmark of individual agency and the market is the only space of freedom and unshackled individual subjectivity, because individuals there can exchange goods—the primary act of free agency—without an overarching vision of the good life to guide their behavior. Deregulation offloads social and economic risk from powerful elites and corporate entities to poor and underserved communities, marking those communities as expendable in the widening search for new markets, especially those communities in cities where public space is part of the fabric of daily life. On freedom as the organizing language of neoliberalism, see Bogues, *Empire of Liberty*, 8.

6 Brown, *Undoing the Demos*; Peck, *Constructions of Neoliberal Reason*; Wacquant, *Punishing the Poor*; Wolin, *Democracy Incorporated*.

7 See Dean, *Communist Horizon*; McKean, *Disorienting Neoliberalism*; Žižek, *Year of Dreaming Dangerously*; Hardt and Negri, *Commonwealth*; Graeber, *Democracy Project*; Piketty, *Capital in the Twenty-first Century*; Gourevich and Robin, "Freedom Now."

8 Harabin, "10 Questions with David Simon."

9 For analysis of *The Wire* in this vein, see La Berge, "Capitalist Realism and Serial Form."

10 On the productivity of failure, see J. Jack Halberstam, *Queer Art of Failure*; Maxwell, *Public Trials*; and the conclusion in Anker, *Orgies of Feeling*.

11 Berlant, *Cruel Optimism*. See also Goldberg, *Dread*. This impasse is itself partly a product of neoliberalism. Neoliberal rationality offers little desire, pleasure, or vision beyond ceaseless risk-taking for economic growth; as capitalism in its liberal-democratic-American-Dream variant lays dying there *is* little vision in mainstream political imaginaries to organize social dreams, because neoliberalism simply doesn't offer one.

12 Benjamin, "Theses on the Philosophy of History."

13 For blueprints of radical futures that specifically counteract neoliberal visions, see, among others, Srnicek and Williams, *Inventing the Future*; Dean, *Communist Horizon*; Mbembe, *Out of the Dark Night*; Gilroy, *Postcolonial Melancholia*. Robin D. G. Kelley's *Freedom Dreams* argues that visions of radical freedom have been there all along, especially Black imaginaries of liberation—they just operate under the radar of dominant critical theoretical approaches and thus have not been acknowledged to guide large-scale visions.

14 I thank Jodi Dean for conversations on this point.

15 On this point, see Corkin, *Connecting "The Wire,"* 9.

16 Linda Williams, *On "The Wire."*

17 These different strategies counter the popular narrative of neoliberalism as state retreat, and reflect what Jamie Peck describes as the twinned neoliberal strategies of "roll-back" and "roll-out"—of market freedom through the roll-back of deregulation paired with the roll-out of increased governmental forms of surveillance. Peck, *Constructions of Neoliberal Reason.*

18 Garland, *Culture of Control*, 175.

19 Vitale, *End of Policing.*

20 As Nikhil Singh writes of policing, gesturing to its connection to freedom, it "determines, finally, who must be subjected to discipline so that others can pursue their self-interest." Singh, *Race and America's Long War*, 39.

21 Gilmore, *Golden Gulag.*

22 See Jordan Camp, *Incarcerating the Crisis*; Duggan, *Twilight of Equality.*

23 To see how police and military rule expand together in a joint project of race war, see Singh, *Race and America's Long War.* An excellent dissertation that traces the long development of the US carceral state is Lindsay Davis, "Lessons in Captivity."

24 Kotef, *Movement and the Ordering of Freedom.*

25 See Gottschalk, *Caught*; Soss, Fording, and Schram, *Disciplining the Poor.*

26 Spence, *Knocking the Hustle*; Goldberg, *The Threat of Race.*

27 Lowndes and HoSang, *Producers, Parasites, Patriots*; Passavant, *Policing Protest.*

28 Linda Williams, *On "The Wire."* See also Jagoda, "Wired."

29 See Schaub, *"The Wire."*

30 Passavant, "Strong Neo-Liberal State."

31 On this point see Corkin, *Connecting "The Wire."*

32 As the show notes, many city resources are transferred from the War on Drugs to the War on Terror, though even as the latter gets more sophisticated equipment, it proves just as ineffective.

33 See Honig, *Public Things.*

34 Boger, "The Meaning of Neighborhood in the Modern City."

35 Malka, *Men of Mobtown.*

36 Muhammad, *Condemnation of Blackness.*

37 For an alternative argument that *The Wire* does not attend to the history of entrenched racism, see Lipsitz, *How Racism Takes Place.*

38 Kelley, "Thug Nation," 28.

39 Moten, *Stolen Life*, 138–39.

40 Brown, *Undoing the Demos*; Foucault, *Birth of Biopolitics*; Dardot and Laval, *New Way of the World.*

41 Feher, "Self-Appreciation." See also Brown, *Undoing the Demos.*

42 Foucault, *Birth of Biopolitics.*

43 Brown, *Undoing the Demos*, 31.

44 As producer Ed Burns notes in the commentary to this scene, "There is an industry that makes a lot of money on this."

45 For a longer argument about the character Stringer Bell's relationship to neoliberalism, see Anker, "Limits of Neoliberalism."

46 Brown, *Undoing the Demos*, 22.

47 Duggan, *Mean Girl*.

48 Foucault, *Birth of Biopolitics*, lectures 9–12.

49 Gibbon and Henricksen make this precise point in "Standard Fit for Neoliberalism."

50 Beer, *Metric Power*.

51 Wacquant, *Punishing the Poor*.

52 Friedman and Szasz, *Friedman and Szasz on Liberty and Drugs*.

53 Friedman, *Capitalism and Freedom*.

54 Sheehan and Sweeney, "*The Wire* and the World."

55 As Wacquant suggests, many neoliberal tactics, like corporate structuring and performance metrics, bolster other logics besides neoliberal ones.

56 See Pinson and Journel, *Debating the Neoliberal City*; Peck and Theodore, *Fast Policy*. For a site-specific focus, see MacLaren and Kelly, *Neoliberal Urban Policy*.

57 Linda Williams, *On "The Wire,"* 83.

58 Bourdieu, "Essence of Neoliberalism."

59 Hornby, "Interview with David Simon."

60 For a classic study, see McDougall, *Black Baltimore*. See also Gomez, *Race, Class, Power, and Organizing*; Ahmann, "It's Exhausting to Create." See also Van Smith, "Campaign to Undermine."

61 Murakawa, *First Civil Right*, 67; Angela Davis, "Meaning of Freedom," 135.

62 Purnell and Stahly-Butts, "Politics Can't Solve the Problem."

63 See Burch, *Trading Democracy for Justice*.

64 Jackman, "Baltimore's 'Tough on Crime' Era Ends."

65 Zirin, "'Game Done Changed.'"

CHAPTER FOUR. FREEDOM AS CLIMATE DESTRUCTION

1 Kolbert, *Sixth Extinction*; and Peter Brannen's challenge to it, *Ends of the World*.

2 Moore, *Capitalism in the Web of Life*; Malm, *Fossil Capital*.

3 See Lewis and Maslin, *Human Planet*; Davis and Todd, "On the Importance of a Date." On eliminationism, see Wolfe, *Traces of History*.

4 Whyte, "Our Ancestors' Dystopia Now."

5 Goeman, "Land as Life"; Sze, *Environmental Justice in a Moment of Danger*. Rob Nixon insists, "Image, idiom and narrative are themselves powerful, if unpredictable, resources" for combatting the slow violence of environmental destruction. Nixon, *Slow Violence*, 36. For a book that bridges indigenous studies and environmental humanities, see DeLoughrey, *Allegories of the Anthropocene*. There are long-standing debates on the origins of the domination over nature. Is it a biblical inheritance from Genesis, a Hellenistic concept, a modern outgrowth of the dethroning of Church hierarchy, a renaissance and enlightenment ideal that focuses on the individual as the locus of the social, or is it specific to settler colonialism and the rise of the industrial age? I am less concerned here with finding the real or true origin story than in tracing

the specific link between freedom and the conquest of nature as it plays out in the present.

6 Davis and Todd, "On the Importance of a Date," 722, 770.

7 Wynter, "Unsettling the Coloniality of Being/Power/Truth/Freedom." On the practice of nonhuman politics, see Ferguson, "What Was Politics to the Denisovan?" On more-than-human politics, see Frost, *Biocultural Creatures*.

8 TallBear, "Caretaking Relations, Not American Dreaming." See also Deloria and Wildcat, *Power and Place*; Coulthard, "Place against Empire."

9 Luciano and Chen, "Has the Queer Ever Been Human?"

10 Kath Weston articulates these kinds of transmatter relations: "people (but not only people) throw their bodies into the mix by viscerally engaging with a socially manufactured, recursively constituted 'environment' that is also, crucially, them." Weston, *Animate Planet*, 8.

11 See especially Frost, *Biocultural Creatures*; Bennett, *Vibrant Matter*; Connolly, *Facing the Planetary*.

12 TallBear, "Indigenous Reflection," 234.

13 Taiaiake Alfred writes that different indigenous thought systems are "based on the notion that people, communities, and the other elements of creation coexist as equals—human beings as either individuals or collectives do not have a special priority in deciding the justice of a situation." "Sovereignty," 48.

14 Rushing, *Virtues of Vulnerability*.

15 Kuznia, "Rich Californians Balk at Limits."

16 Mick Smith, *Against Ecological Sovereignty*.

17 On the dangers of contemporary iterations of individualism for democracy, see Urbanati, *Tyranny of the Moderns*.

18 Dean, *Crowds and Party*, 75.

19 For an excellent elaboration of this see Connolly, *Facing the Planetary*, 7–8.

20 Du Bois, *Darkwater*, 18.

21 This freedom is tied up in violently racist views of Black and brown bodies as having increased capacity to suffer from drought, or ration water, or be exposed to chemicals. See Yusoff, *Billion Black Anthropocenes or None*.

22 Neel Ahuja writes that "any version of freedom in today's global North . . . is imbricated in racialized forms of carbon privilege that disperse social and biological precarity." "Intimate Atmospheres," 367.

23 Tonino, "Two Ways of Knowing." See also Bruyneel, *Settler Memory*.

24 Locke, *Second Treatise*, Sec. 50.

25 Wendy Brown writes, "freedom dirempted from the social becomes not just unlimited, but legitimately exercised without concern for social context or consequences, without restraint, civility, or care for a society as a whole or individuals in it." *In the Ruins of Neoliberalism*, 42.

26 Lizabeth Cohen, *Consumers' Republic*.

27 On the role of consumption in the history of Lockean property, see Kotef, *Movement and the Ordering of Freedom*, 104.

28 Horkheimer and Adorno, *Dialectic of Enlightenment*, 206.

29 Berry, "Faustian Economics," 35.

30 On the neoliberal power of the opt-out, see Honig, *Shell-Shocked*.

31 Foucault, *Birth of Biopolitics*; Brown, *Undoing the Demos*.

32 Schlosberg and Coles, "New Environmentalism of Everyday Life"; Cannavo, "Vulnerability and Limits."

33 Sharon Krause's argument on nonsovereignty is relevant here (even as, different from the case here, it is committed to individual agency). Krause, *Freedom beyond Sovereignty*. On relational freedom, see Marso, *Politics with Beauvoir*.

34 Roy Scranton suggests that to successfully attend to climate change, Americans must learn to die in the Anthropocene. In my interpretation of his provocation, he means that without the death of an entire way of life—one based in large part on a neoliberal carbonized era of consumptive sovereignty powered primarily by industrialized centers on dispossessed land—we will face the end of the human species. In the spirit of Scranton's call, the different imaginaries of political subjectivity explored here call for the death of the sovereign and endlessly consumptive subject of freedom, a subject already on a self-consumptive path toward annihilation. They harness different visions of agency and freedom that move from ceaseless consumption to co-constitution, from domination to dependence, from isolation and hierarchy to enmeshment and equality. Yet in distinction from Scranton's argument, the subjectivities I explore suggest that survival requires acknowledging, forging, and deepening alliances and solidarities beyond the boundaries of the human, motivated not only by fear of death but also by a commitment to life. Scranton, *Learning to Die*.

35 See Cocks, *On Sovereignty*.

36 Haraway, *Staying with the Trouble*, 100.

37 Robb Dunn, *Never Home Alone*, 214; Pennisi, "Right Gut Microbes."

38 Cryan and Dinan, "More Than a Gut Feeling"; "Gut Feelings: Can the Microbiota Talk to the Brain?"; Peter Andrey Smith, "Can the Bacteria in Your Gut Explain Your Mood?"

39 Yong, *I Contain Multitudes*; Collen, *10% Human*; MacAuliffe, *Your Brain on Parasites*. As feminist theorist Elizabeth Wilson argues when discussing the work of microbes in the gut, "the gut is an organ of the mind . . . it ruminates, deliberates, comprehends." *Gut Feminism*, 5.

40 Hobbes, *Leviathan*.

41 "Microbes don't just rule the world, they make every life-form possible." McFall-Ngai, "Noticing Microbial Worlds," M59.

42 Schneider, "Parts and Wholes," 210.

43 Alfred, "Sovereignty."

44 That agency is conditioned by the world is a key insight of disability studies, in which bodies are always enabled by others, by techniques and accoutrements that support movement. Disability studies shows how freedom as individual self-reliance is an abelist fantasy that disavows differentiated forms of support always required to navigate the world and thrive within it. This account of microbiota allies with these insights and draws sustenance from them, while pointing to microbiota shows how this happens in ways that draw on the commons inside bodies for that support.

45 Haraway, *Staying with the Trouble*.

46 Haraway, *Staying with the Trouble*, 4, 19.

47 Watts, "Indigenous Place-Thought and Agency", 23. See also Todd, "An Indigenous Feminist's Take."

48 Arendt, "What Is Freedom?"

49 Coglan, "Gut Microbiota Spotted Eating Brain Chemicals."

50 Gilbert et al., "A Symbiotic View of Life," 336.

51 Dean, *Communist Horizon*, 20.

52 Tsing, *Mushroom at the End of the World*, 28.

53 This also aligns with the laboring subject of political economy in Marx. Marx is often taken to task for drawing upon Locke's theory of labor; for Locke when labor mixes with natural substance it becomes the property of the individual, and this ownership is a hallmark of freedom. Free activity is to turn nature into an object owned by an individual. There are many moments when Marx seems to presume ownership over the product of one's labor, and his critique of alienated labor and commodity fetishism can be read to rest in part on the claim that the laboring object belongs to the subject. Yet at other moments Marx is actually describing something quite different with labor, and this could be instructive for reimagining the political subject of freedom. In part of the *1844 Manuscripts*, it seems less that labor turns nature into an object, but that labor extends the subject into nature. Labor is less an acquisition of nature than an *extrusion* of the self into the world through the labor process. Marx's political economy of labor is not a cordoning off of nature from others but a seepage and a shedding from the laboring body *as nature*, *into* a constructed assemblage which resides somewhere between and within them all. Marx's model, on this reading, is not about labor appropriation but subjective extrusion. Labor is the seepage of "the self" into the world. It offers a vision of radical enmeshment in the world, in the way labor mixes subjects into the world through their very activity.

54 Wollheben, *Hidden Life of Trees*, 61.

55 Oleiwi et al., "Relative DNA-Shedding Propensity"; Oldoni, Castella, and Hall, "Shedding Light"; Phipps and Petricevic, "Tendency of Individuals."

56 Rob Dunn, *Never Home Alone*, 39.

57 Shedding skin challenges what Megan Glick describes as iterations of subjectivity as an isolated entity, "that have sought solace in the construction of a singular corporeality bound by the skin." Glick, *Infrahumanisms*, 201. See also Frost, *Biocultural Creatures*.

58 Gopinath, *Unruly Visions*, 133.

59 Douglas, *Purity and Danger*.

60 Gopinath emphasizes the queerness of these nonnormative intimacies that are not predicated on heterosexual coupling but on affective "relationality between subjects and communities without recourse to claims of biological reproduction and patrilineal genealogy . . . that open the door to new ways of conceptualizing the self and others." Gopinath, *Unruly Visions*, 128–29.

61 William Cohen, "Introduction: Locating Filth", ix–x.

62 Mbembe, *Critique of Black Reason*, 60, 71.

63 Microchimerism is a source of tissue repair. In one study, a woman whose liver was damaged had a large chunk of healthy liver made up of non-self fetal cells from a pregnancy terminated twenty years prior; the liver cells had different DNA with XY chromosomes, which is how the discovery was initially made. Another mother had her adult son's DNA cells repairing her damaged thyroid. K. L. Johnson et al., "Fetal Cell Microchimerism."

64 Aryn Martin notes, in looking at studies of microchimerism, that even the researchers' presumption that cells "belong" to a fetus and not a mother is a fallacy: "The unproblematic recognition, among virtually all researchers, doctors and journalists, that these cells 'belong' to the fetus regardless of where they are found reaffirms and reifies notions of fetal (genetic) independence and autonomy from the mother." Microchimerism shifts traditional descriptions of mother-fetal relations—as sacrificial on the mother's part, and usurping on the fetus's part (as the fetus supposedly saps the resources of the mother)—to instead show how fetal cells contribute to the health and vitality of a biological mother far into the future. Indeed, fetal cells become the parent. Martin, "Microchimerism in the Mother(land)," 27.

65 Anzaldúa, *Borderlands/La Frontera*.

66 Bennett, *Vibrant Matter*, Chapter 4.

67 Fox, *Older Than the Stars*.

68 As Patchen Markell might note, *Older Than the Stars* decomposes individual sovereignty as a form of self-mastery. Markell, "Decomposing Sovereignty."

69 TallBear, "Beyond the Life/Not-Life Binary."

70 Joseph Pugliese describes a related indigenous worldview as a "kincentric vision in which both sentient and nonsentient entities are inscribed in an affective and ethical ecology." Pugliese, *Biopolitics of the More-Than-Human*, 32–33.

71 Kelly, "Dupont's Deadly Deceit"; Rich, "The Lawyer Who Became DuPont's Worst Nightmare"; Lerner, "Teflon Toxin." DuPont has known for decades that perfluorochemicals are poisonous to living creatures but has not been obligated, under laws of private property and free industry, to make its findings public or to act on them. In addition, its vast capital wealth makes most legal challenges to perfluorochemicals unfeasible.

72 Wylie, *Fractivism*.

73 Murphy, "Distributed Reproduction, Chemical Violence."

74 Chen, "Toxic Animacies, Inanimate Affections," 267. See also Chen, *Animacies*.

75 Loboiron et al., "Toxic Politics."

76 Pulido, "Flint, Environmental Racism, and Racial Capitalism"; Sze, *Environmental Justice in a Moment of Danger*, 51–75.

77 Robin Kelley's public lecture quote is cited in Sze, *Environmental Justice in a Moment of Danger*, 10.

78 Shotwell, *Against Purity*, 70.

79 Even stories about toxicity lean on and reveal racial, nationalist, and class hierarchies, as Chen shows, delineating people and places who don't deserve

to be poisoned—those who are white and privileged US citizens—and others who seemingly do, people of color residing in extractible lands worth ravaging. This reflects what Kathryn Yusoff describes as "the presumed absorbent qualities of black and brown bodies to take up the bodily burdens of toxicities and buffer the violence of the earth," which justifies both dumping and racial hierarchy. This presumption extends the plantation master's freedom from chapter 1, presuming that certain sovereign bodies (white, able-bodied, rich, successful) should be protected from the violence and poison afflicting racialized others and that they can gain control by transferring exposure or buffering their borders. Yusoff, *Billion Black Anthropocenes*, xiii.

80 For Chen, the response to toxic deterritorialization should be sympathetic concern, a position that aims to share toxic burdens while countering racial blame for them. I agree but add that it can be more. Can the "coming here" of toxicity in "private" spaces and "sovereign" bodies ground widespread solidarity and affiliation? Chen hints at this possibility: "In perhaps its best versions, toxicity propels, not repels, queer loves, especially once we release it from exclusively human hosts, disproportionately inviting disability, industrial labor, biological targets—inviting loss and its 'losers,' and trespassing containers of animacy." Chen, "Toxic Animacies, Inanimate Affections," 281.

81 Ahuja, "Intimate Atmospheres," 365.

82 Goeman, "Land as Life," 86.

83 Karen Barad writes of "matter's ongoing experimenting with itself—the queer dance of being-time indeterminacy, the imaginative play of presence/absence, here/there, now/then, that holds the disparate parts together-apart," which is refracted in the work of Baassiri's *Dust Series*. Barad, "Transmaterialities," 407.

84 Gopinath, *Unruly Visions*, 133.

85 Casid, "Doing Things with Being Undone," 92.

86 For a thorough analysis of the indigenous-led #NODAPL movement, see Estes, *Our History Is the Future*.

87 Larsen and Johnston, *Being Together in Place*, 2. On political responsibility in an interconnected world, see Rothberg, *The Implicated Subject*. On inconvenience as a social relation, see Berlant, *On the Inconvienience of Other People*.

bibliography

Abbott, Elizabeth. *Sugar: A Bittersweet History.* New York: Abrams, 2010.

Adorno, Theodor. *Aesthetic Theory.* Translated by Robert Hullot-Kentor. Minneapolis: University of Minnesota Press, 1998.

Ahmann, Chloe. "It's Exhausting to Create an Event Out of Nothing: Slow Violence and the Manipulation of Time." *Cultural Anthropology* 33:1 (2018): 142–71.

Ahuja, Neel. "Intimate Atmospheres: Queer Theory in a Time of Extinctions." *GLQ* 21:2–3 (June 2015): 365–85.

Alexander, Michelle. *The New Jim Crow: Mass Incarceration in the Age of Colorblindness.* New York: New Press, 2010.

Alfred, Taiaiake. "Sovereignty." In *Sovereignty Matters,* edited by Joanne Barker, 33–50. Lincoln: University of Nebraska Press, 2006.

Amussen, Susan. *Caribbean Exchanges: Slavery and the Transformation of English Society, 1640–1700.* Chapel Hill: University of North Carolina Press, 2007.

Anker, Elisabeth. "The Cinematic Dream Life of American Politics." *Political Theory* 44:2 (May 2016): 207–18.

Anker, Elisabeth. "The Liberalism of Horror." *Social Research* 81:4 (Winter 2014): 795–823.

Anker, Elisabeth. "The Limits of Neoliberalism: The Wire and Market Rationality." In *The Politics of HBO's "The Wire": Everything Is Connected,* edited by Jonathan Havercroft and Shirin Deylami, 106–26. London: Routledge, 2014.

Anker, Elisabeth. "Mobile Sovereigns." In *The Lives of Guns*, edited by Jonathan Obert, Austin Sarat, and Andrew Poe, 21–40. New York: Oxford University Press, 2019.

Anker, Elisabeth. *Orgies of Feeling Melodrama and the Politics of Freedom*. Durham, NC: Duke University Press, 2014.

Anker, Elisabeth. "A Tale of Two Protests: Anti-Maskers, Black Lives Matter, and the Specter of Multiracial Democracy." In *The Long 2020*, edited by Richard Grusin and Maureen Ryan. Minneapolis: University of Minnesota, forthcoming.

Anker, Elisabeth. "Three Emancipations: *Manderlay*, Slavery, and Racialized Freedom." *Theory and Event* 18:2 (May 2015).

Anker, Elisabeth. "Three Emancipations: *Manderlay* and Racialized Freedom." In *Politics, Theory, and Film: Critical Encounters with Lars von Trier*, edited by Bonnie Honig and Lori J. Marso, 216–39. New York: Oxford University Press, 2016.

Anker, Elisabeth. "Thwarting Neoliberal Security: Ineptitude, the Retrograde, and the Uninspiring in *The Wire*." *American Literary History* 28:4 (Winter 2016): 759–78.

Anker, Elisabeth. "White and Deadly." *Theory and Event* 23:1 (January 2020): 169–206.

Anzaldúa, Gloria. *Borderlands/La Frontera: The New Mestiza*. San Francisco: Aunt Lute Books, 1987.

Arendt, Hannah. "Freedom and Politics: A Lecture." *Chicago Review* 14:1 (Spring 1960): 28–46.

Arendt, Hannah. *The Human Condition*. Chicago: University of Chicago Press, 1998.

Arendt, Hannah. *On Violence*. New York: Harcourt Brace, 1970.

Arendt, Hannah. "Reflections on Little Rock." *Dissent* 6:1 (Winter 1959): 45–56.

Arendt, Hannah. "What Is Freedom?" In *Between Past and Future*, 142–69. New York: Penguin, 2006.

Aristotle. *Poetics*. Translated by Anthony Kenny. New York: Oxford University Press, 2013.

Armitage, David. "John Locke, Carolina, and the Two Treatises of Government." *Political Theory* 32:5 (October 2004): 602–27.

Armitage, David. "John Locke: Theorist of Empire?" In *Empire and Modern Political Thought*, edited by Sankar Muthu, 84–111. Cambridge, UK: Cambridge University Press, 2005.

Arneil, Barbara. *John Locke and America: The Defence of English Colonialism*. Oxford: Oxford University Press, 1996.

Ashworth, William. *A Short History of the International Economy since 1850*. London: Longman, 1967.

Baldwin, James. "Everybody's Protest Novel." In *Notes of a Native Son*, 13–24. Boston: Beacon, 2012.

Baldwin, James. "The Price of the Ticket." In *Collected Essays*, 830–42. New York: Library of America, 1998.

Barad, Karen. "Transmaterialities: Trans*/Matter/Realities and Queer Political Imaginings." *GLQ* 21:2–3 (June 2015): 387–422.

Barker, Joanne. "For Whom Sovereignty Matters." In *Sovereignty Matters*, edited by Joanne Barker, 1–32. Lincoln: University of Nebraska Press, 2006.

Beckles, Hilary McD. *The First Black Slave Society: Britain's "Barbarity Time" in Barbados, 1636–1876*. Kingston, Jamaica: University of the West Indies Press, 2016.

Beckles, Hilary McD. *A History of Barbados: From Amerindian Settlement to Caribbean Single Market*. Cambridge, UK: Cambridge University Press, 2007.

Beckles, Hilary McD, and Andrew Downes. "The Economics of Transition to the Black Labor System in Barbados, 1630–1680." *The Journal of Interdisciplinary History* 18:2 (Autumn 1987): 225–47.

Beer, David. *Metric Power*. New York: Palgrave Macmillan, 2016.

Beer, George Louis. *The Old Colonial System Part 1*. Vol 2. New York: Macmillan, 1913.

Belew, Kathleen. *Bring the War Home: The White Power Movement and Paramilitary America*. Cambridge, MA: Harvard University Press, 2018.

Bell, Duncan. *Reordering the World: Essays on Liberalism and Empire*. Princeton, NJ: Princeton University Press, 2016.

Beltrán, Cristina. *Cruelty as Citizenship: How Migrant Suffering Sustains White Democracy*. Minneapolis: University of Minnesota Press, 2020.

Beltrán, Cristina. "Mestiza Poetics: Walt Whitman, Barack Obama, and the Question of Union." In *A Political Companion to Walt Whitman*, edited by John E. Seery, 59–95. Lexington: University Press of Kentucky, 2011.

Beltrán, Cristina. *The Trouble with Unity: Latino Politics and the Creation of Identity*. New York: Oxford University Press, 2010.

Benjamin, Walter. "Theses on the Philosophy of History." In *Illuminations: Essays and Reflections*, edited by Hannah Arendt, translated by Harry Zohn, 253–64. New York: Schocken, 1969.

Bennett, Jane. *Vibrant Matter: A Political Ecology of Things*. Durham, NC: Duke University Press, 2010.

Berlant, Lauren. *Cruel Optimism*. Durham, NC: Duke University Press, 2011.

Berlant, Lauren and Kathleen Stewart. *The Hundreds*. Durham, NC: Duke University Press, 2019.

Berlant, Lauren. *The Female Complaint: The Unfinished Business of Sentimentality in American Culture*. Durham, NC: Duke University Press, 2008.

Berlant, Lauren. *On the Inconvenience of Other People*. Durham, NC: Duke University Press, forthcoming.

Berlin, Ira. "American Slavery in History and Memory." In *Slavery, Resistance, Freedom*, edited by Gabor Boritt and Scott Hancock, 1–20. Oxford: Oxford University Press, 2007.

Berlin, Isaiah. "Two Concepts of Liberty." In *Liberty*, 166–217. Oxford: Oxford University Press, 2002.

Bernasconi, Robert, and Anika Maaza Mann. "The Contradictions of Racism: Locke, Slavery, and the Two Treatises." In *Race and Racism in Modern Philosophy*, edited by Andrew Valls, 89–107. Ithaca: Cornell University Press, 2005.

Berry, Wendell. "Faustian Economics: Hell Hath No Limits." *Harper's Magazine*, May 2008, 35–42.

Binder, Guyora. "The Slavery of Emancipation." *Cardozo Law Review* 17:6 (May 1996): 2063–102.

Boger, Gretchen. "The Meaning of Neighborhood in the Modern City: Baltimore's Residential Segregation Ordinances, 1910–1913." *Journal of Urban History* 35:2 (January 2009): 236–58.

Bogues, Anthony. *Empire of Liberty: Power, Desire, and Freedom.* Hanover, NH: Dartmouth College Press, 2011.

Bonilla, Yarimar. *Non-Sovereign Futures: French Caribbean Politics in the Wake of Disenchantment.* Chicago: University of Chicago Press, 2015.

Bourdieu, Pierre. "The Essence of Neoliberalism." *Le Monde Diplomatique*, English edition, December 1998. https://mondediplo.com/1998/12/08bourdieu.

Brannen, Peter. *The Ends of the World: Volcanic Apocalypses, Lethal Oceans, and Our Quest to Understand Earth's Past Mass Extinctions.* New York: Ecco, 2018.

Brown, Wendy. *In the Ruins of Neoliberalism: The Rise of Anti-Democratic Politics in the West.* New York: Columbia University Press, 2019.

Brown, Wendy. *Politics Out of History.* Princeton, NJ: Princeton University Press, 2001.

Brown, Wendy. "Resisting Left Melancholy." *boundary 2* 26:3 (Fall 1999): 19–27.

Brown, Wendy. *States of Injury: Power and Freedom in Late Modernity.* Princeton, NJ: Princeton University Press, 1995.

Brown, Wendy. *Undoing the Demos: Neoliberalism's Stealth Revolution.* New York: Zone, 2014.

Brown, Wendy. *Walled States, Waning Sovereignty.* New York: Zone, 2010.

Browne, Simone. *Dark Matters: On the Surveillance of Blackness.* Durham, NC: Duke University Press, 2015.

Bruyneel, Kevin. *Settler Memory: The Disavowal of Indigeneity and the Politics of Race in the United States.* Chapel Hill: University of North Carolina Press, 2021.

Burch, Traci. *Trading Democracy for Justice: Criminal Convictions and the Decline of Neighborhood Political Participation.* Chicago: University of Chicago Press, 2013.

Butler, Judith. *Notes toward a Performative Theory of Assembly.* Cambridge, MA: Harvard University Press, 2015.

Byrd, Jodi. *The Transit of Empire: Indigenous Critiques of Colonialism.* Minneapolis: University of Minnesota Press, 2011.

Calhoun, John C. "Slavery a Positive Good: February 6, 1837." *Teaching American History*, https://teachingamericanhistory.org/library/document/slavery-a-positive-good/

Calhoun, John C. "Speech of January 10, 1838." In *Slavery Defended: The Views of the Old South*, edited by Eric McKitrick, 18–19. Englewood Cliffs, NJ: Prentice Hall, 1963.

Califano, Joseph A., Jr. "The Movie 'Selma' Has a Glaring Flaw." *Washington Post*, December 26, 2014.

Camp, Jordan. *Incarcerating the Crisis: Freedom Struggles and the Rise of the Neoliberal State.* Berkeley: University of California Press, 2016.

Camp, Stephanie M. H. *Closer to Freedom: Enslaved Women and Everyday Resistance in the Plantation South.* Chapel Hill: University of North Carolina Press, 2004.

Campos-Pons, Maria Magdalena. "Interview on 'Sugar/Bittersweet' at Smith College of Art," 2012, YouTube video, https://youtu.be/82fb_uummHU.

Cannavò, Peter F. "Vulnerability and Nondomination: A Republican Perspective on Natural Limits." *Critical Review of International Social and Political Philosophy*. (December 2019), http://doi.org/10.1080/13698230.2019.1698155.

Casid, Jill. "Doing Things with Being Undone." *Journal of Visual Culture* 18:1 (2019): 30–52.

Chen, Mel Y. *Animacies: Biopolitics, Racial Mattering, and Queer Affect.* Durham, NC: Duke University Press, 2012.

Chen, Mel Y. "Toxic Animacies, Inanimate Affections." GLQ 17:2–3 (2011): 265–86.

Ciccariello-Maher, George. "'So Much the Worse for Whites': Dialectics of the Haitian Revolution." *Journal of French and Francophone Philosophy* 12:1 (2014): 19–39.

Cocks, Joan. *On Sovereignty and Other Political Delusions.* London: Bloomsbury, 2014.

Coghlan, Andy. "Gut Microbiota Spotted Eating Brain Chemicals for the First Time." *New Scientist*, July 1, 2016. https://www.newscientist.com/article/2095769-gut-bacteria-spotted-eating-brain-chemicals-for-the-first-time/.

Cohen, Cathy. "Deviance as Resistance: A New Research Agenda for the Study of Black Politics." *Du Bois Review* 1:1 (March 2004): 27–45.

Cohen, Lizabeth. *A Consumers' Republic: The Politics of Mass Consumption in Postwar America.* New York: Vintage, 2003.

Cohen, William. "Introduction: Locating Filth." In *Filth: Disgust, Dirt, and Modern Life*, edited by William Cohen and Ryan Johnson, vi–xxxviii. Minneapolis: University of Minnesota Press, 2004.

Connolly, William. *Facing the Planetary: Entangled Humanism and the Politics of Swarming.* Durham, NC: Duke University Press, 2017.

Corkin, Stanley. *Connecting "The Wire": Race, Space, and Postindustrial Baltimore.* Austin: University of Texas Press, 2017.

Costa, M. Victoria. "Is Neo-Republicanism Bad for Women?" *Hypatia* 28:4 (Fall 2013): 921–36.

Coulthard, Glen. "Place against Empire: Understanding Indigenous Anti-Colonialism." *Affinities: A Journal of Radical Theory, Culture and Action* 4:2 (Fall 2010): 79–83.

Cryan, John, and Timothy Dinan. "More Than a Gut Feeling." *Neuropsychopharmacology* 40 (January 2015): 41–42.

Curtin, Philip. *The Rise and Fall of the Plantation Complex: Essays in Atlantic History.* Cambridge, UK: Cambridge University Press, 1998.

Dardot, Pierre and Christian Laval, *The New Way of the World: On Neoliberal Society.* Translated by Gregory Elliott. London: Verso, 2013.

Davis, Angela. *The Meaning of Freedom: And Other Difficult Dialogues.* San Francisco: City Lights Books, 2012.

Davis, Heather, and Zoe Todd. "On the Importance of a Date, or, Decolonizing the Anthropocene." *ACME: An International Journal for Critical Geographies* 16 (4): 761–80.

Davis, Lindsay. "Lessons in Captivity: A Cultural History of Women and Incarceration in America, 1931–1972." PhD diss., George Washington University, 2018.

Davis, Ralph. *The Rise of the Atlantic Economies*. Ithaca, NY: Cornell University Press, 1973.

Dean, Jodi. *The Communist Horizon*. London: Verso, 2012.

Dean, Jodi. *Crowds and Party*. London: Verso, 2016.

De Dijn, Annelien. *Freedom: An Unruly History*. Cambridge, MA: Harvard University Press, 2020.

Deloria, Vine, Jr., and Daniel R. Wildcat. *Power and Place: Indian Education in America*. Golden, CO: Fulcrum, 2001.

Derrida, Jacques. *Given Time: 1. Counterfeit Money*. Chicago: University of Chicago Press, 1994.

Der Spiegel. "Spiegel Interview with Lars von Trier: 'We Are All Products of the United States,'" *Der Spiegel International*, November 15, 2005. https://www.spiegel.de/international/spiegel/spiegel-interview-with-filmmaker-lars-von-trier-we-are-all-products-of-the-united-states-a-384939.html.

Desmond, Matthew. *Evicted: Poverty and Profit in the American City*. New York: Broadway Books, 2017.

Dilts, Andrew. "To Kill a Thief: Punishment, Proportionality, and Criminal Subjectivity in Locke's Political Theory." *Political Theory* 40:1 (January 2012): 58–83.

Dilts, Andrew. "The Ugliness of Freedom's Practices." *Theory and Event* 23:1 (January 2020): 215–26.

Douglas, Mary. *Purity and Danger: An Analysis of Concepts of Pollution and Taboo*. London: Routledge, 2002.

Douglass, Frederick. "The Present and the Future of the Colored Race in America." In *African American Social and Political Thought 1820–1920*, edited by Howard Brotz, 267–76. London: Routledge, 2017.

Dubois, Laurent, and Richard Lee Turits. *Freedom Roots: Histories from the Caribbean*. Chapel Hill: University of North Carolina Press, 2019.

Du Bois, W. E. B. *Black Reconstruction in America: An Essay toward a History of the Part Which Black Folk Played in the Attempt to Reconstruct Democracy in America, 1860–1880*. New York: Oxford University Press, 2007.

Du Bois, W. E. B. *Darkwater: Voices from within the Veil*. New York: Dover, 1999.

Du Bois, W. E. B. "The Souls of White Folk." In *Darkwater: Voices from within the Veil*, 17–29. New York: Dover, 1999.

Duggan, Lisa. *Mean Girl: Ayn Rand and the Culture of Greed*. Berkeley: University of California Press, 2019.

Duggan, Lisa. *Twilight of Equality: Neoliberalism, Cultural Politics, and the Attack on Democracy*. Boston: Beacon, 2004.

"Dumpster of Liberty Lighting Ceremony." Facebook, Accessed June 24, 2020. https://www.facebook.com/events/the-deltaplex-arena/operation-incinerator-the-recall-revolution-begins/180754769909900/.

Dunn, Richard. *Sugar and Slaves: The Rise of the Planter Class in the English West Indies, 1624–1713*. New York: Norton, 1973.

Dunn, Rob. *Never Home Alone: From Microbes to Millipedes, Camel Crickets, and Honeybees, the Natural History of Where We Live*. New York: Basic, 2018.

Eco, Umberto. *On Ugliness*. Milan: Rizzoli Libri, 2011.

"Education Freedom Scholarships." Accessed June 24, 2020. https://sites.ed.gov
/freedom/2019/0/.

Estes, Nick. *Our History Is the Future: Standing Rock Versus the Dakota Access Pipeline,
and the Long Tradition of Indigenous Resistance.* London: Verso, 2019.

Eze, Emmanuel Chukwudi. "The Color of Reason: The Idea of 'Race' in Kant's
Anthropology." *Bucknell Review* 38:2 (January 1995): 200–241.

Fanon, Frantz. *Toward the African Revolution.* Translated by Haakon Chevalier.
New York: Grove, 1994.

Fanon, Frantz. *The Wretched of the Earth.* Translated by Richard Philcox. New
York: Grove, 2005.

Farr, James. "Locke, Natural Law, and New World Slavery." *Political Theory* 36:4
(August 2008): 495–522.

Feher, Michel. "Self-Appreciation; or, the Aspirations of Human Capital." *Public
Culture* 21:1 (2009): 21–41.

Feimster, Crystal. *Southern Horrors: Women and the Politics of Rape and Lynching.*
Cambridge, MA: Harvard University Press, 2011.

Ferguson, Kennan. "Beholden: From Freedom to Debt." *Theory and Event* 24:2
(2021): 574–91.

Ferguson, Kennan. "What Was Politics to the Denisovan?" *Political Theory* 42:2
(2014): 167–87.

Ferguson, Roderick. *Aberrations in Black: Toward a Queer of Color Critique.* Minneapolis: University of Minnesota Press, 2004.

Fitzhugh, George. "Sociology for the South." In *Slavery Defended: The Views of the
Old South,* edited by Eric McKitrick, 34–50. Englewood Cliffs, NJ: Prentice
Hall, 1963.

Fitzmaurice, Andrew. *Sovereignty, Property, and Empire, 1500–2000.* Cambridge, UK:
Cambridge University Press, 2014.

Follett, Richard. "Legacies of Enslavement: Plantation Identities and the Problem
of Freedom." In *Slavery's Ghost: The Problem of Freedom in an Age of Emancipation* by Eric Foner, Richard Follett, and Walter Johnson, 50–84. Baltimore:
Johns Hopkins University Press, 2011.

Follett, Richard. *The Sugar Masters: Planters and Slaves in Louisiana's Cane World.*
Baton Rouge: Louisiana State University Press, 2005.

Foner, Eric. *The Story of American Freedom.* New York: Norton, 1999.

Forster, Ian. "The Making of Kara Walker's Sugar Sphinx." *Art21 Magazine,* May 23,
2014. https://magazine.art21.org/2014/05/23/the-making-of-kara-walkers
-sugar-sphinx.

Foucault, Michel. *Birth of Biopolitics: Lectures at the Collège de France 1978–1979.*
Translated by Graham Burchell. New York: Picador, 2010.

Foucault, Michel. *History of Sexuality.* Vol. 1, *An Introduction.* Translated by Robert
Hurley. New York: Vintage, 1990.

Fox, Karen. *Older Than the Stars.* Illustrated by Nancy Davis. New York: Charles-
bridge, 2011.

Frank, Jason. "Democracy and Disgust." *J19: The Journal of Nineteenth-Century
Americanists* 5:2 (Fall 2017): 396–403.

Frank, Jason. "The Living Image of the People." *Theory and Event* 18:1 (2015).

Franklin, Benjamin. "Observations Concerning the Increase of Mankind, 1751." Founders Online, National Archives, https://founders.archives.gov /documents/Franklin/01-04-02-0080. Original source: *The Papers of Benjamin Franklin*. Vol. 4, July 1, 1750, through June 30, 1753, edited by Leonard W. Labaree, 225–34. New Haven, CT: Yale University Press, 1961.

Franklin, John Hope. *Runaway Slaves: Rebels on the Plantation*. Oxford: Oxford University Press, 2000.

Freeburg, Christopher. *Counterlife: Slavery after Resistance and Social Death*. Durham, NC: Duke University Press, 2021.

Friedman, Milton. *Capitalism and Freedom*. Chicago: University of Chicago Press, 2002.

Friedman, Milton, and Thomas Szasz. *Friedman and Szasz on Liberty and Drugs: Essays on the Free Market and Prohibition*. Washington, DC: Drug Policy Foundations Press, 1992.

Frost, Samantha. *Biocultural Creatures: Toward a New Theory of the Human*. Durham, NC: Duke University Press, 2016.

Fuente, Alejandro de la. "On Sugar, Slavery, and the Pursuit of (Cuban) Happiness." In *Sugar: Maria Campos-Pons*, edited by Linda Muelid, 36–45. Northampton, MA: Smith College Museum of Art, 2010.

Fuentes, Marisa. *Dispossessed Lives: Enslaved Women, Violence, and the Archive*. Philadelphia: University of Pennsylvania Press, 2016.

Fundamental Constitutions of Carolina, The: March 1, 1669. The Avalon Project, Yale Law School. http://avalon.law.yale.edu/17th_century/nc05.asp.

FundingUniverse. "Domino Sugar Corporation History." Accessed May 15, 2021. http://www.fundinguniverse.com/company-histories/domino-sugar -corporation-history/.

Galloway, J. H. *The Sugar Cane Industry: An Historical Geography from Its Origins to 1914*. Cambridge, UK: Cambridge University Press, 2005.

Garland, David. *The Culture of Control: Crime and Social Order in Contemporary Society*. Chicago: University of Chicago Press, 2001.

Gibbon, Peter, and Lasse Henricksen. "A Standard Fit for Neoliberalism." *Comparative Studies in Society and History* 54:2 (2012): 275–307.

Gilbert, Scott, Jan Sapp, and Alfred Tauber. "A Symbiotic View of Life: We Have Never Been Individuals." *Quarterly Review of Biology* 87:4 (December 2012): 325–41.

Gilmore, Ruth Wilson. *The Golden Gulag: Prisons, Surplus, Crisis, and Opposition in Globalizing California*. Berkeley: University of California Press, 2007.

Gilroy, Paul. *The Black Atlantic: Modernity and Double-Consciousness*. Cambridge, MA: Harvard University Press, 1993.

Gilroy, Paul. *Postcolonial Melancholia*. New York: Columbia University Press, 2006.

Glausser, Wayne. "Three Approaches to Locke and the Slave Trade." *Journal of the History of Ideas* 52:2 (1990): 199–216.

Glenn, Evelyn Nakano. *Unequal Freedom: How Race and Gender Shaped American Citizenship and Labor*. Cambridge, MA: Harvard University Press, 2004.

Glick, Megan. *Infrahumanisms: Science, Culture, and the Making of Modern Non/person-hood*. Durham, NC: Duke University Press, 2018.

Glickman, Lawrence. "'Buy for the Sake of the Slave': Abolitionism and the Origins of American Consumer Activism." *American Quarterly* 56:4 (December 2004): 889–912.

Goeman, Mishuana. "Land as Life: Unsettling the Logics of Containment." In *Native Studies Keywords*, edited by Stephanie Nohelani Teves, Andrea Smith, and Michelle Raheja, 71–89. Tucson: University of Arizona Press, 2015.

Goffe, Tao Leigh. "Sugarwork: The Gastropoetics of Afro-Asia after the Plantation." *Asian Diasporic Visual Cultures and the Americas* 5 (April 2019): 31–56.

Goldberg, David Theo. *Dread: Facing Futureless Futures*. Cambridge, UK: Polity, 2021.

Goldberg, David Theo. *The Threat of Race: Reflections on Racial Neoliberalism*. Malden, MA: Wiley-Blackwell, 2008.

Goldstein, Alyosha. "The Ground Not Given: Colonial Dispositions of Land, Race and Hunger." *Social Text* 36:2 (June 2018): 83–106.

Goldstein, Alyosha. "Possessive Investment: Indian Removals and the Affective Entitlements of Whiteness." *American Quarterly* 66:4 (2014): 1077–94.

Goldstein, Darra. *The Oxford Companion to Sugar and Sweets*. New York: Oxford University Press.

Gomez, Marisela. *Race, Class, Power, and Organizing in East Baltimore: Rebuilding Abandoned Communities in America*. Lanham, MD: Lexington Books, 2013.

Gómez-Barris, Macarena. *The Extractive Zone: Social Ecologies and Decolonial Perspectives*. Durham, NC: Duke University Press, 2017.

Gonzalez, Johnhenry. *Maroon Nation: A History of Revolutionary Haiti*. New Haven, CT: Yale University Press, 2019.

Gopinath, Gayatri. *Unruly Visions: The Aesthetic Practices of Queer Diaspora*. Durham, NC: Duke University Press, 2018.

Gordon, Jane. *Creolizing Political Theory: Reading Rousseau through Fanon*. New York: Fordham University Press, 2014.

Gottschalk, Marie. *Caught: The Prison State and the Lockdown of American Politics*. Princeton, NJ: Princeton University Press, 2015.

Gourevich, Alex. *From Slavery to the Cooperative Commonwealth: Labor and Republican Liberty in the Nineteenth Century*. Cambridge, UK: Cambridge University Press, 2015.

Gourevich, Alex, and Corey Robin. "Freedom Now." *Polity* 52.3 (2020): 384–98.

Goveia, Elsa V. *The West Indian Slave Laws of the 18th Century*. Barbados: Caribbean Universities Press, 1970.

Graeber, David. *The Democracy Project: A History, a Crisis, a Movement*. New York: Spiegel and Grau, 2013.

Greeson, Jennifer Rae. "The Prehistory of Possessive Individualism." *PMLA* 127:4 (October 2012): 918–24.

"Gut Feelings: Can the Microbiota Talk to the Brain?" Press release. *Gut Microbiota for Health*, February 25, 2013. http://www.gutmicrobiotaforhealth.com /en/press-release-gut-feelings-can-the-microbiota-talk-to-the-brain/.

Hahn, Steven. *A Nation under Our Feet: Black Political Struggles in the Rural South from Slavery to the Great Migration.* Cambridge, MA: Harvard University Press, 2004.

Halberstam, J. Jack. Introduction to *The Undercommons: Fugitive Planning and Black Study* by Fred Moten and Stefano Harney. London: Minor Compositions, 2013.

Halberstam, J. Jack. *The Queer Art of Failure.* Durham, NC: Duke University Press, 2011.

Hancock, Ange-Marie. *The Politics of Disgust: The Public Identity of the Welfare Queen.* New York: New York University Press, 2004.

Harabin, Virginia. "10 Questions with David Simon." Politics and Prose Bookstore (website), last accessed May 15, 2021. https://www.politics-prose.com/book -notes/10-questions-david-simon.

Haraway, Donna. *Staying with the Trouble: Making Kin in the Chthulucene.* Durham, NC: Duke University Press, 2016.

Hardt, Michael, and Antonio Negri. *Commonwealth.* Cambridge, MA: Harvard University Press, 2011.

Harpham, Geoffrey. *On the Grotesque: Strategies of Contradiction in Art and Literature.* Princeton, NJ: Princeton University Press, 1982.

Harris, Cheryl. "Whiteness as Property." *Harvard Law Review* 106:8 (June 1993): 1707–91.

Hartman, Saidiya. *Scenes of Subjection: Terror, Slavery, and Self-Making in Nineteenth Century America.* Berkeley: University of California Press, 1997.

Hartman, Saidiya. "The Time of Slavery." *South Atlantic Quarterly* 101:4 (Fall 2002): 757–77.

Hartman, Saidiya. "Venus in Two Acts." *Small Axe: A Journal of Caribbean Criticism* 12:2 (June 2008): 1–14.

Hartman, Saidiya. *Wayward Lives, Beautiful Experiments: Intimate Histories of Riotous Black Girls, Troublesome Women, and Queer Radicals.* New York: Norton, 2019.

Harvey, David. *A Brief History of Neoliberalism.* Oxford: Oxford University Press, 2007.

Hayek, Friedrich. *The Constitution of Liberty.* Chicago: University of Chicago Press, 1978.

Hayek, Friedrich. *The Road to Serfdom.* Chicago: University of Chicago Press, 1994.

Heap, Chad. *Slumming: Sexual and Racial Encounters in American Nightlife, 1885–1940.* Chicago: University of Chicago Press, 2010.

Helton, Laura, Justin Leroy, Max Mischler, Samantha Seeley, and Shauna Sweeney, eds. "The Question of Recovery: Slavery, Freedom, and the Archive." Special issue, *Social Text* 33:4 (December 2015).

Henderson, Gretchen. *Ugliness: A Cultural History.* London: Reaktion, 2015.

Hinshelwood, Brad. "The Carolinian Context of John Locke's Theory of Slavery." *Political Theory* 41:4 (2013): 562–90.

Hirschmann, Nancy. *The Subject of Liberty: Toward a Feminist Theory of Freedom.* Princeton, NJ: Princeton University Press, 2003.

Hobbes, Thomas. *Leviathan*. Edited by Richard Tuck. Cambridge, UK: Cambridge University Press, 1996.

Hochman, Leah. *The Ugliness of Moses Mendelssohn: Aesthetics, Religion and Morality in the Eighteenth Century*. New York: Routledge, 2014.

Hoffer, Peter. *Cry Liberty: The Great Stono River Slave Rebellion of 1739*. Oxford: Oxford University Press, 2011.

Honig, Bonnie. *Antigone, Interrupted*. Cambridge, UK: Cambridge University Press, 2013.

Honig, Bonnie. *Democracy and the Foreigner*. Princeton, NJ: Princeton University Press, 2001.

Honig, Bonnie. *Public Things: Democracy in Disrepair*. New York: Fordham University Press, 2017.

Honig, Bonnie. *Shell-Shocked: Feminist Criticism after Trump*. New York: Fordham University Press, 2021.

Hooker, Juliet. *Theorizing Race in the Americas: Douglass, Sarmiento, Du Bois, and Vasconcelos*. New York: Oxford University Press, 2017.

Horkheimer, Max, and Theodor Adorno. *Dialectic of Enlightenment*. Stanford, CA: Stanford University Press, 2007.

Hornby, Nick. "Interview with David Simon." *The Believer*, no. 46 (August 2007). http://www.believermag.com/issues/200708/?read=interview_simon.

Horne, Gerald. *The Apocalypse of Settler Colonialism: The Roots of Slavery, White Supremacy, and Capitalism in Seventeenth-Century North America and the Caribbean*. New York: Monthly Review Press, 2018.

Howes, Dustin. *Freedom without Violence: Resisting the Western Tradition*. New York: Oxford University Press, 2016.

Hsueh, Vicki. *Hybrid Constitutions: Challenging Legacies of Law, Privilege, and Culture in Colonial America*. Durham, NC: Duke University Press, 2010.

Immerwahr, Daniel. *How to Hide an Empire: A History of the Greater United States*. Cambridge, MA: Harvard University Press, 2019.

Ince, Onur Ulas. *Colonial Capitalism and the Dilemmas of Liberalism*. New York: Oxford University Press, 2018.

Irving, Sarah. *Natural Science and the Origins of the British Empire*. Cambridge, UK: Cambridge University Press, 2008.

Jackman, Tom. "Baltimore's 'Tough on Crime' Era Ends," *Washington Post*, March 27, 2021, A1.

Jackson, Zakiyyah Iman. *Becoming Human: Matter and Meaning in an Antiblack World*. New York: New York University Press, 2020.

Jagoda, Patrick. "Wired." *Critical Inquiry* 38 (Autumn 2011): 189–99.

James, C. L. R. *Black Jacobins: Toussaint L'Ouverture and the San Domingo Revolution*. New York: Vintage, 1989.

Jealous, Benjamin. "Freedom." *American History* 47:5 (December 2012): 55.

Johnson, K. L., J. L. Nelson, D. E. Furst, P. A. McSweeney, D. J. Robert, D. K. Zhen, and D. W. Bianchi. "Fetal Cell Microchimerism in Tissue from Multiple Sites in Women with Systemic Sclerosis." *Arthritis Rheumatology* 44:8 (August 2001): 1848–54.

Johnson, Walter. "Agency: A Ghost Story." In *Slavery's Ghost: The Problem of Freedom in the Age of Emancipation*, by Eric Foner, Richard Follet, and Walter Johnson, 8–30. Baltimore: Johns Hopkins University Press, 2011.

Johnson, Walter. *River of Dark Dreams: Slavery and Empire in the Cotton Kingdom.* Cambridge, MA: Harvard University Press, 2013.

Johnson, Walter. "Slavery, Reparations, and the Mythic March of Freedom." *Raritan* 27:2 (Fall 2007): 41–67.

Johnston, Steven. *The Truth about Patriotism.* Durham, NC: Duke University Press, 2007.

Jones, Cecily. *Engendering Whiteness: White Women and Colonialism in Barbados and South Carolina, 1627–1865.* Manchester, UK: Manchester University Press, 2007.

Jones, Norrece T. "Rape in Black and White: Sexual Violence in the Testimony of Enslaved and Free Americans." In *Slavery and the American South: Essays and Commentaries*, edited by Winthrop Jordan, 93–116. Jackson: University Press of Mississippi, 2003.

Jones-Rogers, Stephanie E. *They Were Her Property: White Women as Slave Owners in the American South.* New Haven, CT: Yale University Press, 2019.

Kamugisha, Aaron. *Beyond Coloniality: Citizenship and Freedom in the Caribbean Intellectual Tradition.* Bloomington: Indiana University Press, 2019.

Kazanjian, David. *The Brink of Freedom: Improvising Life in the Nineteenth-Century Atlantic World.* Durham, NC: Duke University Press, 2016.

Kelley, Robin D. G. *Freedom Dreams: The Black Radical Imagination.* New York: Penguin, 2002.

Kelley, Robin D. G. "Thug Nation: On State Violence and Disposability." In *Policing the Planet: Why the Policing Crisis Led to Black Lives Matter*, edited by Christina Heatherton and Jordan Camp, 15–33. London: Verso 2016.

Kelly, Sharon. "DuPont's Deadly Deceit: The Decades-long Cover-up behind the 'World's Most Slippery Material.'" *Salon*, January 4, 2016. https://www.salon.com/2016/01/04/teflons_toxic_legacy_partner/.

Kimmerer, Robin Wall. *Braiding Sweetgrass: Indigenous Wisdom, Scientific Knowledge, and the Teachings of Plants.* Minneapolis: Milkweed Editions, 2013.

Kindley, Evan. "The End of Freedom: How America Lost Its Fervor for Its Defining Ideal." *The New Republic,* May 2021, 54–57.

King, Lovalerie. *Race, Theft, and Ethics: Property Matters in African American Literature.* Baton Rouge: Louisiana State University Press, 2007.

Kolbert, Elizabeth. *The Sixth Extinction: An Unnatural History.* New York: Henry Holt, 2014.

Kotef, Hagar. *The Colonizing Self: Or, Home and Homelessness in Israel/Palestine.* Durham, NC: Duke University Press, 2020.

Kotef, Hagar. *Movement and the Ordering of Freedom: On Liberal Governances of Mobility.* Durham, NC: Duke University Press, 2015.

Kramer, Paul. *The Blood of Government: Race, Empire, the United States, and the Philippines.* Chapel Hill: University of North Carolina Press, 2006.

Krause, Sharon. *Freedom beyond Sovereignty: Reconstructing Liberal Individualism.* Chicago: University of Chicago Press, 2015.

Kuznia, Rob. "Rich Californians Balk at Limits: 'We're Not All Equal When It Comes to Water.'" *Washington Post*, June 13, 2015.

La Berge, Leigh Claire. "Capitalist Realism and Serial Form: The Fifth Season of *The Wire*." *Criticism* 52:3–4 (Summer and Fall 2010): 547–67.

Larsen, Soren, and Jay Johnston. *Being Together in Place: Indigenous Coexistence in a More Than Human World*. Minneapolis: University of Minnesota Press, 2017.

Lerner, Sharon. "The Teflon Toxin." *Intercept*, August 11–20, 2015. https://theintercept.com/series/the-teflon-toxin/.

Lewis, Simon, and Mark Maslin. *The Human Planet: How We Created the Anthropocene*. New Haven, CT: Yale University Press, 2018.

Liboiron, Max, Manuel Tironi, and Nerea Calvillo. "Toxic Politics: Acting in a Permanently Polluted World." *Social Studies of Science* 48:3 (July 2018): 331–49.

Lightfoot, Natasha. *Troubling Freedom: Antigua and the Aftermath of British Emancipation*. Durham, NC: Duke University Press, 2017.

Ligon, Richard. *A True and Exact History of the Island of Barbados*. 1657. New York: Hackett, 2011.

Lipsitz, George. *How Racism Takes Place*. Philadelphia: Temple University Press, 2011.

Lloyd, Vincent. *The Problem with Grace: Reconfiguring Political Theology*. Stanford, CA: Stanford University Press, 2011.

Locke, John. "Letter 254." In *The Correspondence of John Locke*, Vol. 1, edited by E. S. De Beer, 355–56. Oxford: Oxford University Press, 2010.

Locke, John. *Two Treatises of Government*. Edited by Peter Laslett. Cambridge, UK: Cambridge University Press, 1988.

Loichot, Valerie. "Kara Walker's Blood Sugar." *Southern Spaces*, July 8, 2014.

Loury, Glenn. "Ferguson Won't Change Anything: What Will?" *Boston Review*, January 5, 2015.

Lowe, Lisa. "Colonial Pasts and Conditional Futures." Lecture given at the Centre for Comparative Politics, School of Oriental and African Studies, University of London, October 2018.

Lowe, Lisa. *The Intimacies of Four Continents*. Durham, NC: Duke University Press, 2015.

Lowndes, Joseph, and Daniel HoSang. *Producers, Parasites, Patriots: Race and the New Right-Wing Politics of Precarity*. Minneapolis: University of Minnesota Press, 2019.

Luciano, Dana, and Mel Y. Chen. "Has the Queer Ever Been Human?" *GLQ* 21:2–3 (June 2015): 183–207.

MacAuliffe, Kathleen. *This Is Your Brain on Parasites: How Tiny Creatures Manipulate Our Behavior and Shape Society*. Boston: Mariner, 2017.

MacGilvray, Eric. *The Invention of Market Freedom*. Cambridge, UK: Cambridge University Press, 2011.

MacLaren, Andrew, and Sinéad Kelly. *Neoliberal Urban Policy and the Transformation of the City: Reshaping Dublin*. New York: Palgrave Macmillan, 2014.

MacPherson, C. B. *The Political Theory of Possessive Individualism: Hobbes to Locke*. Oxford: Oxford University Press, 2011.

Makalani, Minkah. "Black Lives Matter and the Limits of Formal Black Politics." *South Atlantic Quarterly* 116:3 (July 2017): 529–52.

Malka, Adam. *The Men of Mobtown: Policing Baltimore in the Age of Slavery and Emancipation*. Chapel Hill: University of North Carolina Press, 2018.

Malm, Andreas. *Fossil Capital: The Rise of Steam Power and the Roots of Global Warming*. London: Verso, 2016.

Mamdani, Mahmood. *Neither Settler nor Native: The Making and Unmaking of Permanent Minorities*. Cambridge, MA: Harvard University Press, 2020.

Markell, Patchen. "Decomposing Sovereignty." Paper delivered at The End of Sovereignty Conference at the Potomac Center for Modernity 2015 Lecture, September 2015.

Markell, Patchen. "The Insufficiency of Non-Domination." *Political Theory* 36:1 (2008): 9–36.

Marshall, Stephen H. "The Political Life of Fungibility." *Theory and Event* 15:3, (2012).

Marso, Lori. *Politics with Beauvior: Freedom in the Encounter*. Durham, NC: Duke University Press, 2017.

Martel, James. *Textual Conspiracies: Walter Benjamin, Idolatry, and Political Theory*. Ann Arbor: University of Michigan, 2012.

Martin, Aryn. "Microchimerism in the Mother(land): Blurring the Borders of Body and Nation." *Body and Society* 16:3 (September 2010): 23–50.

Marwah, Inder S. *Liberalism, Diversity and Domination: Kant, Mill and the Government of Difference*. Cambridge, UK: Cambridge University Press, 2019.

Marx, Karl. *Grundrisse: Foundations of the Critique of Political Economy*. Translated by Martin Nicolaus. New York: Penguin, 1993.

Marx, Karl. "On the Jewish Question." In *Karl Marx: Early Writings*, translated by Rodney Livingstone, 211–42. New York: Penguin, 1992.

Maxwell, Lida. "The Pleasures of Freedom." *Theory and Event* 23:1 (January 2020): 207–14.

Maxwell, Lida. *Public Trials: Burke, Zola, Arendt, and the Politics of Lost Causes*. New York: Oxford University Press, 2014.

Mbembe, Achille. *Critique of Black Reason*. Translated by Laurent Dubois. Durham, NC: Duke University Press, 2017.

Mbembe, Achille. *Out of the Dark Night: Essays on Decolonization*. New York: Columbia University Press, 2021.

Mbembe, Achille. *Necropolitics*. Durham, NC: Duke University Press, 2019.

Mbembe, Achille, and David Theo Goldberg. "In Conversation: Achille Mbembe and David Theo Goldberg on 'Critique of Black Reason.'" *Theory, Culture and Society* (blog), July 3, 2018. https://www.theoryculturesociety.org/blog /interviews-achille-mbembe-david-theo-goldberg-critique-black-reason.

McDougall, Harold. *Black Baltimore: A New Theory of Community*. Philadelphia: Temple University Press, 1993.

McFall-Ngai, Margaret. "Noticing Microbial Worlds: The Postmodern Synthesis in Biology." In *Arts of Living on a Damaged Planet: Ghosts and Monsters of the Anthropocene*, edited by Anna Tsing, Heather Swanson, Elaine Gan, and Nils Bubandt, M51–M69. Minneapolis: University of Minnesota Press, 2017.

McKean, Benjamin. *Disorienting Neoliberalism: Global Justice and the Outer Limit of Freedom*. New York: Oxford University Press, 2020.

McLeod, Allegra. "Law, Critique, and the Undercommons." In *A Time for Critique*, edited by Didier Fassin and Bernard Harcourt, 252–270. New York: Columbia University Press, 2019.

Mehta, Uday. *Liberalism and Empire: A Study in Nineteenth-Century British Liberal Thought*. Chicago: University of Chicago Press, 1999.

Menard, Russell. *Sweet Negotiations: Sugar, Slavery, and Plantation Agriculture in Early Barbados*. Charlottesville: University of Virginia Press, 2014.

Merleaux, April. *Sugar and Civilization: American Empire and the Cultural Politics of Sweetness*. Chapel Hill: University of North Carolina Press, 2015.

Mill, John Stuart. "Civilization." In *Essays on Politics and Society*, edited by J. M. Robson, 119–47. London: Routledge and Keegan Paul, 1977.

Mill, John Stuart. *On Liberty and Other Writings*. Cambridge, UK: Cambridge University Press, 1989.

Miller, Monica Carol. *Being Ugly: Southern Women Writers and Social Rebellion*. Baton Rouge: Louisiana State University Press, 2017.

Mills, Charles. "Kant's *Untermenschen*." In *Race and Racism in Modern Philosophy*, edited by Andrew Valls, 169–93. Ithaca, NY: Cornell University Press, 2005.

Mills, Charles. *The Racial Contract*. Ithaca, NY: Cornell University Press, 1997.

Mintz, Sidney. "Plantations and the Rise of a New Food Economy." *Review (Fernand Braudel Center)* 34:2 (2011): 3–14.

Mintz, Sydney. *Sweetness and Power: The Place of Sugar in Modern History*. New York: Penguin, 1986.

Mirzoeff, Nicholas. *The Right to Look: A Counterhistory of Visuality*. Durham, NC: Duke University Press, 2011.

Monahan, Michael. *The Creolizing Subject: Race, Reason, and the Politics of Purity*. New York: Fordham University Press, 2011.

Moore, Jason. *Capitalism in the Web of Life: Ecology and the Accumulation of Capital*. London: Verso, 2015.

Morefield, Jeanne. *Empires without Imperialism. Anglo-American Decline and the Politics of Deflection*. New York: Oxford University Press, 2014.

Moreton-Robinson, Aileen. *The White Possessive: Property, Power, and Indigenous Sovereignty*. Minneapolis: University of Minnesota Press, 2015.

Morgan, Edmund. *American Slavery, American Freedom*. New York: Norton, 2003.

Morgan, Jennifer. *Laboring Women: Reproduction and Gender in New World Slavery*. Philadelphia: University of Pennsylvania Press, 2004.

Moten, Fred. *Stolen Life*. Durham, NC: Duke University Press, 2018.

Moten, Fred, and Stefano Harney. *The Undercommons: Fugitive Planning and Black Study*. London: Minor Compositions, 2013.

Muhammad, Khalil Gibran. *The Condemnation of Blackness: Race, Crime, and the Making of Modern Urban America*. Cambridge, MA: Harvard University Press, 2011.

Municipal Art Society of New York. "Save Brooklyn's Industrial Heritage." Website, saveindustrialbrooklyn.org. Accessed May 16, 2021. https://web.archive.org/web/20101110210945/http://saveindustrialbrooklyn.org/domino.html.

Murakawa, Naomi. *The First Civil Right: How Liberals Built Prison America*. New York: Oxford University Press, 2014.

Murphy, Michelle. "Distributed Reproduction, Chemical Violence, and Latency." *Scholar and Feminist Online* 11:3 (2013). Accessed September 1, 2021. https://sfonline.barnard.edu/life-un-ltd-feminism-bioscience-race/distributed-reproduction-chemical-violence-and-latency/

Musser, Amber. "Queering Sugar: Kara Walker's Sugar Sphinx and the Intractability of Black Female Sexuality." *Signs* 42:1 (2016): 153–74.

Musser, Amber. *Sensual Excess: Queer Femininity and Brown Jouissance*. New York: New York University Press, 2018.

Myers, Ella. "Beyond the Psychological Wage: Du Bois on White Dominion." *Political Theory* 47:1 (February 2019): 6–31.

Newman, Simon. *A New World of Labor: The Development of Plantation Slavery in the British Atlantic*. Philadelphia: University of Pennsylvania Press, 2013.

Ngai, Sianne. *Ugly Feelings*. Cambridge, MA: Harvard University Press, 2007.

Nguyen, Mimi Thi. *The Gift of Freedom: War, Debt, and Other Refugee Passages*. Durham, NC: Duke University Press, 2013.

Nichols, Robert. *Theft as Property! Dispossession and Critical Theory*. Durham, NC: Duke University Press, 2019.

Nicholson, Bradley. "Legal Borrowing and the Origins of Slave Law in the Colonies." *Journal of American Legal History* 38:1 (January 1994): 38–54.

Nixon, Rob. *Slow Violence and the Environmentalism of the Poor*. Cambridge, MA: Harvard University Press, 2010.

Norton, Anne. *On the Muslim Question*. Princeton, NJ: Princeton University Press, 2012.

Nyong'o, Tavia. *Afro-Fabulations: The Queer Drama of Black Life*. New York: New York University Press, 2018.

Obama, Michelle. "Remarks by the First Lady at the Congressional Black Caucus Gala." White House Press Office, September 23, 2012. Accessed August 17, 2020. https://obamawhitehouse.archives.gov/the-press-office/2012/09/23/remarks-first-lady-congressional-black-caucus-gala.

Oldoni, F., V. Castella, and D. Hall. "Shedding Light on the Relative DNA Contributions of Two People Handling the Same Object." *Forensic Science International: Genetics* 24 (September 2016): 148–57.

Oleiwi, Abdulrahman, M. R. Morris, W. M. Schmerer, and R. Sutton. "The Relative DNA-Shedding Propensity of the Palm and Finger Surfaces." *Science and Justice* 55:5 (September 2015): 329–34.

Olson, Joel. *The Abolition of White Democracy*. Minneapolis: University of Minnesota Press, 2004.

Olson, Kevin. *Imagined Sovereignties: The Power of the People and Other Myths of the Modern Age*. New York: Oxford University Press, 2016.

Ortiz, Fernando. *Cuban Counterpoint: Tobacco and Sugar*. Durham, NC: Duke University Press, 1995.

Pagden, Anthony. *Lords of All the World: Ideologies of Empire in Spain, Britain, and France 1500–1800*. New Haven, CT: Yale University Press, 1995.

Panagia, Davide. *The Political Life of Sensation*. Durham, NC: Duke University Press, 2009.

Panagia, Davide. *Rancière's Sentiments*. Durham, NC: Duke University Press, 2019.

Parekh, Bhikhu. "Decolonizing Liberalism: A Critique of Locke and Mill." In *The End of "Isms"? Reflections on the Fate of Ideological Politics after Communism's Collapse*, edited by Alexander Shtromas, 85–103. London: Blackwell, 1994.

Parker, Matthew. *The Sugar Barons: Family, Corruption, Empire, and War in the West Indies*. London: Windmill, 2011.

Passavant, Paul A. *Policing Protest: The Post-Democratic State and the Figure of Black Insurrection*. Durham, NC: Duke University Press, 2021.

Passavant, Paul A. "The Strong Neo-Liberal State: Crime, Consumption, Governance." *Theory and Event* 8:3 (Fall 2006).

Pateman, Carole, and Charles Mills. *The Contract and Domination*. London: Polity, 2013.

Patterson, Orlando. *Freedom*. Vol. 1, *Freedom in the Making of Western Culture*. New York: Basic, 1991.

Patterson, Orlando. *Slavery and Social Death: A Comparative Study*. Cambridge, MA: Harvard University Press, 1982.

Patterson, Orlando. "The Unholy Trinity: Freedom, Slavery, and the American Constitution." *Social Research* 54:3 (Autumn 1987): 543–78.

Peck, Jamie. *Constructions of Neoliberal Reason*. New York: Oxford University Press, 2013.

Peck, Jamie, and Nic Theodore. *Fast Policy: Experimental Statecraft at the Thresholds of Neoliberalism*. Minneapolis: University of Minnesota Press, 2016.

Pennisi, Elizabeth. "The Right Gut Microbes Help Infants Grow." *Science*, February 18, 2016. http://www.sciencemag.org/news/2016/02/right-gut-microbes -help-infants-grow.

Pettit, Philip. *Republicanism: A Theory of Freedom and Government*. Oxford: Oxford University Press, 1999.

Phipps, Matthew, and Susan Petricevic. "The Tendency of Individuals to Transfer DNA to Handled Items." *Forensic Science International* 168:2–3 (2007): 162–68.

Piketty, Thomas. *Capital in the Twenty-first Century*. Cambridge, MA: Harvard University Press, 2013.

Pinson, Gilles, and Christelle Journel, eds. *Debating the Neoliberal City*. London, Routledge, 2017.

Pitts, Jennifer. *A Turn to Empire: The Rise of Imperial Liberalism in Britain and France*. Princeton, NJ: Princeton University Press, 2006.

Povinelli, Elizabeth. *Economies of Abandonment: Social Belonging and Endurance in Late Liberalism*. Durham, NC: Duke University Press, 2011.

Powers, Nicholas. "Why I Yelled at the Kara Walker Exhibit." *The Indypendant*, June 30, 2014. https://indypendent.org/2014/06/why-i-yelled-at-the-kara -walker-exhibit/.

Puar, Jasbir. *The Right to Maim: Debility, Capacity, Disability*. Durham, NC: Duke University Press, 2017.

Puckrein, Gary. *Little England: Plantation Society and Anglo-Barbadian Politics, 1627–1700*. New York: New York University Press, 1987.

Pugliese, Joseph. *Biopolitics of the More-Than-Human: Forensic Ecologies of Violence*. Durham, NC: Duke University Press: 2020.

Pulido, Laura. "Flint, Environmental Racism, and Racial Capitalism." *Capitalism, Nature, Socialism* 27:3 (2016): 1–16.

Purnell, Derecka, and Marbre Stahly-Butts. "The Police Can't Solve the Problem. They Are the Problem." *New York Times*, September 26, 2019.

Quarles, Benjamin. *Black Abolitionists*. Boston: De Capo Press, 1991.

Ramgotra, Manjeet. "Republic and Empire in Montesquieu's *Spirit of the Laws*." *Millennium: Journal of International Studies* 42:3 (2014): 790–816.

Rana, Aziz. *The Two Faces of American Freedom*. Cambridge, MA: Harvard University Press, 2010.

Rancière, Jacques. *The Politics of Aesthetics: Distribution of the Sensible*. London: Continuum, 2006.

Reddy, Chandan. *Freedom with Violence: Race, Sexuality, and the US State*. Durham, NC: Duke University Press, 2011.

Reinhardt, Mark. "Vision's Unseen: On Sovereignty, Race, and the Optical Unconscious." In *Photography and the Optical Unconscious*, edited by Shawn Michelle Smith, 174–222. Durham, NC: Duke University Press, 2017.

Rich, Nathaniel. "The Lawyer Who Became DuPont's Worst Nightmare." *New York Times Magazine*, January 6, 2016.

Robbins, Bruce. *The Beneficiary*. Durham, NC: Duke University Press, 2017.

Roberts, Neil. *Freedom as Marronage*. Chicago: University of Chicago Press, 2015.

Robertson, David. *Denmark Vesey: The Buried Story of America's Largest Slave Rebellion and the Man Who Led It*. New York, Vintage, 2009.

Robin, Corey. *The Reactionary Mind: Conservatism from Edmund Burke to Sarah Palin*. London: Oxford University Press, 2013.

Rodriguez, Dylan. *Suspended Apocalypse: White Supremacy, Genocide, and the Filipino Condition*. Minneapolis: University of Minnesota Press, 2009.

Roediger, David. *Seizing Freedom: Slave Emancipation and Liberty for All*. London: Verso, 2015.

Roediger, David. *The Wages of Whiteness: Race and the Making of the American Working Class*. London: Verso, 1991.

Rogers, Melvin. "Difference, Domination, and Republicanism." *Difference without Domination*, edited by Danielle Allen and Rohini Somanathan, 59–90. Chicago: University of Chicago Press, 2020.

Rogin, Michael. *Ronald Reagan, the Movie, and Other Episodes in Political Demonology*. Berkeley: University of California Press, 1988.

Rooney, Kara. "A Sonorous Subtlety: Kara Walker with Kara Rooney." *Brooklyn Rail*, May 2014. https://brooklynrail.org/2014/05/art/kara-walker-with-kara-rooney.

Rosenkranz, Karl. *Aesthetics of Ugliness: A Critical Edition*. London: Bloomsbury, 2015.

Rothberg, Michael. *The Implicated Subject: Beyond Victims and Perpetrators*. Stanford, CA: Stanford University Press, 2019.

Rugemer, Edward, "The Development of Mastery and Race in the Comprehensive Slave Codes of the Greater Caribbean during the Seventeenth Century." *The William and Mary Quarterly* 70:3 (July 2013): 429–58.

Rugemer, Edward. *Slave Law and the Politics of Resistance in the Early Atlantic World.* Cambridge, MA: Harvard University Press, 2018.

Rushing, Sara. *The Virtues of Vulnerability: Humility, Autonomy, and Citizen-Subjectivity.* New York: Oxford University Press, 2020.

Schaub, Joseph. "*The Wire*: Big Brother Is Not Watching You in Body-more, Murda-land." *Journal of Popular Film and Television* 38:3 (September 2010): 122–32.

Scherer, Matthew. *Beyond Church and State: Democracy, Secularism, and Conversion.* Cambridge, UK: Cambridge University Press, 2013.

Schlosberg, David, and Romand Coles. "The New Environmentalism of Everyday Life: Sustainability, Material Flows, and Movements." *Contemporary Political Theory* 15 (May 2016): 160–81.

Schneider, Gregory. "Parts and Wholes: The Human Microbiome, Ecological Ontology, and the Challenges of Community." *Perspectives in Biology and Medicine* 57:2 (March 2014): 208–23.

Schoolman, Morton. *A Democratic Enlightenment: The Reconciliation Image, Aesthetic Education, Possible Politics.* Durham, NC: Duke University Press, 2020.

Schwartz, Stuart. "A Commonwealth Within Itself: The Early Brazilian Sugar Industry 1550–1670." In *Tropical Babylons: Sugar and the Making of the Atlantic World, 1450–1680,* edited by Stuart Schwartz, 158–200. Chapel Hill: University of North Carolina Press, 2004.

Schweik, Susan. *Ugly Laws: Disability in Public.* New York: New York University Press, 2010.

Scott, David. *Conscripts of Modernity: The Tragedy of Colonial Enlightenment.* Durham, NC: Duke University Press, 2004.

Scott, David. *Omens of Adversity: Tragedy, Time, Memory, Justice.* Durham, NC: Duke University Press, 2014.

Scott, James C. *Weapons of the Weak: Everyday Forms of Peasant Resistance.* New Haven, CT: Yale University Press, 1985.

Scranton, Roy. *Learning to Die in the Anthropocene.* San Francisco: City Lights, 2015.

Sexton, Jared. *Amalgamation Schemes: Antiblackness and the Critique of Multiracialism.* Minneapolis: University of Minnesota Press, 2009.

Sharpe, Christina. *In the Wake: On Blackness and Being.* Durham, NC: Duke University Press, 2016.

Sheehan, Helena, and Sheamus Sweeney. "*The Wire* and the World: Narrative and Metanarrative." *JumpCut: A Journal of Contemporary Media* 51 (Spring 2009). https://www.ejumpcut.org/archive/jc51.2009/Wire/.

Sheller, Mimi. *Consuming the Caribbean: From Arawaks to Zombies.* London: Routledge, 2003.

Sheridan, Richard. *Sugar and Slavery: An Economic History of the West Indies 1623–1775.* Baltimore: Johns Hopkins University Press, 1974.

Sheth, Falguni. *Toward a Political Philosophy of Race.* Albany: SUNY Press, 2009.

Shotwell, Alexis. *Against Purity: Living Ethically in Compromised Times*. Minneapolis: University of Minnesota Press, 2016.

Shulman, George. "A Flight from the Real." *New Literary History* 45:4 (2014): 549–73.

Simon, Joshua. *The Ideology of Creole Revolution: Imperialism and Independence in American and Latin American Political Thought*. Cambridge: Cambridge University Press, 2017.

Simpson, Audra. *Mohawk Interruptus: Political Life across the Borders of Settler States*. Durham, NC: Duke University Press, 2014.

Simpson, Audra. "Savage States: Settler Governance in an Age of Sorrow." Lecture delivered at the George Washington University, Washington, DC, March 1, 2018.

Simpson, Leanne Betasamosake. *As We Have Always Done: Indigenous Freedom through Radical Resistance*. Minneapolis: University of Minnesota Press, 2017.

Singh, Nikhil Pal. "The Pervasive Power of the Settler Mindset." *Boston Review*, November 26, 2019. http://bostonreview.net/war-security-race/nikhil-pal-singh-pervasive-power-settler-mindset.

Singh, Nikhil Pal. *Race and America's Long War*. Berkeley: University of California Press, 2017.

Sirmans, M. Eugene. *Colonial South Carolina: A Political History 1663–1763*. Chapel Hill: University of North Carolina Press, 2012.

Skinner, Quentin. *Liberty before Liberalism*. Cambridge, UK: Cambridge University Press, 2012.

Smith, Henry A. M. "The Colleton Family in South Carolina." *South Carolina Historical and Genealogical Magazine* 1:4 (October 1900): 325–41.

Smith, Michelle. "Affect and Respectability Politics." *Theory and Event* 17:3 (2014).

Smith, Mick. *Against Ecological Sovereignty: Ethics, Biopolitics, and Saving the Natural World*. Minneapolis: University of Minnesota Press, 2011.

Smith, Peter Andrey. "Can the Bacteria in Your Gut Explain Your Mood?" *New York Times Magazine*, June 23, 2015.

Smith, Roberta. "Sugar? Sure, But Salted with Meaning." *New York Times*, May 11, 2014.

Smith, Van. "A Campaign to Undermine a Controversial Baltimore Waste-burning Power Plant Appears to Be Working." *Baltimore Sun*, February 24, 2015.

Soss, Joe, Richard C. Fording, and Sanford F. Schram. *Disciplining the Poor: Neoliberal Paternalism and the Persistent Power of Race*. Chicago: University of Chicago Press, 2011.

Spence, Lester. *Knocking the Hustle: Against the Neoliberal Turn in Black Politics*. Santa Barbara, CA: Punctum Books, 2015.

Srnicek, Nick, and Alex Williams. *Inventing the Future: Postcapitalism and a World without Work*. London: Verso, 2016.

Stanley, Amy Dru. *From Bondage to Contract: Wage Labor, Marriage, and the Market in the Age of Slave Emancipation*. Cambridge, UK: Cambridge University Press, 1998.

Stow, Simon. *American Mourning: Tragedy, Democracy, Resilience*. Cambridge, UK: Cambridge University Press, 2017.

"Sugar Farming's Toll on the Environment." *World Wildlife Federation Magazine,* Summer 2015. https://www.worldwildlife.org/magazine/issues/summer-2015/articles/sugarcane-farming-s-toll-on-the-environment.

Sze, Julie. *Environmental Justice in a Moment of Danger.* Berkeley: University of California Press, 2020.

TallBear, Kim. "Beyond the Life/Not-Life Binary: A Feminist-Indigenous Reading of Cryopreservation, Interspecies Thinking, and the New Materialisms." In *Cryopolitics: Frozen Life in a Melting World,* edited by Joanna Radin and Emma Kowal, 179–202. Cambridge, MA: MIT Press, 2017.

TallBear, Kim. "Caretaking Relations, Not American Dreaming." *Kalfou* 6:1 (2019): 24–41.

TallBear, Kim. "An Indigenous Reflection on Working Beyond the Human/Nonhuman." *GLQ* 21:2–3 (2015): 230–35.

Theoharis, Jeanne. *A More Beautiful and More Terrible History: The Uses and Misuses of Civil Rights History.* Boston: Beacon, 2018.

Tocqueville, Alexis de. *Democracy in America.* Translated by Henry Reeves. New York: Norton, 2007.

Tompkins, Kyla Wazana. *Racial Indigestion: Eating Bodies in the Nineteenth Century.* New York: New York University Press, 2012.

Tompkins, Kyla Wazana. "Sweetness, Capacity, Energy." *American Quarterly* 71:3 (September 2019): 849–56.

Tonino, Leath. "Two Ways of Knowing: Robin Wall Kimmerer on Scientific and Native American Views of the Natural World." *Sun Magazine,* April 2016, 4–14.

Tsing, Anna. *The Mushroom at the End of the World: On the Possibility of Life in Capitalist Ruins.* Princeton, NJ: Princeton University Press, 2016.

Tuck, Richard. *The Rights of War and Peace.* Oxford: Oxford University Press, 2001.

Tully, James. *An Approach to Political Philosophy: Locke in Contexts.* Cambridge, UK: Cambridge University Press, 1993.

Urbanati, Nadia. *The Tyranny of the Moderns.* New Haven, CT: Yale University Press, 2015.

"Ugly, adj. adv. and n." *Oxford English Dictionary Online.* Oxford: Oxford University Press, 2019.

Uzgalis, William. "An Inconsistency Not to Be Excused: On Locke and Racism." In *Philosophers on Race: Critical Essays,* edited by Julie Ward and Tommy Lott, 81–100. Oxford: Blackwell, 2008.

Vermeulen, Heather. "Thomas Thistlewood's Libidinal Linnean Project: Slavery, Ecology, and Knowledge Production." *Small Axe* 22:1 (2018): 18–38.

Vitale, Alex. *The End of Policing.* London: Verso, 2017.

Wacquant, Loïc. *Punishing the Poor: The Neoliberal Government of Social Insecurity.* Durham, NC: Duke University Press, 2009.

Walvin, James. *Sugar: The World Corrupted.* New York: Little, Brown, 2018.

Warren, Calvin. *Ontological Terror: Blackness, Nihilism, and Emancipation.* Durham, NC: Duke University Press, 2017.

Warren, Dorian. "Response to Ferguson." *Boston Review,* January 5, 2015.

Watts, Vanessa. "Indigenous Place-Thought and Agency amongst Humans and Non-Humans (First Woman and Sky Woman go on a European World Tour!)." *Decolonization: Indigeneity, Education, and Society* 2:1 (2013): 20–34.

Wedeen, Lisa. *Authoritarian Apprehensions: Ideology, Judgment, and Mourning in Syria.* Chicago: University of Chicago, 2019.

Wehiliye, Alexander. *Habeas Viscus: Racializing Assemblages, Biopolitics, and Black Feminist Theories of the Human.* Durham, NC: Duke University Press, 2014.

Weinbaum, Alys. *The Afterlife of Reproductive Slavery: Biocapitalism and Black Feminism's Philosophy of History.* Durham, NC: Duke University Press, 2019.

Wells, Ida B. "Lynch Law in America" (1900). In *The Light of Truth: Writings of an Anti-Lynching Crusader*, edited with an introduction and notes by Mia Bay, 394–403, New York: Penguin Classics, 2014.

Weston, Kath. *Animate Planet: Making Visceral Sense of Living in a High-Tech Ecologically Damaged World.* Durham, NC: Duke University Press, 2017.

Whyte, Kyle Powys. "Our Ancestors' Dystopia Now: Indigenous Conservation and the Anthropocene." In *Routledge Companion to the Environmental Humanities*, edited by Ursula K. Heise, Jon Christensen, and Michelle Niemann, 206–15. London: Routledge, 2017.

Wilder, Gary. *Freedom Time: Negritude, Decolonization, and the Future of the World.* Durham, NC: Duke University Press, 2015.

Wilderson, Frank. *Red, White, and Black: Cinema and the Structure of U.S. Antagonisms.* Durham, NC: Duke University Press, 2010.

Wilderson, Frank, and Esther Armah. "The Lady with the Whip: Gendered Violence and Social Death in *Manderlay* and *Django Unchained*." Lecture given at Barnard College, March 6, 2013. Vimeo, http://vimeo.com/61345252.

Wilderson, Frank, and Aria Dean. "Frank B. Wilderson III in Conversation with Aria Dean." *November* 2 (2020). https://novembermag.com/contents/2.

Williams, David. *I Freed Myself: African American Self-Emancipation in the Civil War Era.* Cambridge, UK: Cambridge University Press, 2014.

Williams, Eric. *Capitalism and Slavery.* Chapel Hill: University of North Carolina Press, 1994.

Williams, Eric. *From Columbus to Castro: The History of the Caribbean 1492–1969.* New York: Vintage, 1984.

Williams, Linda. *On "The Wire."* Durham, NC: Duke University Press, 2014.

Williams, Linda. *Playing the Race Card: Melodramas of Black and White from Uncle Tom to O. J. Simpson.* Princeton, NJ: Princeton University Press, 2001.

Williams, Raymond. *Modern Tragedy.* Stanford, CA: Stanford University Press, 1966.

Wilson, Elizabeth. *Gut Feminism.* Durham, NC: Duke University Press, 2015.

Wilson, Thomas. *The Ashley Cooper Plan: The Founding of Carolina and the Origins of Southern Political Culture.* Chapel Hill: University of North Carolina Press, 2016.

Wingrove, Elizabeth Rose. *Rousseau's Republican Romance.* Princeton, NJ: Princeton University Press, 2000.

Wolfe, Patrick. *Traces of History: Elementary Structures of Race.* London: Verso, 2016.

Wolin, Sheldon. *Democracy Incorporated: Managed Democracy and the Specter of Inverted Totalitarianism.* Princeton, NJ: Princeton University Press, 2010.

Wolin, Sheldon. *The Presence of the Past: Essays on the State and the Constitution.* Baltimore: Johns Hopkins University Press, 1989.

Wollheben, Peter. *The Hidden Life of Trees: What They Feel, How They Communicate—Discoveries from a Secret World.* Minneapolis, MN: Greywolf, 2017.

Wood, Betty. *The Origins of American Slavery: Freedom and Bondage in the English Colonies.* New York: Hill and Wang, 1997.

Wood, Peter. *Black Majority: Negroes in Colonial South Carolina from 1670 through the Stono Rebellion.* New York: Norton, 1996.

Woodly-Davis, Deva. *Reckoning: Black Lives Matter and the Democratic Necessity of Social Movements.* New York: Oxford University Press, 2021.

World Wildlife Federation. "Sugarcane Farming's Toll on The Environment." *World Wildlife Federation Magazine,* Summer 2015.

Wylie, Sarah. *Fractivism: Corporate Bodies and Chemical Bonds.* Durham, NC: Duke University Press, 2018.

Wynter, Sylvia. "Unsettling the Coloniality of Being/Truth/Power/Freedom: Towards the Human, after Man, Its Overrepresentation—An Argument." CR: *The New Centennial Review* 3:3 (Fall 2003): 257–337.

Yong, Ed. *I Contain Multitudes: The Microbes within Us and a Grander View of Life.* New York: Ecco, 2016.

Younge, Gary. "Liberty? No, Thanks." *Guardian,* February 23, 2006.

Yudkin, John. *Pure, White and Deadly.* New York: Viking, 1972.

Yusoff, Kathryn. *A Billion Black Anthropocenes or None.* Minneapolis: University of Minnesota Press, 2018.

Zerilli, Linda. "Critique as a Political Practice of Freedom." In *A Time for Critique,* edited by Didier Fassin and Bernard Harcourt, 36–51. New York: Columbia University Press, 2019.

Zerilli, Linda. *Feminism and the Abyss of Freedom.* Chicago: University of Chicago Press, 2005.

Zirin, Dave. "'The Game Done Changed': Reconsidering 'The Wire' amidst the Baltimore Uprising." *Nation,* May 4, 2015.

Žižek, Slavoj. *The Year of Dreaming Dangerously.* London: Verso, 2012.

index

gang-style slavery, 45. *See also* slavery
gender, 20–21, 26, 54–55, 71–75, 97–100,
    107–8, 143–44, 149. *See also* patriarchy;
    racial domination
geochemical subjects, 168–73
gift-giving, 95–96, 111–12, 181n8, 196n41
Gilbert, Scott, 163
Gilmore, Ruth Wilson, 120–21
Gilroy, Paul, 182n18, 199n13
Goeman, Mishuana, 172–73, 178
Goldstein, Alyosha, 187n14, 193n135
Gómez-Barris, Macarena, 46
Goose Creek Men, 193n134
Gopinath, Gayatri, 166, 175, 204n60
Greeson, Jennifer Rae, 188n45
gun ownership, 10, 154
gut microbiota, 12, 16, 33–34, 160–65

Haitian revolution, 64, 79, 193n140
Halberstam, Jack, 108
Haraway, Donna, 46, 160, 162–63
harm principle, 10–11, 21–22
Harney, Stefano, 92, 106, 109, 124–25
Harris, Cheryl, 104, 188n45
Hartman, Saidiya, 5, 15, 19, 32, 70, 76,
    79–80, 89, 94–95, 99, 103, 186n2, 198n66,
    198n69
Hawai'i, 65, 193n142
health freedom, 8–9
Henry VIII, 44, 68
heroism, 143–47, 150–52, 172, 184n54
Hobbes, Thomas, 161
Hochman, Leah, 13
Hoffer, Peter, 192n131
Hollywood, 93, 106, 196n43
homo economicus, 126, 131, 134, 157–58
Honig, Bonnie, 101, 203n30
Horkheimer, Max, 19, 157
housing groups, 145–47
Howes, Dustin, 184nn55–56
Hsueh, Vicki, 192n129
Hudson River School, 150–51
human capital, theory of, 126–27,
    130–33
human exceptionalism, 5–6, 18, 33–34,
    149–52, 155, 158–60, 173–80, 183n43,
    206n83

ideal theory, 19, 29–30
imperialism: disavowal and, 6–7, 13, 20–23,
    30, 89–90, 101; freedom's legitimation
    of, 4–5, 21, 24, 28–29; slave regimes and,
    44–49, 59, 65. *See also* civilization dis-
    courses; despotism; racial domination;
    settler colonialism; slavery
indentured servitude, 45
indigenous peoples, 56; land theft from, 3,
    56–57, 60–62, 64–65, 193n134; sugar plan-
    tations and, 37, 193n134; thought systems
    of, 34–35, 156, 202n13. *See also* despotism;
    dispossession; indigenous political
    thought; Locke, John; *specific peoples*
indigenous political thought, 7, 18, 34–35,
    47, 150–53, 163–64, 169, 172, 178, 202n13.
    See also specific thinkers
individualism: ableism of, 203n44; bound-
    aries of, 11, 18, 33, 150–55, 160–68, 170–76,
    180; collective agency and, 152–63, 168–
    73, 177–80; consumptive sovereignty
    and, 158–60; dust wipes and, 175–77; as
    freedom practice, 3–5, 37–38, 94–95; mi-
    crobiota and, 12; misplaced burdens of,
    93–99; nature's destruction and, 38–40,
    168–73; negative freedom and, 20–21,
    183n47; neoliberalism and, 116–18, 126–37,
    143–47; private property and, 39–40,
    103–8, 155–65; relationality and, 150–52,
    164, 168–80, 204n60; resistance and, 29,
    137–42, 146–47; self-directed labor and,
    20, 23–24; self-mastery and, 43, 66–73,
    83, 100–112, 155, 163–64, 172, 205n68;
    self-possession and, 160–65; slavery as
    opposite of, 186n77, 196n35; tragedy
    and, 143–47. *See also* agency; collective
    subjects; liberal theory; sovereignty
Iraq War, 4

James, C. L. R., 41, 46, 79, 187n8
Jamestown (colony), 187n21.
Jealous, Benjamin, 77
Jefferson, Thomas, 31
Johnson, Jay, 179
Johnson, Lyndon, 196n43
Johnson, Walter, 81–82, 186n77
Johnston, Steven, 194n4

postcolonial studies, 28–29, 32, 78–80

principal-agent problem, 142

private property: boundaries and, 11, 18, 33, 150–55, 160–68, 170–76, 180; consumptive sovereignty and, 155–58; dust wipes and, 175–77; freedom and, 5, 9, 29, 38, 48–49, 60–65, 94–95, 149, 187n14, 198n66; human exceptionalism and, 5–6, 18, 33–34, 149–55, 158–60, 173–80, 183n43, 206n83; Locke on, 55–57, 60–62, 101, 155; mastery and, 4–5, 10, 18, 31, 38–43, 49, 53–56, 65–76, 80–88, 98–112, 155, 160–80; neoliberalism and, 9–10, 32–33, 117–18, 125–37, 199n5; racialization of, 4, 39–40, 59, 100–108, 155–56, 193n134. *See also* dispossession; neoliberalism; possession; sovereignty

privatization, 33, 113–18, 120–25, 137–42, 149, 182n19

Puar, Jasbir, 184n50

Puckrein, Gary, 50

Puerto Rico, 65, 193n142

Pugliese, Joseph, 205n70

quantification. *See* bureaucracy; neoliberalism; statistical juking

queer inhumanisms, 152–53, 166–67, 172

queer vulnerability, 73

racial contract, 86, 89–90, 93–99, 102–3, 106, 195n26

racial domination: Afropessimism and, 32, 81, 91, 96; agency and, 15, 19, 76, 82–83, 93–99, 186n77, 196n43; colonial practices and, 5–7, 16, 21, 31, 62–65, 89–108, 165–68, 173–80, 196n34; criminality and, 84, 101–8, 111–12, 116–25, 144–45, 200n20; emancipation and, 11–12, 20, 77–85, 93–99; enlightenment subjects of freedom and, 79–85, 89–90; environmental destruction and, 41, 45–49, 52–55, 60–62, 148–60, 171, 190n88, 191n118, 205n79; filthiness tropes and, 166–68, 173–80; freedom as, 3–4, 24, 29, 32, 62–65, 78, 85–93, 100–108; gender and, 54–55, 71–75, 97–100; Lockean freedom and, 49–65, 190n97; mastery and, 4–5, 10, 18, 31, 38–43, 49, 51–56, 65–76, 80–88, 98–112; neoliberalism and, 9–10, 115–18; sexuality and, 72–73, 84, 104–8; slave codes and, 53–55, 68; stereotypes and, 94–101; sugar plantations and, 37, 39, 44–55. *See also* agency; colonialism; dispossession; mastery; racial contract; slavery; sovereignty

Rana, Aziz, 56

Rancière, Jacques, 13, 70

rape, 54–55, 71–72

rationality, 5–6, 125–37, 155–57, 185n71, 198n1

Rebecca (du Maurier), 107

recognition, 27–29

Reddy, Chandan, 11

refusal, 24–26, 29, 131–32, *132*, 132–33, 137, 146–47

reproductive labor, 54–55, 71

republican theory, 21–23. *See also* nondomination

resistance: agency and, 25–26, 33, 82–83, 98, 116–117, 146, 186n77; Black freedom and, 30, 78–84, 90–99, 102–5, 110–12, 124, 196n43; individualism and, 29, 137–42, 146–47; neoliberal governmentality and, 11–12, 16, 115–25, 145–47; to settler colonialism, 64–66. *See also* agency; Black freedom; colonialism; policing; racial domination; slavery; taking (freedom as)

revolutionary politics, 23, 26, 79, 85, 108–9, 115, 129

Roberts, Neil, 66, 70

Rogin, Michael, 104

romance (revolutionary), 32, 79, 85, 109–12

Roman Republic, 21–22

Royal Africa Company, 56

Rugemer, Edward, 53

rule of law, 3, 5, 9–10, 23–24, 37

Sapp, Jan, 163

Schneider, Gregory, 161

Scott, David, 32, 78, 83, 89, 108–9

Scott, James C., 26, 145

Scranton, Roy, 203n34

Second Treatise of Government (Locke), 56–59

self-mastery, 43, 66–73, 83, 100–112, 155, 163–64, 172, 205n68

59–65, 80–81, 97–99, 149, 155–56, 189n53, 191n117; private property and, 101–9, 188n45; slave codes and, 53–55; sovereignty and, 89; sugar as metaphor of, 65–76. *See also* civilization discourses; dispossession; mastery; private property; possession; racial domination; settler colonialism

Wilderson, Frank, 81

Williams, Eric, 45, 48, 142, 144, 188n29

Williams, Linda, 121, 142

Williams, Raymond, 80

Wilson, Darren, 77

wipes (dusting), 175–77

Wire, The (show), 33, 115–18, 122, 125–37, *128, 135,* 137–47

Wood, Betty, 42–43

worldmaking, 19, 22–23, 28, 75–76, 104, 164, 167–68, 173–80, 184n54

Wynter, Sylvia, 48, 53, 91, 152

xenophobia, 8, 27

Yamahsee, 64

yeoman farmer, 31, 42–43

Yusoff, Kathryn, 205n79

Zerilli, Linda, 92